Real World Camera Raw
with Adobe Photoshop CS

Real World Camera Raw with Adobe Photoshop CS

Industrial-Strength Production Techniques

Bruce Fraser

Peachpit Press

Adobe

To all those who love photons and who make the decision
to capture a frozen instant in time.

Real World Camera Raw with Adobe Photoshop CS

Bruce Fraser

Copyright ©2005 by Bruce Fraser

Peachpit Press
1249 Eighth Street
Berkeley, CA 94710
510/524-2178
Fax: 510/524-2221

Find us on the World Wide Web at www.peachpit.com.

Peachpit Press is a division of Pearson Education.
Real World Camera Raw with Adobe Photoshop CS is published in association with Adobe Press.

Interior design by Stephen F. Roth/Open House
Cover Design: Aren Howell
Cover Illustration: Ben Fishman, Artifish, Inc.
Image credits and permissions, page 219

ISBN 0-321-27878-X
9 8 7 6 5 4 3 2

Printed and bound in the United States of America

Overview
The Big Picture

Contents

What's Inside

Preface

Real World Raw

If you're reading this book because you want to be told that digital really is better than film, look elsewhere. Those discussions tend to generate a lot more heat than light, and if you aren't at least contemplating shooting digital for some or all of your work, this book isn't relevant. If you want to be told that shooting digital raw is better than shooting JPEG, you'll have to read between the lines—what this book does is to explain how raw *differs* from JPEG, and how you can exploit those differences.

But if you're looking for solid, tested, proven techniques for dealing with hundreds or thousands of raw images a day—moving them from the camera to the computer, making initial selects and sorts, optimizing the raw captures, enriching them with metadata, and processing them into deliverable form—this is the book for you. My entire reason for writing this book was to throw a lifebelt to all those photographers who find themselves drowning in gigabytes of data.

The combination of Photoshop's File Browser and Camera Raw plug-in offers a fast, efficient, and extremely powerful workflow for dealing with raw digital captures, but the available information tends to be short on answers to questions such as the following.

▶ What special considerations should I take into account when shooting digital raw rather than film or JPEG?

► What edits should I make in Camera Raw?

► How and where are my Camera Raw settings saved?

► How can I fine-tune Camera Raw's color performance to better match my camera's behavior?

► How can I set up the File Browser to speed up making initial selects from a day's shoot?

► How can I make sure that every image I deliver contains copyright and rights management notices?

► How do I make sure that all the work I do in the File Browser, ranking or flagging images, entering keywords and other metadata, and sorting in a custom order, doesn't suddenly disappear?

► What are my alternatives to editing each individual image by hand?

► How can I automate the conversion of raw images to deliverable files?

Raw shooters face these questions, and many others, every day. Unfortunately, the answers are hard to find in the gazillion Photoshop books out there—much less Photoshop's own manuals—and when they're addressed at all they tend to be downplayed in favor of whizzy filter effects. This book answers these questions, and the other daily workflow issues that arise, head-on, and focuses on everything you need to do *before* you get your images open in Photoshop.

Teach a Man to Fish

The old saw goes, "Give a man a fish, and you give him a meal; teach a man to fish, and you give him a living." By that reckoning, my goal is to make you, gentle reader, a marine biologist—teaching you not only how to fish, but also to understand fish, how they think, where they hang out, and how to predict their behavior.

Digital photography holds immense promise, but if you're on a deadline and suddenly find that all your raw images are mysteriously being processed at camera default settings rather than the carefully optimized ones you've applied, or your images insist on displaying in order of file name rather than the custom sort order you spent an hour constructing, you can easily be forgiven for contemplating a return to rush processing at your friendly local lab and sorting on a light table with a grease pencil.

My hope is that you'll turn to this book instead.

You Are the Lab

One of the best things about shooting raw is the freedom it confers in imposing your preferred interpretation on your images. The concomitant downside is that if you don't impose your preferred interpretation on the images, you'll have to settle for one imposed by some admittedly clever software that is nonetheless a glorified adding machine with no knowledge of tone and color, let alone composition, aesthetics, or emotion.

With raw capture, you have total control, and hence total responsibility. A great many photographers wind up converting all their raw images at default settings and then try to fix everything in Photoshop, because Photoshop is something they know and understand. You'd be hard pressed to find a bigger Photoshop fan than I am—I've been living and breathing Photoshop for over a dozen years—but the fact is that Camera Raw allows you to do things that simply cannot be replicated in Photoshop. If you don't use Camera Raw to optimize your exposure and color balance, you'll wind up doing a lot more work in Photoshop than you need to, and the quality of the results will almost certainly be less than you'd obtain by starting from an optimized raw conversion rather than a default one.

Drowning in Data

If you had to edit every single image by hand, whether in Photoshop or in Camera Raw, you'd quickly find that digital is neither faster nor cheaper than film. A day's shoot may produce six or seven gigabytes of image data, and it all has to get from the camera to the computer before you can even start making your initial selects. Building an efficient workflow is critical if you want to make the digital revolution survivable, let alone enjoyable. So just about every chapter in this book contains key advice on building a workflow that lets you work smarter rather than harder.

Making Images Smarter

We're already living science fiction, and the future arrived quite a while ago. One of the most-overlooked aspects of digital imaging is the opportunities offered by metadata. Your camera already embeds a great deal of potentially useful information in the image—the date and time of shooting, the ISO speed, the exposure and aperture settings, the focal length, and so on—but the File Browser makes it easy to enrich your images still further with keywords and other useful metadata and lets you protect your intellectual property by embedding copyright and rights management.

Metadata is a means of adding value to your images. Camera metadata provides unambiguous image provenance, while keywords make it much likelier that your images will be selected by clients you've yet to meet. An image with no metadata is simply a collection of pixels, while an image that has been enriched by metadata is a digital asset that can keep earning for a lifetime.

Starting Out Right

The reason for doing a lot of work in Camera Raw and the File Browser is simple. If you do the work correctly right at the start of the workflow, you never have to do it again later. When you attach your preferred Camera Raw setting to a raw image, those settings will be used every time you open that raw image, with no further work required on your part. And any metadata you apply to the raw image will automatically be embedded in every converted image you create from that raw image unless you take steps to remove it (and yes, I'll show you how to do that too). Not only do you only have to do the work once, you greatly reduce the likelihood that it will be undone later.

Understanding and Hubris

It took a great deal of nerve for me to write this book. I confess to being the world's worst photographer, and it takes a certain amount of hubris for me to advise photographers who are hugely more skilled than I am on how to ply their trade. But I've been lucky enough to enjoy a close and fruitful relationship with the wonderful group of people who have made Photoshop the incredibly powerful tool it has become, and in the process I've had the opportunity to look longer and deeper at its inner workings than most people who use it to earn their livelihood.

Some of those inner workings are probably what my friend and colleague Fred Bunting likes to term "more interesting than relevant," but others—such as where and how your ranking or flagging information, your hand-tuned image settings, and your color-correct previews get stored—are pieces of vital information for anyone who entrusts their work to the tools discussed by this book. If conveying that information helps much better photographers than I to realize their vision, I consider the effort worthwhile.

How the Book Is Organized

A significant problem I faced in writing this book is that everything in the workflow affects everything else in the workflow, so some circularity is inherent.

That said, I've tried to impose some order. The first three chapters look at images one at a time. Chapter 1, *Digital Camera Raw*, looks at the fundamental nature of raw images—what they are, and the advantages and pitfalls of shooting them. Chapter 2, *How Camera Raw Works*, looks at the specific advantages that Camera Raw offers over other raw converters. In Chapter 3, *Using Camera Raw*, I look in depth at Camera Raw's controls and how to use them to get the best out of your raw captures.

But working photographers need to deal with not one, but hundreds if not thousands of images at a time, so the remainder of the book is devoted to handling images in quantity. Chapter 4, *The File Browser*, introduces you to your virtual digital light table, explains its component parts, and describes its functionality. Chapter 5, *It's All About the Workflow*, explains how to use the features described in Chapter 4 to process large collections of images quickly and efficiently, as well as showing you how to trouble-shoot should problems arise. Chapter 6, *Understanding Metadata*, looks at the inner workings of the various metadata schemes used by Camera Raw and the File Browser and shows you how to make them work for you. Finally, Chapter 7, *Exploiting Automation*, show you how to leverage the work done in Camera Raw and the File Browser to produce converted images that require minimal work in Photoshop and contain the metadata you want them to.

A Word to Windows Users

This book applies to both Windows and Macintosh. But I've been using Macs for 20 years, so all the dialog boxes, menus, and palettes are illustrated using screen shots from the Macintosh version. Similarly, when discussing the many keyboard shortcuts in the program, I cite the Macintosh versions. In almost every case, the Command key translates to the Ctrl key and the Option key translates to the Alt key. In the very few exceptions to this rule, I've spelled out both the Macintosh and the Windows versions explicitly. I apologize to all you Windows users for the small inconvenience, but because Photoshop is so close to being identical on both platforms, I picked the one I know and ran with it.

Thank You!

I owe thanks to the many people who made this book possible. My first vote of thanks must go to Thomas Knoll, first for creating Photoshop, second for building Camera Raw, and third for taking the time to provide feedback on the chapters while they were under construction and for preventing me from making a number of egregious errors. Thanks also go to my other peer reviewers. Russell Preston Brown not only provided his unique insight but came up with the idea of doing this book in the first place. Jeff Schewe patiently pointed out and then did his best to fill the gaps in my understanding of photography, and called me on explanations that made no sense. Any errors or inadequacies that remain in the book are despite their best efforts and are solely my responsibility.

Rebecca Gulick, my editor at Peachpit Press, kept me on track and made me meet my deadlines, with patience and grace; production coordinator Hilal Sala and my other friends at Peachpit turned my virtual creation into a manufactured reality. Tiffany Taylor painstakingly combed the manuscript for typos and inconsistencies, and uncovered an embarrassingly large number of them. Those that may remain are entirely my fault. Caroline Parks provided the comprehensive index to make sure that everyone can find the information they need.

This book would be a much weaker effort without the generosity of the great photographers who contributed their images. To Jim Caulfield, Peter Fox, Greg Gorman, Jay Maisel, Eric Meola, Seth Resnick, Jack Reznicki, Jeff Schewe, David Stoecklein, Michel Tcherevkoff, and Art Wolfe, my thanks and my respect.

Special thanks go to Stephen Johnson and Michael Kieran for being great human beings and even better friends—you contributed to this book in more ways than you know.

Last but by no stretch of the imagination least, I must thank my lovely wife, Angela, not only for putting up with the insane hours, the abstracted gazes, and the glassy incomprehension that greeted perfectly sensible questions like "have you fed the cat?"—but also for making my life such a very happy one.

Bruce Fraser
San Francisco, June 2004

1

Digital Camera Raw

Exploiting the Digital Negative

Perhaps the greatest challenge that faces shooters who have made, or are in the process of making, the transition to digital is just dealing with the gigabytes of captured data. You can make some gross judgments about the image from a camera's on-board LCD display; but to separate the hero images from the junk, you have to copy the images from the camera media to a computer with a decent display, which is less convenient and more challenging than getting rush-processed chromes back from the lab and sorting them on the light table.

Digital raw files present a further bottleneck, since they require processing before you can even see a color image. This book tells you how to deal with raw images quickly and efficiently, so that you can exploit the very real advantages of raw capture over JPEG, yet still have time to have a life. The key is in unlocking the full power of three vital features in Adobe Photoshop CS—the Adobe Camera Raw plug-in, the File Browser, and Photoshop actions. Together, these three features can help you build an efficient workflow based on raw captures, from making the initial selects, through rough editing for client approval, to final processing of selected images.

In this first chapter, though, we'll focus on raw captures themselves, their fundamental nature, their advantages, and their limitations. So the first order of business is to understand just what a raw capture is.

What Is a Digital Raw File?

Fundamentally, a digital raw file is a record of the raw sensor data from the camera, accompanied by some camera-generated *metadata* (literally, data about data). I'll discuss metadata in great detail in Chapter 6, *Metadata*, but for now, all you need to know is that the camera metadata supplies information about the way the image was captured, including ISO setting, shutter speed and aperture value, white balance setting, and so on.

Different camera vendors may encode the raw data in different ways, apply various compression strategies, and in some cases even apply encryption, so it's important to realize that "digital camera raw" isn't a single file format. Rather, it's a catch-all term that encompasses Canon .CRW, Minolta .MRW, Nikon .NEF, Olympus .ORF, and all the other raw formats on the ever-growing list that's readable by Adobe Camera Raw. But all the various flavors of raw files share the same basic properties and offer the same basic advantages. To understand these, you need to know a little something about how digital cameras work.

The Camera Sensor

A raw file is a record of the sensor data, so let's look at what the sensor in a digital camera actually captures. A number of different technologies get lumped into the category of "digital camera," but virtually all the cameras supported by the Camera Raw plug-in are of the type known as "mosaic sensor" or "color filter array" cameras ("virtually all" because versions 2.2 and later of Camera Raw also support the Sigma cameras based on Foveon's X3 technology—see "The Foveon X3 Difference," later in this chapter). The first key point is that striped-array raw files are grayscale!

Color filter array cameras use a two-dimensional area array to collect the photons that are recorded in the image. The array is made up of rows and columns of photosensitive detectors—typically using either CCD (charge-coupled device) or CMOS (complementary metal oxide semiconductor) technology—to form the image. In a typical setup, each element of the array contributes one pixel to the final image (see Figure 1-1).

Figure 1-1
An area array

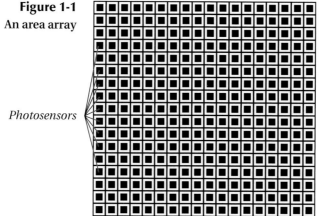

Photosensors

Each photosensor contributes one pixel to the image.

But the sensors in the array, whether CCD or CMOS, just count photons—they produce a charge proportional to the amount of light they receive—without recording any color information. The color information is produced by color filters that are applied over the individual elements in the array in a process known as "striping"—hence the term "striped array." Most cameras use a Bayer pattern arrangement for the color filter array, alternating green, red, green, blue filters on each consecutive element, with twice as many green as red and blue filters (because our eyes are most sensitive in the green region). See Figure 1-2.

Figure 1-2
Bayer pattern

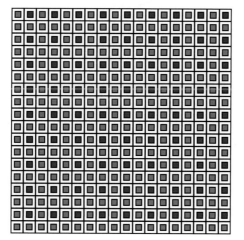

In a Bayer Pattern color filter array, each photosensor is filtered so that it captures only a single color of light: red, green, or blue. Twice as many green filters are used as red or blue because our eyes are most sensitive to green light.

Other color filter array configurations are possible—some cameras use a cyan, magenta, yellow arrangement instead of the GRGB configuration in the classic Bayer pattern, while still others may use four colors in an attempt to improve color fidelity. But unless you plan on designing your own cameras, you needn't worry about the details of this or that filter setup.

Raw Files Are Grayscale

No matter what the filter arrangement, the raw file simply records the luminance value for each pixel, so the raw file is a grayscale image. It contains color *information*—the characteristics of the color filter array are recorded, so raw converters know whether a given pixel in the raw file represents red, green, or blue luminance (or whatever colors the specific camera's filter array uses)—but it doesn't contain anything humans can interpret as color.

Obtaining a color image from the raw file is the job of a raw converter such as Camera Raw. The raw converter interpolates the missing color information for each pixel from its neighbors, a process known as *demosaicing*, but it does much more, too. Besides interpolating the missing color information, raw converters control all of the following.

▶ **White balance.** The white balance indicates the color of the light under which the image was captured. Our eyes automatically adapt to different lighting situations—to oversimplify slightly, we interpret the brightest thing in the scene as white, and judge all the other colors accordingly. Cameras—whether film or digital—have no such adaptation mechanism, as anyone who has shot tungsten film in daylight has learned the hard way, so digital cameras let us set a white balance to record the color of the light.

But the on-camera white balance setting has no effect on the raw capture. It's saved as a metadata tag, and applied by the raw converter as part of the conversion process.

▶ **Colorimetric interpretation.** Each pixel in the raw file records a luminance value for either red, green, or blue. But "red," "green," and "blue" are pretty vague terms. Take a hundred people and ask them to visualize "red." If you could read their minds, you'd almost certainly see a hundred different shades of red.

Many different filter sets are in use with digital cameras. So the raw converter has to assign the correct, specific color meanings to the "red," "green," and "blue" pixels, usually in a colorimetrically defined color space such as CIE XYZ, which is based directly on human color perception.

▶ **Gamma correction.** Digital raw captures have linear gamma (gamma 1.0), a very different tonal response from that of either film or the human eye. So the raw converter applies gamma correction to redistribute the tonal information so that it corresponds more closely to the way our eyes see light and shade. I discuss the implications of linear gamma on exposure in the sidebar, "Exposure and Linear Gamma," later in this chapter.

▶ **Noise reduction, antialiasing, and sharpening.** When the detail in an image gets down to the size of individual pixels, problems can arise. If the detail is only captured on a red-sensing pixel or a blue-sensing pixel, its actual color can be difficult to determine. Simple demosaicing methods also don't do a great job of maintaining edge detail, so raw converters perform some combination of edge-detection, antialiasing to avoid color artifacts, noise reduction, and sharpening.

All raw converters perform each of these tasks, but each one may use different algorithms to do so, which is why the same image can appear quite different when processed through different raw converters.

The Foveon X3 Difference

Foveon X3 technology, embodied in the Sigma SD-9 and SD-10 SLR cameras, is fundamentally different from striped-array cameras.

The Foveon X3 direct image sensor captures color by exploiting the fact that blue light waves are shorter than green light waves, which in turn are shorter than red ones. It uses three layers of photosensors on the same chip.

The front layer captures the short blue waves, the middle layer captures the green waves, while only the longest red waves penetrate all the way to the third layer, which captures red.

The key benefit claimed by the X3 sensor is that it captures full color data, red, green, and blue, for every pixel in the image. As a result, .X3F files—Foveon X3 raws—don't require demosaicing. But they do need all the other operations a raw converter carries out—white balance, colorimetric interpretation, gamma correction, and detail control—so Camera Raw is as applicable to files from Foveon X3-equipped cameras as it is to those from the more common striped array cameras.

Exposure and Linear Gamma

One final topic is key to understanding digital capture in general, not just digital raw. Digital sensors, whether CCD or CMOS, respond to light quite differently than does either the human eye or film. Most human perception, including vision, is nonlinear.

If we place a golf ball in the palm of our hand, then add another one, it doesn't feel twice as heavy. If we put two spoonfuls of sugar in our coffee instead of one, it doesn't taste twice as sweet. If we double the acoustic power going to our stereo speakers, the resulting sound isn't twice as loud. And if we double the number of photons reaching our eyes, we don't see the scene as twice as bright—brighter, yes, but not twice as bright.

count photons in a linear fashion. If a camera uses 12 bits to encode the capture, producing 4,096 levels, then level 2,048 represents half the number of photons recorded at level 4,096. This is the meaning of linear gamma—the levels correspond exactly to the number of photons captured.

Linear capture has important implications for exposure. If a camera captures six stops of dynamic range, half of the 4,096 levels are devoted to the brightest stop, half of the remainder (1,024 levels) are devoted to the next stop, half of the remainder (512 levels are devoted to the next stop, and so on. The darkest stop, the extreme shadows, is represented by only 64 levels—see Figure 1-3.

rect exposure in the digital realm means keeping the highlights as close to blowing out, without actually doing so, as possible.

In this regard, it's worth emphasizing that the on-camera histogram shows the histogram of the conversion to JPEG: a raw histogram would be a rather strange-looking beast, with all the data clumped at the shadow end, so cameras show the histogram of the image after processing using the camera's default settings. Most cameras apply a fairly strong S-curve to the raw data so that the JPEGs have a more film-like response, with the result that the on-camera histogram often tells you that your highlights are blown when in fact they aren't.

Figure 1-3   Linear gamma

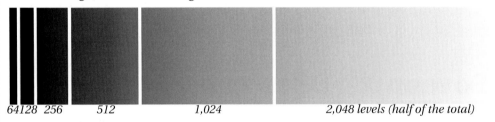

64 128 256   512   1,024   2,048 *levels (half of the total)*

This built-in compression lets us function in a wide range of situations without driving our sensory mechanisms into overload—we can go from subdued room lighting to full daylight without our eyeballs catching fire! But the sensors in digital cameras lack the compressive nonlinearity typical of human perception. They just

It may seem tempting to underexpose images to avoid blowing out the highlights, but if you do, you're wasting a lot of the bits the camera can capture, and you'll run a significant risk of introducing noise in the midtones and shadows. Correct exposure is at least as important with digital capture as it is with film, but cor-

The response of a camera set to ISO 100 may be more like ISO 125 or even ISO 150 (or, for that matter, ISO 75). It's well worth spending some time determining your camera's real sensitivity at different speeds, then dialing in an appropriate exposure compensation to make sure that you're making the best use of the available bits.

Why Shoot Raw?

The answer to the above question is simply, control over the interpretation of the image. When you shoot JPEG, the camera's on-board software carries out all the tasks listed earlier to produce a color image, then compresses it using JPEG compression. Some cameras let you set parameters for this conversion—typically, a choice of sRGB or Adobe RGB as color space, a sharpness value, and perhaps a tone curve or contrast setting—but unless your shooting schedule is atypically leisurely, you probably can't adjust these parameters on an image-by-image basis, so you're locked into the camera's interpretation of the scene. JPEGs offer fairly limited editing headroom—large moves to tone and color tend to exaggerate the 8-by-8-pixel blocks that form the foundation of JPEG compression—and while JPEG does a pretty good job of preserving luminance data, it really clobbers the color, leading to problems with skin tones and gentle gradations.

When you shoot raw, however, *you* get to control the scene interpretation through all the aforementioned aspects of the conversion. With raw, the *only* on-camera settings that have an effect on the captured pixels are the ISO speed, shutter speed, and aperture. Everything else is under your control when you convert the raw file. You can reinterpret the white balance, the colorimetric rendering, the tonal response, and the detail rendition (sharpening and noise reduction) with a great deal of freedom, and, within limits, you can even reinterpret the exposure compensation (see the sidebar, "Exposure and Linear Gamma").

Using All the Bits

Most of today's cameras capture at least 12 bits per channel per pixel, for a possible 4,096 levels in each channel. More bits translates directly into editing headroom, but the JPEG format is limited to 8 bits per channel per pixel: So when you shoot JPEG, you trust the camera's built-in conversions to throw away one-third of your data in a way that does justice to the image.

When you shoot raw, though, you have, by definition, captured everything the camera can deliver, so you have considerably more freedom in shaping the overall tone and contrast for the image. You also produce a file that can withstand a great deal more editing in Photoshop than can an 8-bit per channel JPEG.

Edits in Photoshop are "destructive"—when you use a tool such as Levels, Curves, Hue/Saturation, or Color Balance, you change the actual pixel values, creating the potential for either or both of two problems.

▶ Posterization can occur when you stretch a tonal range. Where the levels were formerly adjacent, they're now stretched apart, so instead of a gradation from, for example, level 100 through 101, 102, 103, 104, to 105, the new values may look more like 98, 101, 103, 105, 107. On its own, such an edit is unlikely to produce visible posterization— it usually takes a gap of four or five levels before you see a visible jump instead of a smooth gradation—but subsequent edits can widen the gaps, inducing posterization.

▶ Detail loss can occur when you compress a tonal range. Where the levels were formerly different, they're now compressed into the same value, so the differences, which represent potential detail, are tossed irrevocably into the bit-bucket, never to return.

Figure 1-4 shows how the compression and expansion of tonal ranges can affect pixel values. Don't be overly afraid of losing levels—it's a normal and necessary part of image editing, and its effect can be greatly reduced by bringing images into Photoshop as 16-bit/channel files rather than 8-bit/channel ones—but simply be aware of the destructive potential of Photoshop edits.

White Balance Control

I'll go into much more detail on how Camera Raw's white balance controls actually work in Chapter 2, *How Camera Raw Works*. For now, I want to make the key point that adjusting the white balance on a raw file is fundamentally different from attempting to do so on an already-rendered image in Photoshop.

As Figure 1-4 shows, Photoshop edits are inherently destructive— you wind up with fewer levels than you started out with. But when you change the white balance as part of the raw conversion process, the edit is much less destructive, because instead of changing pixel values by applying curves, you're gently scaling one or two channels to match the third. There may be very few free lunches in this world, but white balance control in Camera Raw is a great deal cheaper, in terms of losing data, than anything you can do to the processed image in Photoshop.

Figure 1-4
Destructive editing

This tonal range is
being expanded...

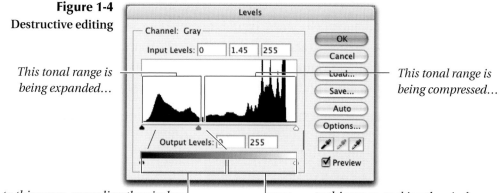

This tonal range is
being compressed...

...to this range, spreading the pixels
out and making them more different,
so detail is more apparent.

...to this range, making the pixels more
similar (and in some cases, identical), so
detail is less visible or completely lost.

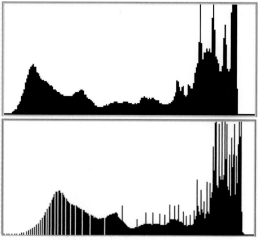

Before-and-after histograms show the loss of levels. The top histogram shows
the state of the unedited image; the bottom one shows the state of the image
after editing. The gaps indicate lost levels where the tonal range was stretched,
and the spikes indicate lost differences where the tonal range was compressed.

Colorimetric Interpretation

When you shoot JPEG, you typically have a choice between capturing images in either sRGB or Adobe RGB (1998). Yet the vast majority of today's cameras can capture colors that lie outside the gamut of either of these spaces, especially in the case of saturated yellows and cyans, and those colors get clipped when you convert to sRGB or Adobe RGB.

Raw converters vary in their ability to render images into different color spaces, but Adobe Camera Raw offers four possible destinations. One of these, ProPhoto RGB, encompasses all colors we can capture, and the vast majority of colors we can see—if you see color clipping on a conversion to ProPhoto RGB, you're capturing something other than visible light!

Figure 1-5 shows a quite unexceptional image rendered to ProPhoto RGB, and plotted against the gamuts of sRGB and Adobe RGB. Notice just how much of the captured color lies outside the gamut of both spaces.

Figure 1-5
Color spaces and clipping

The gamut plots below, produced using Chromix ColorThink, plot color in Lab space. You're looking at a side elevation of the color space, with the Lightness axis running vertically. The a* axis, from red to green, runs almost straight toward you out of the page; the b* axis, from blue to yellow, runs from left to right.

Even an innocuous image like the one at right can contain colors that lie well outside the range that either Adobe RGB (1998) or sRGB can represent.

The image above plotted (as squares) against the color gamut of Adobe RGB (1998) (shaded solid)

These dark yellows and oranges lie outside the gamut of Adobe RGB (1998) or sRGB

The image above plotted (as squares) against the color gamut of sRGB (shaded solid)/

Exposure

As with white balance adjustments, exposure adjustments performed as part of the raw conversion are lossless (unless you clip highlights to white or shadows to black), unlike tonal adjustments made in Photoshop on the rendered image (see Figure 1-3). In practice, however, you have somewhat less freedom to adjust exposure than you do white balance.

The main limitation on exposure adjustments is that when you try to open up significantly underexposed images, you'll probably see noise or posterization in the shadows. It's not that the edit is destructive—you just didn't capture enough shadow information in the first place.

Completely blown highlights are also beyond recovery, but Camera Raw goes a good bit further than other raw converters in rescuing highlight detail even when only one channel contains data. Depending on the camera and the white balance chosen, you may be able to recover up to one stop of highlight detail. Nevertheless, good exposure is still highly desirable—see the sidebar, "Exposure and Linear Gamma," earlier in this chapter.

Detail and Noise

When you shoot JPEG, the sharpening and noise reduction are set by the on-camera settings (most cameras let you make a setting for sharpness, but few do for noise reduction). When you shoot raw, you have control over both sharpening and noise reduction—Camera Raw even lets you handle luminance noise and color noise separately.

This confers several advantages. You can tailor the noise reduction to different ISO speeds, apply quick global sharpening for rough versions of images, or convert images with no sharpening at all so that you can apply more nuanced localized sharpening to the rendered image in Photoshop.

Raw Limitations

While raw offers significant advantages over JPEG, it also has some limitations. For the majority of work, I believe that the advantages outweigh the disadvantages, but I'd be remiss if I didn't point out the downsides. So in the interests of full disclosure, let's look at the limitations of raw.

Processing Time

Perhaps the biggest limitation is also the main strength of raw files—you gain a huge amount of control in the conversion process, but you have to take the time to process the raw file to obtain an image. Camera Raw lets you convert raw images very efficiently, particularly once you learn to use it in conjunction with Photoshop's automation features, but each image still takes some time—a few seconds—to process.

If you digest and implement all the techniques, tips, and tricks offered in this book, you'll find that the bulk of the time spent on raw conversions is computer time—you can set up batch conversions and go do something more interesting while the computer crunches the images. But any way you slice it, raw files aren't as immediately available as JPEGs, and they require one more step in the workflow.

File Size

Raw files are larger than JPEGs—typically somewhere between two and four times as large. Storage is cheap and getting cheaper every year, but if you need to fit the maximum number of images on a camera's storage card, or you need to transmit images as quickly as possible over a network or the Web, the larger size of raw files may be an issue.

In most cases, a modicum of planning makes file size a non-issue—just make sure you have enough storage cards, and leave yourself enough time for file transmission.

Tip: Two small cards are better than one large one. High-capacity Compact Flash cards command premium prices compared to lower-capacity ones—a 4GB card costs more than double the price of a 2GB one, which in turn costs more than double the price of a 1GB one. But using two smaller cards rather than one bigger one lets you hand off the first card to an assistant who can then start copying the files to the computer, archiving them, and perhaps even doing rough processing, while you continue to shoot with the second card. Multiple smaller, cheaper cards give you much more flexibility than one big one.

Longevity

There's one other issue with raw files. Currently, many camera vendors use proprietary formats for raw files, raising a concern about their long-term readability. Hardware manufacturers don't have the best track record when it comes to producing updated software for old hardware—I have cupboards full of ancient orphaned weird junk to prove it—so it's entirely legitimate to raise the question of how someone will be able to read the raw files you capture today in 10 or 100 years time.

I don't have a crystal ball, but Adobe's commitment to making Camera Raw a universal converter for raw images is clear. At the same time, it's no secret that some camera vendors are less than supportive of Adobe's efforts in this regard. If you're concerned about long-term support for your raw files, you need to make your camera vendor aware of the fact. You can also support any initiatives to produce an open, documented file format for raw captures, and, if necessary, use your wallet to vote against vendors who resist such initiatives.

Adobe Camera Raw

If you've read this far, I hope I've convinced you of the benefits of shooting raw. In the remainder of this chapter, let's examine the reasons for making Adobe Camera Raw the raw converter of choice.

Universal Converter

Unlike the raw converters supplied by the camera vendors, Camera Raw doesn't limit its support to a single brand of camera. Adobe has made a commitment to add support for new cameras on a regular basis, and so far, they seem to be doing a good job. So even if you shoot with multiple cameras from different vendors or add new cameras regularly, you have to learn only one user interface and only one set of controls. This translates directly into savings of that most precious commodity, time.

Industrial-strength Features

Camera Raw is one of the most full featured raw converters in existence. It offers fine control over white balance, exposure, noise reduction, and sharpness, but unlike most other raw converters, it also has controls for eliminating chromatic aberration (digital capture is brutal at revealing lens flaws that film masks) and for fine-tuning the color response for individual camera models.

Thanks to the magic of metadata, Camera Raw can identify the specific camera model on which an image was captured. You can create Calibration settings for each camera model, which Camera Raw then applies automatically. Of course, you can also customize all the other Camera Raw settings and save them as Camera Defaults—so each camera model can have its own set of custom settings.

Integration with Photoshop

As soon as you point Photoshop's File Browser at a folder full of raw images, Camera Raw goes straight to work, generating thumbnails and previews so that you can make your initial selects quickly.

The File Browser's automation features let you apply custom settings on a per-image basis, then batch-convert images to Web galleries, PDF presentations, or virtual contact sheets. And when it's time to do serious manual editing on selected images, Camera Raw delivers them right into Photoshop, where you need them.

The Digital Negative

If you've digested this chapter, you'll doubtless have concluded that, like most analogies, the one that equates digital raw with film negative isn't perfect—raw capture doesn't offer the kind of exposure latitude we expect from negative film. But in a great many other respects, it holds true.

Both offer a means for capturing an unrendered image, providing a great deal of freedom in how you render that image post-capture. Both allow you to experiment and produce many different renderings of the same image, while leaving the actual capture unchanged.

In the next chapter, *How Camera Raw Works*, we'll look at some of the technological underpinnings of Camera Raw. If you're the impatient type who just wants to jump in with both feet, feel free to skip ahead to Chapter 3, *Using Camera Raw Controls*, where you'll learn how to use the various buttons and sliders to interpret your images. But if you want to understand *why* these buttons and sliders work the way they do, and why you should use them rather than try to fix everything in Photoshop, it's worth setting aside part of a rainy afternoon to understanding just what Camera Raw actually does.

2 How Camera Raw Works

What Lies Under the Hood

Despite the title of this chapter, I promise to keep it equation-free and relatively non-technical. Camera Raw offers functionality that at a casual glance may seem to replicate that of Photoshop. But some operations are much better carried out in Camera Raw, while with others, the choice between making the edits in Camera Raw and in Photoshop may be as much about workflow and convenience as it is about quality.

To understand which ones are which, it helps to know a little about how Camera Raw performs its magic. If you're the type who would rather learn by doing, feel free to skip ahead to the next chapter, where you'll be introduced to the nitty-gritty of actually using all the controls in Camera Raw; but if you take the time to digest the contents of this chapter, you'll have a much better idea of what the controls actually do, and hence a better understanding of how and when to use them.

To use Camera Raw effectively, you must first realize that computers and software applications like Photoshop and Camera Raw don't know anything about tone, color, truth, beauty, or art. They're really just glorified and incredibly ingenious adding machines that juggle ones and zeroes to order. I won't go into the intricacies of binary math except to note that there are 10 kinds of people in this world, those who understand binary math and those who don't! You don't need to learn to count in binary or hexadecimal, but you do need to understand some basic stuff about how numbers can represent tone and color.

15

Digital Image Anatomy

Digital images are made up of numbers. The fundamental particle of a digital image is the pixel—the number of pixels you capture determines the image's size and aspect ratio. It's tempting to use the term *resolution*, but doing so often confuses matters more than it clarifies them. Why?

Pixels and Resolution

Strictly speaking, a digital image in its pure Platonic form doesn't have resolution—it simply has pixel dimensions. It only attains the attribute of resolution when we realize it in some physical form—displaying it on a monitor, or making a print. But resolution isn't a fixed attribute.

If we take as an example a typical six-megapixel image, it has the invariant property of pixel dimensions, specifically, 3,072 pixels on the long side of the image, 2,048 pixels on the short one. But we can display and print those pixels at many different sizes. Normally, we want to keep the pixels small enough that they don't become visually obvious, so the pixel dimensions essentially dictate how large a print we can make from the image. As we make larger and larger prints, the pixels become more and more visually obvious until we reach a size at which it just isn't rewarding to print.

Just as it's possible to make a 40-by-60 inch print from a 35mm color neg, it's possible to make a 40-by-60 inch print from a six-megapixel image, but neither of them is likely to look very good. With the 35mm film, you end up with grain the size of golf balls, and with the digital capture, each pixel winds up being just under $1/50^{th}$ of an inch square—big enough to be obvious.

Different printing processes have different resolution requirements, but in general, you need not less than 100 pixels per inch, and rarely more than 360 pixels per inch to make a decent print. So the effective size range of our six-megapixel capture is roughly from 20 by 30 inches downward, and 20 by 30 is really pushing the limits. The basic lesson is that you can print the same collection of pixels at many different sizes, and as you do so, the resolution—the number of pixels per inch—changes, but the number of pixels does not. At 100 pixels per inch, our 3072-by-2048 pixel image will yield a 30.72-by-20.48 inch print. At 300 pixels per inch, the same image will make a 10.24-by-6.83 inch print. So resolution is a fungible quality—you can spread the same pixels over a smaller or larger area.

To find out how big an image you can produce at a specific resolution, divide the pixel dimensions by the resolution. Using pixels per inch (ppi) as the resolution unit and inches as the size unit, if you divide 3,072 (the long pixel dimension) by 300, you obtain the answer 10.24 inches for the long dimension and if you divide 2,048 (the short pixel dimension) by the same quantity, you get 6.826 inches for the short dimension. At 240 ppi, you get 12.8 by 8.53 inches. Conversely, to determine the resolution you have available to print at a given size, divide the pixel dimensions by the size, in inches. The result is the resolution in pixels per inch. For example, if you want to make a 10-by-15 inch print from your six-megapixel, 3,072-by 2,048 pixel image, divide the long pixel dimension by the long dimension in inches, or the short pixel dimension by the short dimension in inches. In either case, you'll get the same answer, 204.8 pixels per inch.

Figure 2-1 shows the same pixels printed at 50 pixels per inch, 150 pixels per inch, and 300 pixels per inch.

Figure 2-1
Image size and resolution

50 ppi   *150 ppi*   *300 ppi*

But each individual pixel is defined by a set of numbers, and these numbers also impose limitations on what you can do with the image, albeit more subtle limitations than those dictated by the pixel dimensions.

Bit Depth, Dynamic Range, and Color

We use numbers to represent a pixel's tonal value—how light or dark it is—and its color—red, green, blue, yellow, or any of the myriad gradations of the various rainbow hues we can see.

Bit Depth. In a grayscale image, each pixel is represented by some number of bits. Photoshop's 8-bit/channel mode uses 8 bits to represent each pixel, and its 16-bit/channel mode uses 16 bits to represent each pixel. An 8-bit pixel can have any one of 256 possible tonal values, from 0 (black) to 255 (white), or any of the 254 intermediate shades of gray. A 16-bit pixel can have any one of 32,769 possible tonal values, from 0 (black) to 32,768 (white), or any of the 32,767 intermediate shades of gray. If you're wondering why 16 bits in Photoshop gives you 32,769 shades instead of 65,536, see the sidebar "High-Bit Photoshop," later in this chapter (if you don't care, skip it). So while pixel dimensions describe the two-dimensional height and width of the image, the bits that describe the pixels produce a third dimension that describes how light or dark each pixel is—hence the term *bit depth*.

Dynamic Range. Some vendors try to equate bit depth with dynamic range. This is largely a marketing ploy, because while there *is* a relationship between bit depth and dynamic range, it's an indirect one. Dynamic range in digital cameras is an analog limitation of the sensor.

The brightest shade the camera can capture is limited by the point at which the current generated by a sensor element starts spilling over to its neighbors—a condition often called "blooming"—and produces a featureless white blob. The darkest shade a camera can capture is determined by the more subjective point at which the noise inherent in the system overwhelms the very weak signal generated by the small number of photons that hit the sensor—the subjectivity lies in the fact that some people can tolerate a noisier signal than others.

One way to think of the difference between bit depth and dynamic range is to imagine a staircase. The dynamic range is the height of the staircase. The bit depth is the number of steps in the staircase. If we want our staircase to be reasonably easy to climb, or if we want to preserve the illusion of a continuous gradation of tone in our images, we need more steps in a taller staircase than we do in a shorter one, and we need more bits to describe a wider dynamic range than a narrower one. But more bits, or a larger number of smaller steps, doesn't increase the dynamic range, or the height of the staircase.

High-Bit Photoshop

If an 8-bit channel consists of 256 levels, a 10-bit channel consists of 1,024 levels, and a 12-bit channel consists of 4,096 levels, doesn't it follow that a 16-bit channel should consist of 65,536 levels?

Well, that's certainly one way that a 16-bit channel could be constructed, but it's not the way Photoshop does it. Photoshop's implementation of 16 bits per channel uses 32,769 levels, from 0 (black) to 32,768 (white). The advantage of this approach is that it provides an unambiguous midpoint between white and black, useful in many imaging operations, that a channel comprising 65,536 levels lacks.

To those who would claim that Photoshop's 16-bit color is really more like 15-bit color, I simply point out that it takes 16 bits to represent, and by the time capture devices that can actually capture more than 32,769 levels are at all common, we'll all have moved on to something like 32-bit floating point channels rather than 16-bit integer ones.

Color. RGB color images comprise three 8-bit or 16-bit grayscale images, or *channels*, one representing shades of red, the second representing shades of green, and the third representing shades of blue. Red, green, and blue are the primary colors of light, and combining them in different proportions allows us to create any color we can see. So an 8-bit/channel RGB image can contain any of 16.7 million unique color definitions (256 x 256 x 256), while a 16-bit/channel image can contain any of some 35 *trillion* unique color definitions.

Either of these may sound like a heck of a lot of colors, and indeed, they are. Estimates of how many unique colors the human eye can distinguish vary widely, but even the most liberal estimates are well shy of 16.7 million and nowhere close to 35 trillion. Why then do we need all this data?

We need it for two quite unrelated reasons. The first one, which isn't particularly significant for the purposes of this book, is that 8-bit/channel RGB contains 16.7 million color *definitions*, not 16.7 million perceivable colors. Many of the color definitions are redundant: Even on the very best display, you'd be hard pressed to see the difference between RGB values of 0,0,0 and 0,0,1 or 0,1,0 or 1,0,0, or for that matter between 255,255,255 and 254, 255, 255 or 255, 254, 255 or 255, 255, 254. Depending on the specific flavor of RGB you choose, you'll find similar redundancies in different parts of the available range of tone and color.

The second reason, which is *extremely* significant for the purposes of this book, is that we need to edit our images—particularly our digital raw images, for reasons that will become apparent later—and every edit we make has the effect of reducing the number of unique colors and tone levels in the image. A good understanding of the impact of different types of edits is the best basis for deciding where and how you apply edits to your images.

Gamma

To understand the key difference between shooting film and shooting digital, you need to get your head around the concept of gamma encoding. As I explained in Chapter 1, digital cameras respond to photons quite differently from either film or our eyes. The sensors in digital cameras simply count photons and assign a tonal value in direct proportion to the number of photons detected—they respond linearly to incoming light.

Human eyeballs, however, do not respond linearly to light. Our eyes are much more sensitive to small differences in brightness at low levels than at high ones. Film has traditionally been designed to respond to light approximately the way our eyes do, but digital sensors simply don't work that way.

Gamma encoding is a method of relating the numbers in the image to the perceived brightness they represent. The sensitivity of the camera sensor is described by a gamma of 1.0—it has a linear response to the incoming photons. But this means that the captured values don't correspond to the way humans see light. The relationship between the number of photons that hit our retinas and the sensation of lightness we experience in response is described by a gamma of somewhere between 2.0 and 3.0 depending on viewing conditions. Figure 2-2 shows the approximate difference between what the camera sees and what we see.

Figure 2-2
Digital capture and
human response

How the camera sees light

How the human eye sees light

I promised that I'd keep this chapter equation-free—if you want more information about the equations that define gamma encoding, a Google search on "gamma encoding" will likely turn up more than you ever wanted to know—so I'll simply cut to the chase and point out the practical implications of the linear nature of digital capture.

Digital captures devote a large number of bits to describing differences in highlight intensity to which our eyes are relatively insensitive, and a relatively small number of bits to describing differences in shadow intensity to which our eyes are very sensitive. As you're about to learn, all our image-editing operations have the unfortunate side effect of reducing the number of bits in the image. This is true for all digital images, whether scanned from film, rendered synthetically, or captured with a digital camera, but it has specific implications for digital capture.

With digital captures, darkening is a much safer operation than lightening, since darkening forces more bits into the shadows, where our eyes are sensitive, while lightening takes the relatively small number of captured bits that describe the shadow information and spreads them across a wider tonal range, exaggerating noise and increasing the likelihood of posterization. With digital, you need to turn the old rule upside down—you need to expose for the highlights, and develop for the shadows!

Image Editing and Image Degradation

Just about anything you do to change the tone or color of pixels results in some kind of data loss. If this sounds scary, rest assured that it's a normal and necessary part of digital imaging. The trick is to make the best use of the available bits you've captured to produce the desired image appearance, while preserving as much of the original data as possible. Why keep as much of the original data as possible if you're going to wind up throwing it away later? Very simply, it's all about keeping your options open.

The fact is, you don't need a huge amount of data to represent an image. But if you want the image to be editable, you need a great deal more data than you do to simply display or print it. Figure 2-3 shows two copies of the same image. They appear very similar visually, but their histograms are very different. One contains a great deal more data than the other.

Figure 2-3
Levels and appearance

 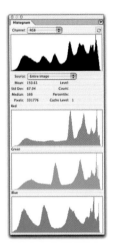

*This image was
produced by making
corrections in Camera
Raw, producing a 16-
bit-per-channel image
in Photoshop.*

 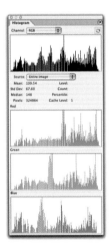

*This image was
produced by converting
at Camera Raw default
settings, producing an
8-bit-per-channel image
that was further edited
in Photoshop.*

*The two images shown above appear quite similar, but the
histograms shown to the right of each image reveal a significant
difference. The lower image contains a great deal less data than
the upper one. Careful examination may reveal subtle differences in hue and detail, but the biggest difference is the amount
of editing headroom each image offers.*

Despite the vast difference in the amount of data they contain, it's hard
to see any significant differences between the two images—you may be
able to see that the one with more data shows more details on the chest
feathers of the top birdie, but it's a pretty subtle difference. Figure 2-4
shows what happens when a fairly gentle curve edit is applied to the images shown in Figure 2-3. The difference is no longer subtle!

Figure 2-4
Levels and editing
headroom

Here you see the images from Figure 2-3 after application of a fairly gentle S-curve (to increase contrast slightly) to both images. The differences between the data-rich (upper) and data-poor (lower) versions are now much more obvious. The data-poor version shows much less detail, and displays some unwanted hue shifts.

The difference between the two images is in the way they were edited. The one with the larger amount of data made full use of Camera Raw to convert the raw file into a 16-bit/channel image in Photoshop. Additional edits were done in 16-bit/channel mode. The one with the smaller amount of data was converted to an 8-bit/channel image at camera default settings, and the edits were performed in 8-bit/channel mode in Photoshop.

Losing Data and Limiting Options

The sad truth is that every edit you make limits the options that are available to you afterward. You can keep many more options open by making full use of Camera Raw controls and by converting to a 16-bit/channel image rather than an 8-bit one. But no matter what you do, edits degrade the data in an image file in three different ways.

Clipping. The black and white input sliders in Photoshop's Levels command and the Exposure and Shadows sliders in Camera Raw are clipping controls. They let you force pixels to pure white (level 255) or solid black (level 0).

Depending on how you use the sliders, you may clip some levels—in fact, it's often desirable to do so. On the highlight end, you normally want to make sure that specular highlights are represented by level 255, so if the image is underexposed, you usually want to take pixels that are darker than level 255 and force them to pure white. But if you go further than that, you may clip some levels—for example, if you have pixels at levels 252, 253, and 254, and you set the white input slider in Levels to level 252, then all the pixels at levels 252, 253, and 254 are forced to 255. Once you make this edit permanent, the differences between those pixels are gone, permanently.

On the shadow end, you often want to clip some levels because typically there's a good deal of noise in the shadows. If everything below level 10 is noise, for example, it makes perfect sense to set the black input slider in Levels to 10, to force everything at level 10 and below to solid black. Again, you lose the distinction between the unedited levels 0 through 10 permanently, but it's not necessarily a bad thing. Figure 2-5 shows how clipping works.

However, if you're used to adjusting clipping in Photoshop's Levels, you'll find that the Exposure and Shadow controls in Camera Raw behave a bit differently from Levels' black and white input sliders, partly because the latter works on linear-gamma data rather than the gamma-corrected data that appears in Photoshop, partly because Camera Raw's Exposure slider can make negative as well as positive moves.

If the camera can capture the entire scene luminance range, as is the case with the image in Figure 2-5, it's usually best to adjust the Exposure and Shadows sliders to near-clipping, leaving a little headroom (unless you actually want to clip to white or black for creative reasons). If the camera can't handle the entire scene luminance range, you'll have to decide whether to hold the highlights or the shadows, and your choice may be dictated by the captured data—if highlights are completely blown, or shadows are completely plugged, there isn't much you can do about it in the raw conversion. See the sidebar "How Much Highlight Detail Can I Recover?" later in this chapter.

Figure 2-5
Black, white, and
saturation clipping

This raw image is under-exposed, but it captures the full luminance range of the scene, with no clipping of highlights or shadows.

highlight clipping

When you increase the Exposure slider value too far, you clip highlight pixels to solid white.

Ideally, you want to adjust the Exposure slider to push the data as far toward the right end of the histogram as possible without actually forcing clipping.

shadow clipping

When you increase the Shadows slider value too far, you clip shadow pixels to solid black.

saturation clipping

In addition to clipping highlights with Exposure or shadows with the Shadows slider, you can force individual channels to clip by adding too much saturation. In this case, increasing the saturation has clipped the blue channel.

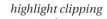

Tonal range compression. When you compress a tonal range, you also lose levels, in a somewhat less obvious way than you do with clipping moves. For example, when you lighten the midtones without moving the white clipping point, the levels between the midtone and the highlight get compressed. As a result, some pixels that were formerly at different levels end up being at the same level, and once you make the edit permanent, you've lost these differences, which may potentially represent detail. See Figure 2-6.

Tonal range expansion. A different type of image degradation occurs when you expand a tonal range. You don't lose any data, but you stretch the data that's there over a broader tonal range, and hence run the danger of losing the illusion of a continuous gradation. Almost everyone who has used Photoshop for more than a week has encountered the experience of pushing edits just a little too far and ending up with banding in the sky or posterization in the shadows. It's simply caused by stretching the data over too broad a range, so that the gaps between the available levels become visibly obvious. See Figure 2-6.

Figure 2-6
Tonal range compression
and expansion

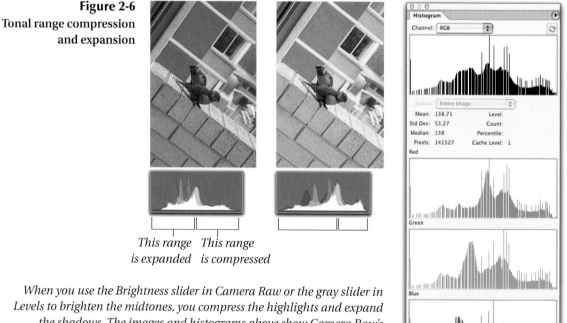

This range   This range
is expanded   is compressed

When you use the Brightness slider in Camera Raw or the gray slider in Levels to brighten the midtones, you compress the highlights and expand the shadows. The images and histograms above show Camera Raw's Brightness control, and the histogram at right shows the results of using the gray input slider in Levels on an 8-bit/channel image. The gaps are from expansion, the spikes from compression.

If all this makes you think that editing images is a recipe for disaster, you've missed the point. You need to edit images to make them look good. Sometimes you *want* to throw away some data—shadow noise being a good example—and the inherent data loss is simply something that comes with the territory. It isn't something to fear, just something of which you should be aware. The importance of the preceding information is that some editing methods allow you more flexibility than others.

Color Space Conversions

One other operation that usually entails all three of the aforementioned types of image degradation is color space conversions. When you convert from a larger gamut to a smaller one, colors present in the source space that are outside the gamut of the destination space get clipped (see Figure 1-5 in the previous chapter for an illustration of gamut clipping).

A significant number of levels also get lost in conversions between spaces with different gammas or tone curves. The bigger the difference between the gammas, the more levels get lost. Figure 2-7 shows what happens when you convert a linear-gamma gradient to a gamma 1.8 working space in both 8-bit/channel and 16-bit/channel modes. Even in 16-bit per channel mode, the shadows get stepped on pretty hard, and in 8-bit per channel mode, about 25 percent of the levels have disappeared.

Figure 2-7
Gamma conversions

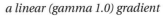

a linear (gamma 1.0) gradient

original data   *16-bit conversion*   *8-bit conversion*
                               to gamma 1.8   *to gamma 1.8*

The Camera Raw Advantage

The reason all this stuff about data loss and image degradation is relevant is that one of the main tasks Camera Raw performs is to convert images from native, linear-gamma camera RGB to a gamma-corrected working space. When you use the controls in Camera Raw, you aren't just editing the pixels you captured, you're also tailoring the conversion. As you saw back in Figures 2-3 and 2-4, it's possible to arrive at the same image appearance with a robust file that contains plenty of data and hence offers plenty of editing headroom, or a very fragile file containing relatively little data that will fall apart under any further editing.

Since the raw conversion is at the beginning of the image-processing pipeline, and the converted images may be subjected to many different color space conversions and many different edits to optimize them for different output processes, you'll save yourself a world of grief if you use Camera Raw's controls to deliver as robust a file as you can muster. If you're skilled in Photoshop, and you avoid exposure problems, you may well be able to arrive at the desired image appearance by converting all your images at camera default settings and doing all the work in Photoshop, but the resulting files will be much more fragile than if you learn to exploit the controls that Camera Raw offers.

From Raw to Color

At long last, we come to the nitty-gritty of the conversion from Camera Raw to gamma-corrected RGB. In the next chapter, *Using Camera Raw Controls*, we'll look at the various ways it makes sense to use the various controls Camera Raw offers. Here, though, we'll look at how they actually apply to the raw conversion.

Demosaicing and Colorimetric Interpretation

The first stage of the process, demosaicing, introduces the color information, turning the grayscale image into an RGB one. This stage is also where the initial colorimetric interpretation occurs—the grayscale is converted to a "native camera space" image, with linear gamma and primaries (usually, but not always, R, G, and B—some cameras add a fourth color filter) defined by the built-in profiles that define each supported camera's color space. (See the sidebar "Camera Raw and Color" for more details on how Camera Raw handles the tricky task of defining camera color.) The demosaicing and colorimetric interpretation happen automatically to produce the default rendering you see in the File Browser and the larger one you see when you open the image in Camera Raw.

Operationally, the first step is the colorimetric interpretation. The demosaicing is then performed in linear-gamma camera space. A little noise reduction, and any chromatic aberration corrections, are also done in the native camera space. (Chromatic aberration corrections could cause unwanted color shifts if they were done later in a non-native space.)

White Balance and Calibrate Adjustments

White Balance (Color Temperature and Tint), in addition to any adjustments made in Camera Raw's Calibrate tab, actually tweak the conversion from native camera space to an intermediate, large-gamut processing space. (This intermediate space uses ProPhoto RGB primaries and white point, but with linear gamma rather than the native ProPhoto RGB gamma 1.8.)

These operations work by redefining the colorimetric definition of the camera RGB primaries and white rather than by redistributing the pixel values. It's simply impossible to replicate these corrections in Photoshop,

Camera Raw and Color

One of the more controversial aspects of Camera Raw is its color-handling, specifically the fact that Camera Raw has no facility for applying custom camera profiles. Having tried most camera profiling software, and having experienced varying degrees of disappointment, I've concluded that unless you're shooting in the studio with controlled lighting and a custom white balance for that lighting, camera profiling is an exercise in frustration if not futility, and I've come to view Camera Raw's incompatibility with custom camera profiles as a feature rather than a limitation.

The way Camera Raw handles color is ingenious and, thus far, unique. For each supported camera, Thomas Knoll, Camera Raw's creator, has created not one but two profiles: one built from a target shot under a D65 (daylight) light source, the other built from the same target shot under an Illuminant A (tungsten) light source. The correct profiles for each camera are applied automatically in producing the colorimetric interpretation of the raw image. Camera Raw's White Balance (Color Temperature and Tint) sliders let you interpolate between, or even extrapolate beyond, the two built-in profiles.

For cameras that write a readable white balance tag, that white balance is used as the "As Shot" setting for the image; for those that don't, Camera Raw makes highly educated guesses. Either way, you can override the initial settings to produce the white balance you desire.

It's true that the built-in profiles are "generic" profiles for the camera model. Some cameras exhibit more unit-to-unit variation than others, and if your camera differs substantially from the unit used to create the profiles for the camera model, the default color in Camera Raw may be a little off. So the Calibrate controls let you tweak the conversion from the built-in profiles to optimize the color for your specific camera. This is a much simpler, and arguably more effective, process in most situations than custom camera profile creation (see "Using the Calibrate Controls" in Chapter 3, *Using Camera Raw*, for a detailed description of the process.

so it's vital that you take advantage of Camera Raw to set the white balance and, if necessary, to tweak the calibration for a specific camera. (I'll save the detailed description of how to use these controls for the next chapter, *Using Camera Raw Controls.*)

The remaining operations are carried out in the intermediate linear-gamma version of ProPhoto RGB. In many cases, it's possible to achieve a similar appearance by editing in Photoshop, but the Camera Raw controls still offer some significant advantages. The Exposure control is a case in point.

Exposure

The Exposure slider is really a white-clipping control, even though it affects the whole tonal range. The big difference between the Exposure slider and the Brightness slider is that the former lets you change the white clipping point, whereas the latter does not. With positive values, the Exposure slider behaves very much like the white input slider in Photoshop's Levels command, clipping levels to white. But since it's operating on linear-gamma data, it tends to be gentler on the midtones and shadows than white clipping in Photoshop on a gamma-corrected image, and it offers much finer control over the white clipping than does the white input slider in Levels on a gamma-corrected image.

With negative values on the Exposure slider, the story is very different. Unlike most raw converters, Camera Raw offers "highlight recovery." Most raw converters treat all pixels where one channel has clipped at the highlights as white, since they lack complete color information, but Camera Raw can recover a surprising amount of highlight detail even when it exists only in a single channel. It does, however, maintain pure white (that is, clipped in all channels) pixels as white, unlike some other converters that let you turn clipped pixels gray, and then it lowers the gamma to darken the rest of the image, using special algorithms to maintain the color of the non-white pixels. See the sidebar "How Much Highlight Detail Can I Recover?" for more technical details, and see Figure 2-8 for a real-world example of highlight recovery.

It's simply impossible to match Camera Raw's highlight detail recovery effectively in Photoshop on a gamma-corrected image. In linear-gamma space, fully half of the captured data describes the brightest f-stop, so you have a large number of bits describing the highlights. Once the image is converted to a gamma-corrected space, you have far fewer highlight bits to play with.

Figure 2-8
Highlight recovery

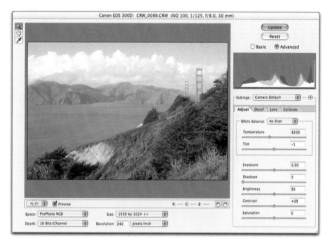

This image is overexposed, as indicated by the white spike at the right end of the histogram.

Reducing the value of the Exposure slider to -0.75 stops brings the highlights back into range. The amount of headroom varies from camera to camera, but this particular camera easily allows a three-quarter stop recovery on this image.

Increasing the Brightness slider value to 60 and the Contrast slider value to 64 counteracts the darkening effect of the Exposure adjustment. Raising the Shadow slider to 6 puts punch back in the shadows.

How Much Highlight Detail Can I Recover?

The answer, of course, is "it depends." If the captured pixel is completely blown out—clipped to white in all three channels—there is no highlight detail to recover. If a single channel, (or, better, two channels) still contain some information, Camera Raw will do its best to recover the detail and attribute natural-looking color to it.

The first stage of highlight recovery is to use any headroom the camera leaves by default—this varies considerably from vendor to vendor, with some leaving no headroom at all. The next stage uses Camera Raw's highlight recovery logic to build color information from the data in one or two unclipped channels. Next, the amount of highlight compression introduced by the Brightness slider is reduced, stretching the available highlight data over a wider tonal range. The final stage is application of a gamma curve to map the midtones and shadows correctly.

Several different factors limit the amount of highlight data you can recover, and these vary from camera model to camera model.

The first is the sensor clipping itself—the point at which all three channels clip. You can recover a lot of highlight data when only one channel contains data, but if you stretch the highlights too far, the transition between the totally blown-out highlights and the recovered ones looks unnatural. Also, some cameras run the sensor chip slightly past its linear range, producing hue shifts near the clipping point, and these hue shifts get magnified by the extended highlight recovery process—if you try to stretch the highlight data too far, you'll get strange colors—so in either case the practical limit may be lower than the theoretical one.

Most cameras use analog gain to provide different ISO speeds, but some use digital gain instead—a high-ISO image from these cameras is essentially just an underexposed image with built-in positive exposure compensation applied—so a lot of highlight data can be recovered by undoing the positive exposure compensation.

The white balance also has an effect on highlight recovery, since it scales the clipped channels to match the unclipped one. When you're attempting extreme highlight recovery it's often a good idea to adjust the Exposure slider before setting white balance, because the white balance is likely to change as you stretch the highlights anyway.

In practice, most cameras will let you recover at least a quarter stop of highlight data if you're willing to compromise a little on the white balance. Many cameras will let you recover at least one stop, possibly more, but the full four-stop range offered by the Exposure slider is beyond the useful range for most cameras. I don't advocate deliberate overexposure, but if you're shooting in changing lighting conditions, the linear-gamma nature of digital captures makes it preferable to err on the side of *slight* overexposure rather than underexposure, because underexposing to hold the highlights will make your shadows noisier than they need be. In these situations, Camera Raw's highlight recovery provides a very useful safety net.

Shadows

The Shadows slider is the black clipping control. It behaves very much like the black input slider in Photoshop's Levels command, but its effect tends to be more drastic, simply because it's operating on linear-gamma data, which devotes very few bits to the deepest shadows. As a result, the Shadows control is a bit of a blunt instrument.

Of all the Camera Raw controls, Shadows is the one that most demands caution. Rather than using it to set a black clipping point, I recommend leaving a little headroom, so that you can fine-tune the black point in Photoshop on the gamma-corrected image, where you can operate with a little more finesse.

Brightness and Contrast

The Brightness and Contrast controls affect the rendering tone curve controlling the conversion from linear-gamma ProPhoto RGB to the final gamma-corrected output space. They work completely differently from the Photoshop controls that share their names—Photoshop's Contrast and Brightness. They behave similarly to Photoshop's Levels and Curves, respectively (Brightness is a gamma adjustment, Contrast is an S-curve) but with one important difference. The Camera Raw controls use an algo-rithm that preserves the original hue, whereas hard curve adjustments to the composite RGB curve in Photoshop can cause slight hue shifts.

If you make little or no adjustment with the Exposure slider, it's prob-ably a wash as to whether you use Camera Raw's Brightness and Contrast sliders or make the adjustments post-conversion using Photoshop's tools. But if you make significant Exposure adjustments, it's well worth using Camera Raw's Brightness and Contrast sliders to fine-tune them, and if you make major Exposure adjustments, using Brightness and Contrast to counteract the extreme lightening or darkening the Exposure adjustments produce is essential (see Figure 2-8, earlier in this chapter).

Saturation

The Saturation slider operates similarly to the master saturation slider in Photoshop's Hue/Saturation command—the slight differences are mostly due to Camera Raw's slider operating on the linear-gamma data while Photoshop's operates on gamma-corrected data. As with the Exposure and Shadows controls, the Saturation slider can introduce clipping, so it's best used with caution, if at all.

Size

Camera Raw allows you to convert images at the camera's native resolution, or at larger or smaller sizes—the specific sizes vary from camera model to camera model, but they generally correspond to 50 percent, 66 percent, 100 percent, 133 percent, 166 percent, and 200 percent of the native size.

For cameras that capture square pixels, there's usually very little difference between resizing in Camera Raw and upsizing in Photoshop using Bicubic Smoother or downsizing in Photoshop using Bicubic Sharper. However, if you need a small file, it's usually more convenient to convert to a smaller size in Camera Raw than to downsample in Photoshop after the conversion.

For cameras that capture non-square pixels, the native size is the one that most closely preserves the original pixel count, meaning that one dimension is upsampled while the other is downsampled. The next size up preserves the pixel count along the higher-resolution dimension, upsampling the lower-resolution dimension to match and create square pixels in the converted image. This size preserves the maximum amount of detail for non-square-pixel cameras, and it will typically produce better results than converting to the smaller size and then upsampling in Photoshop.

The one size up is also useful for Fuji SuperCCD cameras, which use a 45-degree rotated Bayer pattern. The one size up keeps all the original pixels and fills in the holes caused by the 45-degree rotation. The native pixel count size actually uses the rotation and filling in from the one-size-up processing, and then downsamples to the native pixel count.

Sharpening

Camera Raw's sharpening is relatively unsophisticated, with only one parameter: strength. It's handy for doing quick-and-dirty sharpening for preliminary versions of images, but it's not as flexible as Photoshop's sharpening features because it's applied to the entire image, and it lacks a radius control to let you tailor the sharpening to the image content.

Camera Raw offers the option to apply sharpening to the preview image only, leaving the converted image unsharpened. This option can be quite useful in helping you set the overall image contrast, because a completely unsharpened image generally looks flatter than one that has had some sharpening applied.

Some pundits claim that sharpening should always be applied in linear-gamma space (as is Camera Raw's sharpening). Frankly, I've yet to see any major benefit in doing so, and the relative lack of control over sharpening in Camera Raw always leads me to sharpen post-conversion in Photoshop unless speed outweighs quality.

Luminance and Color Noise Reduction

While the Sharpening control is mildly convenient, the Luminance Smoothing and Color Noise Reduction controls in Camera Raw are simply indispensable. Luminance noise manifests itself as random variations in tone, usually in the shadows, though if you shoot at high ISO speeds it can spread all the way up into the midtones. Color noise shows up as random variations in color.

Before the advent of Camera Raw, I used to rely on rather desperate Photoshop techniques that involved converting the image to Lab so that I could address color noise and luminance noise separately, usually by blurring the a and b channels to get rid of color noise, and blurring or despeckling the Lightness channel to get rid of Luminance noise. Compared to the controls offered by Camera Raw, these techniques were very blunt instruments indeed—the round trip from RGB to Lab and back is fairly destructive due to rounding errors, and working on the individual channels is time-consuming.

Thanks to some nifty algorithms, Camera Raw lets you address color noise and luminance noise separately without putting the data through a conversion to Lab—the processing is done in the intermediate large-gamut linear RGB. Camera Raw's noise reduction controls are faster, less destructive, and more effective than anything you can do in Photoshop. So use them!

Watch the Histogram!

The histogram display is one of Camera Raw's most useful but often most-overlooked features. Throughout this chapter, I've harped on the usefulness of the histogram as a tool for analyzing the image, and especially for judging clipping. But the histogram in Camera Raw differs from the histograms you see on-camera in an important way.

Camera Raw's histogram is more trustworthy than the histograms that cameras display—they almost invariably show the histogram of the JPEG you'd get if you shot JPEG at the current camera settings rather than raw. As a result, they're useful as a rough guide to exposure, but not much more. Most camera vendors apply a fairly strong default tone curve to the default, in-camera raw-to-JPEG conversion, perhaps in an effort to produce a default result that more closely resembles transparency film.

Instead, Camera Raw's histogram shows you, dynamically, the histogram of the converted image. It lets you see clipping in its various forms—clipping highlights to white, clipping shadows to black, or clipping one or more channels to totally saturated color. It also lets you see the effect of the various controls on the converted image data. Watching what happens to both the histogram and the preview image as you operate the controls will give you a much better understanding of what's happening to the image than simply looking at the preview alone. In the next chapter, we'll look in detail at the many ways you can use the Camera Raw controls to get the best out of your raw captures. But if you're new to digital imaging, or even if you're just new to digital capture, it's well worth spending some time mulling over the contents of this chapter, because digital capture really is significantly different from film, and understanding how numbers are used to represent images is key to grasping and, eventually, exploiting that difference.

3

Using Camera Raw

Interpreting Raw Images

In this chapter, we'll look at the Camera Raw controls in detail. Camera Raw starts working as soon as you point the file browser at a folder full of raw images, creating thumbnails and previews, but its real power is in the degree of control and flexibility it offers in converting raw images to RGB.

Bear in mind as you go through this fairly lengthy chapter that, while Camera Raw allows you to make painstaking edits on every image, it doesn't force you to do so! Unless you're being paid by the hour, you'll want to take advantage of Camera Raw's ability to let you save custom settings and subsets of settings, and the File Browser's ability to let you apply those saved settings to multiple images without actually opening them in Camera Raw.

But before you can run, you have to learn to walk, and before you can batch-process images with Camera Raw, you need to learn to deal with them one at a time. If raw files are digital negatives, Camera Raw is the digital darkroom that offers all the tools you need to put your own unique interpretation on those digital negatives.

Like negatives, raw files are simply a starting point. The tools in Camera Raw offer much more control over the interpretation of the raw file than any wet darkroom. At first, the sheer number of options may seem overwhelming, but they're presented in a logical order, and you can master them in a fraction of the time it takes to learn traditional darkroom skills.

Camera Raw Anatomy

Camera Raw opens automatically whenever you open a raw image. In addition to the static elements—the Tool palette, the histogram, the RGB readout, the rotate controls—it offers two sets of controls; one static work-flow set that is "sticky" (the settings remain unchanged unless and until you change them) and another dynamic image-specific set that changes depending on which tab is currently selected (see Figure 3-1).

Figure 3-1
Camera Raw controls

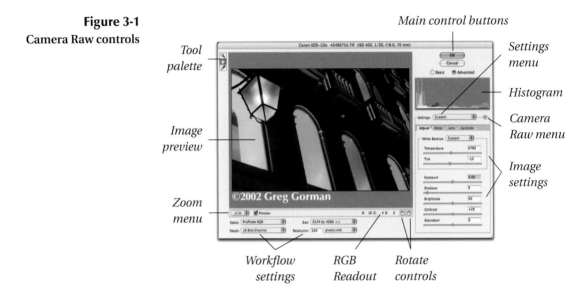

Tool palette

Image preview

Zoom menu

Main control buttons

Settings menu

Histogram

Camera Raw menu

Image settings

©2002 Greg Gorman

Workflow settings   *RGB Readout*   *Rotate controls*

The static elements include the Tool palette, the Zoom menu, the Preview toggle, the main OK and Cancel buttons, the Basic and Advanced radio buttons that let you toggle between Basic and Advanced modes, a live histogram that shows the conversion that the current settings will produce, and a Settings menu that lets you load and save settings. See Figure 3-2.

The workflow controls govern the kind of output Camera Raw will produce—they let you choose the color space, bit depth, size, and resolution of converted images. See Figure 3-3.

The image controls, which apply to individual images, appear immediately below the Settings menu. In Basic mode, Camera Raw offers two separate panels, Adjust and Detail, each with its own set of controls. In Advanced mode, two additional panels, Lens and Calibrate, become available, with more controls. See Figure 3-4.

Figure 3-2
Camera Raw
static elements

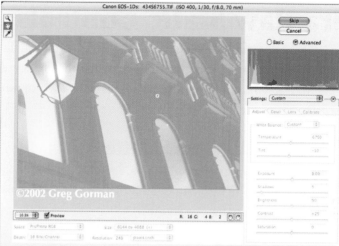

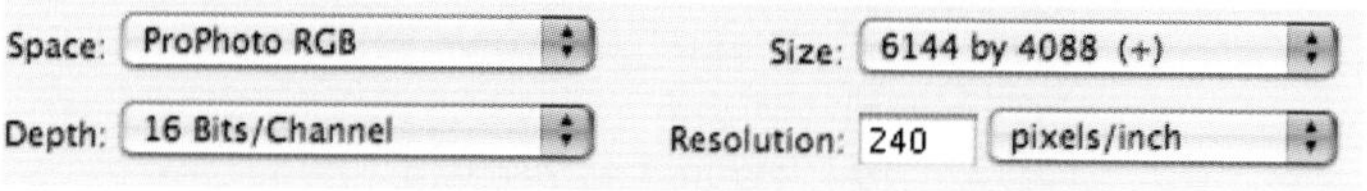

Figure 3-3
Camera Raw workflow
controls

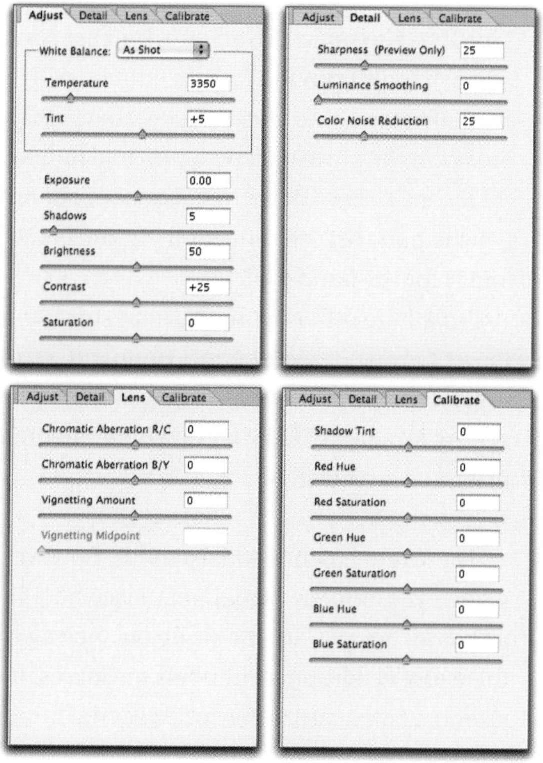

Space:	ProPhoto RGB	Size:	6144 by 4088 (+)
Depth:	16 Bits/Channel	Resolution:	240 pixels/inch

Figure 3-4
Camera Raw
image controls

Adjust Detail Lens Calibrate

White Balance: As Shot

Temperature   3350
Tint   +5

Exposure   0.00
Shadows   5
Brightness   50
Contrast   +25
Saturation   0

Adjust Detail Lens Calibrate

Sharpness (Preview Only)   25
Luminance Smoothing   0
Color Noise Reduction   25

Adjust Detail Lens Calibrate

Chromatic Aberration R/C   0
Chromatic Aberration B/Y   0
Vignetting Amount   0
Vignetting Midpoint

Adjust Detail Lens Calibrate

Shadow Tint   0
Red Hue   0
Red Saturation   0
Green Hue   0
Green Saturation   0
Blue Hue   0
Blue Saturation   0

Camera Raw Static Controls

The static controls, which appear all the time in Camera Raw, fall into several groups: the Tool palette; the preview controls; the rotate controls; the main control buttons; the histogram; the RGB readout; the Settings menu; and the Camera Raw menu. Let's look at each of these in turn.

The Tool Palette

Camera Raw's Tool palette contains three tools. The zoom (magnifying glass) and pan (grabber hand) tools work just like their Photoshop counterparts. See Figure 3-5.

Figure 3-5
Camera Raw tool palette

Zoom tool

Hand (pan) tool

White balance tool

Tip: Use Keyboard Shortcuts for Fast Navigation. Choosing the zoom and pan tools from the Tool palette is strictly for those who get paid by the hour! If you want to work quickly, there are much faster ways to navigate. First, you can always get the zoom tool by holding down the Command key (Mac) or Ctrl key (Windows). To zoom out rather than in, add Option/Alt. For the pan tool, hold down the spacebar. Or, press Z for the zoom tool and H for the hand tool.

But all the other zoom shortcuts for Photoshop also work in Camera Raw. Command -+ zooms in, Command -- (minus) zooms out. Command-0 (zero) fits the entire image in the preview, and Command-Option-0 (zero) zooms to Actual Pixels view, where one image pixel equals one screen pixel. So use them!

The white balance tool (press I), however, works differently from the white eyedroppers that appear elsewhere in Photoshop. The white balance tool lets you set the white balance by clicking on the image. Unlike the white eyedropper in Levels or Curves, it doesn't allow you to choose a source color, and it doesn't affect the luminance of the image. Instead, it lets you set the white balance—the color temperature and tint—for the capture by clicking on pixels you've determined should be neutral.

Don't confuse the white balance tool with the gray balance tool offered by some other raw converters, which are designed to balance a midtone gray. Camera Raw's white balance tool works best on light grays close to diffuse highlight values.

Tip: Click-Balance on Diffuse Highlights. The white balance tool is best used on a diffuse highlight white that still contains detail, rather than on a specular highlight that's pure white—the second-to-lightest gray patch on the old 24-patch Macbeth Color Checker works well, as do bright (but not blown-out) clouds.

Click-balancing with the white balance tool provides a very quick way to set color temperature and tint simultaneously. You can always fine-tune the results using the individual Temperature and Tint controls in the Adjust tab, which we'll cover in due course.

The Preview Controls

Situated immediately below the image preview, the preview controls let you control the zoom level and orientation of the preview, and toggle before-and-after views. See Figure 3-6.

Figure 3-6
Camera Raw
preview controls

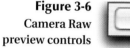

Zoom Level menu. The Zoom Level menu lets you choose a zoom level for the image preview—zoom in to check fine details, zoom out to see the global effects of your adjustments on the image (but see the earlier tip, "Use Keyboard Shortcuts for Fast Navigation").

Preview checkbox. The Preview checkbox toggles the image preview to reflect the current settings or those that were in effect when you opened Camera Raw—it provides the same before-and-after functionality as the Preview checkbox in the Adjustments dialog boxes such as Levels or Curves (press P to toggle Preview on and off).

Rotate controls. The Rotate 90 Degrees Left and Right controls (press L and R, respectively) let you apply a rotation to the preview that will be honored in the final conversion.

The Main Control Buttons

Both the OK and Cancel buttons perform multiple duties. Clicking OK dismisses the Camera Raw dialog box and converts the image using the settings specified in Camera Raw. Clicking Cancel closes Camera Raw, leaving the image unchanged, and no conversion takes place.

When you hold down the Shift key, the OK button changes to Skip. The subtle difference between Skip and Cancel is that if you select multiple images to open with Camera Raw, Cancel cancels the entire process, while Skip simply skips the current image and opens the next one in Camera Raw.

When you hold down the Option key, the OK button changes to Update. When you click Update, the current settings are written to the image's metadata without performing the conversion and opening the image. The Cancel button changes to a Reset button, resetting any changes you've made in Camera Raw and leaving the Camera Raw window open. See Figure 3-7.

The Basic and Advanced radio buttons, unsurprisingly, let you toggle between Basic and Advanced modes. The obvious difference between the two is that the Advanced mode adds two extra sets of image controls, Lens and Calibrate, which I'll discuss later in this chapter. A less obvious difference is that Advanced mode also adds some commands to the Camera Raw menu, which I'll discuss shortly. Since you've bought this book and read this far, I'll assume that you're an advanced user and hence you'll do what I do and keep the Advanced radio button turned on at all times.

Figure 3-7
Camera Raw
main control buttons

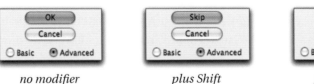

no modifier   *plus Shift*   *plus Option*

The Histogram and RGB Readout

The histogram displays the histograms of the red, green, and blue channels that will be created by the current conversion settings, *not* the histogram of the raw image (which would look strange since digital cameras capture at linear gamma—all the image data would be scrunched over to the left).

The histogram lets you check for black and white, just like the histograms on the Histogram palette, but it also lets you check for clipping caused by colors you've captured that are outside the gamut of your chosen working space (see Figure 1-5 in Chapter 1, *Digital Camera Raw*). If you find that the chosen working space is clipping some colors, you can select a larger one—if your color is clipping in ProPhoto RGB, you're probably capturing something other than visible light!

The histogram is a useful tool both for evaluating the unedited raw capture and for checking your edits to make sure that you don't introduce any unwanted clipping.

The RGB readout shows the RGB values that will result from the conversion at the current settings—it shows the RGB value for the pixel under the cursor. See Figure 3-8. The RGB readout always reads 5-by-5 pixels at the current view resolution, so it may give different values at different zoom levels. When you fit the entire image into Camera Raw's preview, you're sampling an average of a fairly large number of pixels—the exact number depends on both the camera's native resolution and the size you've chosen from the Size menu in the workflow controls (see "Camera Raw Workflow Controls," later in this chapter). You can't really sample a single pixel, but in those rare cases where you'd want to, sampling at 400% view will get you very close.

Figure 3-8
Camera Raw histogram
and RGB readout

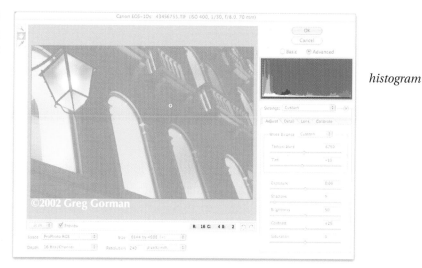

histogram

RGB readout

The Settings Menu

The Settings menu lets you recall and apply any saved Camera Raw settings (see Figure 3-9). The items that always appear are Selected Image, Camera Default, and Previous Conversion, in addition to the filenames of any raw images currently open in the File Browser for which you've saved custom Camera Raw settings. (I've seen situations where older versions of the plug-in listed all raw files open in the File Browser, whether they had associated saved settings or not, and choosing ones that didn't have saved settings just produced an error message.) Choosing an image from the Settings menu loads that image's settings into Camera Raw.

Figure 3-9
Camera Raw
Settings menu

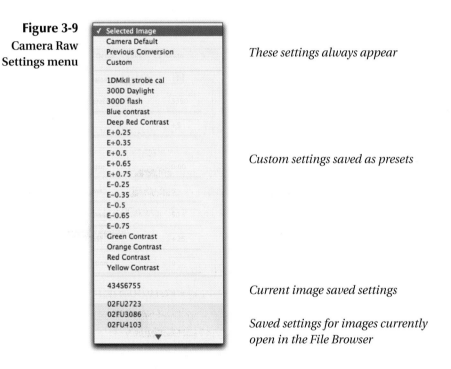

These settings always appear

Custom settings saved as presets

Current image saved settings

Saved settings for images currently open in the File Browser

You can also save your own custom settings as presets, which then become available from this menu. It's easy to overlook the mechanism for doing so, though, because it lives on the final item on the list of general controls, which besides being one of the most important, is also (for reasons unknown) unlabeled.

The Camera Raw Menu

Hidden under the small unlabeled right-facing triangle is the Camera Raw menu, which allows you to load, save, and delete settings or subsets of settings, set default settings for an individual camera, restore Camera Raw's default settings for a camera, and set Preferences. (In Basic mode, the Save Settings Subset and Preferences commands don't appear on the menu, but on Mac OS only, you can still access Camera Raw Preferences from the Photoshop menu when Camera Raw is in the foreground.) See Figure 3-10.

Figure 3-10
Camera Raw menu
(Basic and Advanced)

Load Settings...
Save Settings...
Delete Current Settings

Set Camera Default
Reset Camera Default

*Camera Raw
menu (Basic)*

Load Settings...
Save Settings...
Save Settings Subset...
Delete Current Settings

Set Camera Default
Reset Camera Default

Preferences...

*Camera Raw
menu (Advanced)*

The Load Settings and Save Settings commands let you load and save any settings you make with the any of the image-specific (Adjust, detail, Lens, and Calibrate) controls. If you save settings in the Adobe Photoshop CS/Presets/Camera Raw folder, they appear on the Settings menu. If you save them elsewhere, you can load them using the Load Settings command.

In Advanced mode, the Save Settings Subset command becomes available (see Figure 3-11). This lets you save subsets of the image settings—for example, you can create settings that only adjust the exposure value up or down in 1/4-stop increments such as +0.25, +0.50, -0.25, -0.5, and so on.

Figure 3-11
Save Settings Subset

bset

All Settings
Only White Balance
Subset: ✓ Only Adjustments   Save...
Only Details
✓ Wh   Only Lens   Cancel
✓ Exp   Only Calibration
✓ Shadows Custom Subset
✓ Brightness
✓ Contrast
✓ Saturation

☐ Sharpness
☐ Luminance Smoothing
☐ Color Noise Reduction

☐ Chromatic Aberration
☐ Vignetting

☐ Calibration

*Choose a group of settings
from the menu, or...*

*...use the checkboxes to
save a custom set.*

Camera Raw contains factory default settings for each supported camera model, which are used as the defaults for images originated by that model of camera. But you can create your own defaults—the image metadata tells Camera Raw which default to use for each camera model. The Reset Camera Default command resets the default setting for the camera that shot the current image to Camera Raw's factory default.

The Camera Raw Preferences command (which is also accessible from the Photoshop menu when Camera Raw is in the foreground) contains two items (see Figure 3-12).

Figure 3-12
Camera Raw Preferences

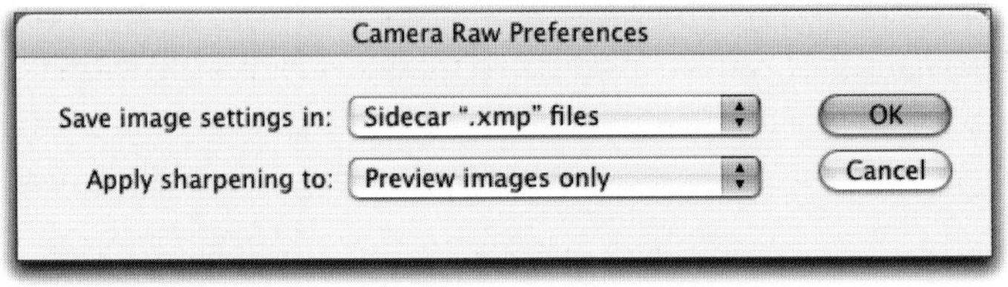

The "Save image settings in" option lets you save settings in the Camera Raw database or in individual sidecar .xmp files. Camera Raw treats the raw images as read-only (which is a Good Thing since your raw images never get overwritten), so any metadata that you add or edit for the image is saved either in a sidecar .xmp file—a small file designed to travel with the image—or in the Camera Raw database.

The Camera Raw database indexes the images by file content rather than name, so if you rename the raw file, the Camera Raw database will still find the correct settings. If you save the settings in sidecar files, make sure that you set the File Browser Preferences to "Keep Sidecar Files with Master Files," and make sure that you include the extension in any Batch Renaming operations—that way the sidecar files will get renamed to match the images, and will travel with the images if you move them using the File Browser. (See "Using Sidecar .xmp Files" in Chapter 4, *The File Browser*.)

The "Apply sharpening to" option lets you choose whether to apply sharpening to the previews *and* to the converted image, or to the previews only. I prefer to apply selective sharpening to the converted images, so I set this option to "Preview images only"—that way I can enjoy reasonably sharp previews, but apply more nuanced sharpening to the converted images. Note that this preference only affects the Sharpness setting, not either of the noise reduction settings, which are found on the same Detail tab as the Sharpness control (see "The Detail Tab," later in this chapter).

Camera Raw Workflow Controls

At the bottom of the dialog box, four controls let you set output parameters for the converted image. See Figure 3-13.

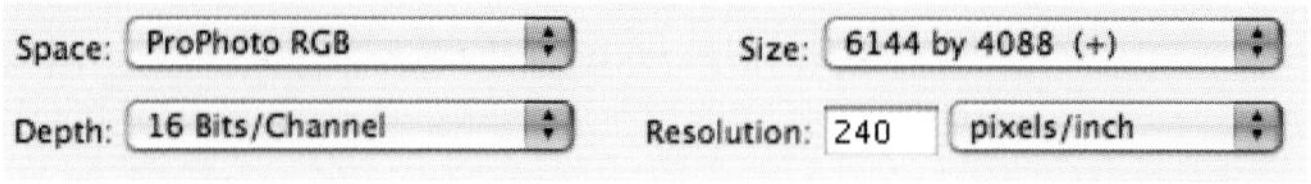

Figure 3-13
Camera Raw
output controls

The settings made using these controls apply to the current image, or to all the images being converted in a batch process. Unlike the settings made with the image-specific controls, these settings aren't saved with images. This is an advantage, because you can set the workflow controls to produce large files in a large-gamut color space for print or final delivery, or change them to produce small files in sRGB for review on the Web or email.

Space lets you choose the destination color space for the conversion from one of four preset working spaces: Adobe RGB (1998), Colormatch RGB, ProPhoto RGB, or sRGB IEC61966-1 (the lattermost being the "standard" flavor of the sRGB standard). See the sidebar "Camera Raw and Color" in Chapter 2, *How Camera Raw Works*, for details on how Camera Raw handles the color management aspect of the conversion.

Depth lets you choose whether to convert to an 8-bit/channel image or a 16-bit/channel one. A 16-bit/channel file requires twice as much storage space on disk as an 8-bit/channel one, but it provides *128 times* as many tonal steps between black and white, so it offers much more editing headroom. See the sidebar "The High-Bit Advantage," later in this chapter, for more on the pros and cons of 8-bit/channel and 16-bit/channel modes.

Size lets you resample the image on the fly, or convert it at the native camera resolution. The actual sizes offered depend on the camera from which the image came, but they correspond to the native resolution; downsampling to 66 percent or to 50 percent; and upsampling to 133 percent, 166 percent, and 200 percent. For a discussion on the pros and cons of resampling in Camera Raw versus resampling in Photoshop, see the sidebar "When to Resample," later in this chapter.

Resolution lets you specify a resolution for the converted image, in pixels per inch or pixels by centimeter, giving you the option to save yourself a trip to the Image Size dialog box once the image is converted. Unlike the Size control, it has no effect on the number of pixels in the converted image—it just specifies a default resolution for the image. You can always override it later using Photoshop's Image Size command.

Camera Raw Image Controls

The image controls—the ones you're likely to change with each image—occupy the rest of the Camera Raw dialog box. In Basic mode, they're split into two tabs, Adjust and Detail. Advanced mode adds two more tabs, Lens and Calibrate, that provide additional controls for the more advanced user. You can toggle quickly between the tabs by pressing Command-1 through Command-4.

These controls are really the meat and potatoes of Camera Raw, offering very precise control over your raw conversions. Some of the controls offer functionality that simply can't be replicated in Photoshop, while with others, the difference between making the adjustments in Camera Raw or in Photoshop is a little less clear-cut, depending to some extent on what you do with the controls that Photoshop can't replicate.

The Adjust Tab

The controls in the Adjust tab let you tweak the white balance, exposure, tonal behavior, and saturation. Three controls in this tab are key: the Temperature, Tint, and Exposure controls let you do things to the image that simply cannot be replicated using Photoshop's tools on the converted image.

The Contrast, Brightness, and Shadows controls provide similar functionality to Photoshop's Levels and Curves, with the important difference that they operate on the high-bit linear-gamma data in the raw capture, rather than on gamma-corrected data post-conversion. If you make major corrections with the Exposure slider, you definitely want to use the Brightness, Contrast, and Shadows controls to shape the raw data the way you want it before converting the raw image. If you don't make big Exposure corrections, it's more a matter of convenience whether you do the major tone-shaping in Camera Raw or in Photoshop.

The Saturation control in Camera Raw offers slightly finer global adjustments than Photoshop's Hue/Saturation command, but unlike the Photoshop command, it doesn't allow you to address different color ranges selectively. See Figure 3-14.

Figure 3-14
The Adjust tab

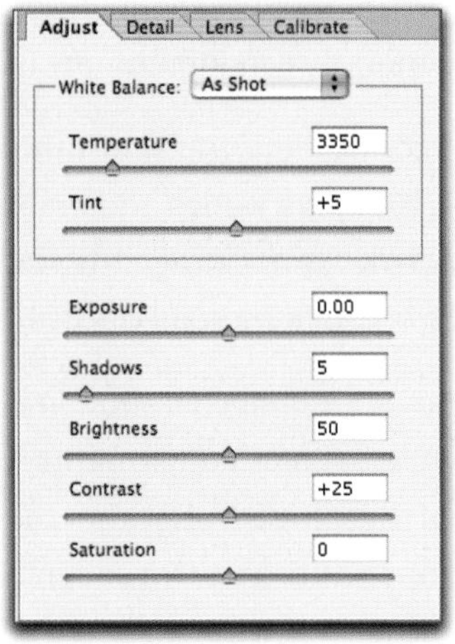

White balance controls

Tonal controls

Saturation control

White Balance. The two controls that set the white balance, Temperature and Tint, are the main tools for adjusting color in the image. If your camera's response to light is reasonably close to the one used to build the profile support for the camera model, then when you set the white balance correctly the rest of the color should more or less fall into place in terms of hue. Note that "correct white balance" includes, but isn't limited to, "accurate white balance." Later in this chapter I'll show some creative uses of the white balance controls.

If you find yourself consistently making the exact same selective color corrections in Photoshop on your processed raws, you may want to visit the Calibrate tab to tweak the color for your specific camera—see "The Calibrate Tab," later in this chapter.

▶ **Temperature.** The Temperature control lets you specify the color temperature of the lighting in Kelvins, thereby setting the blue-yellow color balance. Lowering the color temperature makes the image more blue to compensate for the yellower light; raising the color temperature makes the image more yellow, to compensate for the bluer light. (This may seem counterintuitive—we're used to thinking of higher color temperatures as bluer and lower ones as yellower: the trick is to remember that the temperature control *compensates* for the color temperature of the light, so if you tell Camera Raw that the light is bluer, it makes the image yellower.)

When the Temperature field is selected, the up and down arrow keys adjust the color temperature in increments of 50 Kelvins. Adding Shift adjusts the temperature in increments of 500 Kelvins.

▶ **Tint.** The Tint control lets you fine-tune the color balance along the red-green axis. Negative values add green, positive ones add red. The up and down arrow keys change the tint in increments of 1. Adding Shift changes the tint in increments of 10.

Figure 3-15 shows an image as shot, and the same image with some fairly gentle white balance adjustments that nevertheless greatly alter the character of the image. Notice that the adjustments involve the use of both the Temperature and Tint sliders. Later in this chapter, I'll look at more extreme uses of white balance adjustments.

Tip: Use the White Balance Tool for Rough White Balance, Then Fine-Tune with the Sliders. To get the approximate settings for Temperature and Tint, click the white balance tool on an area of detail white. This automatically sets the Temperature and Tint controls to produce as close to a neutral as possible. Then make small moves with the Temperature (and, if necessary, the Tint) control to fine-tune the results.

Note that you can alter the color balance dramatically with these controls with virtually no image degradation, which you simply can't do on the converted image using Photoshop's tools. Camera Raw's controls alter the colorimetric interpretation of the image in the conversion to gamma-corrected RGB, while Photoshop's Color Balance and Photo Filter features actually stretch or squeeze the levels in individual channels. Compared to making color balance changes in Photoshop, doing so in Camera Raw is almost lossless.

Tone controls. Learning how the four tone controls, Exposure, Shadows, Contrast, and Brightness, interact will save you time. They aren't particularly intuitive at first glance, but the four controls work together to produce a five-point curve adjustment.

Figure 3-15
White Balance
adjustments

White balance as shot

White balance adjusted to cool the image

White balance adjusted to warm the image

Exposure and Shadows set the white and black endpoints, respectively. Brightness adjusts the midpoint. Contrast then applies an S-curve around the midpoint set by Brightness, darkening the values below the midpoint and brightening those above, without affecting the endpoints. Figure 3-16 shows the tonal adjustments translated, approximately, into Photoshop Curves.

Figure 3-16
Tonal adjustments

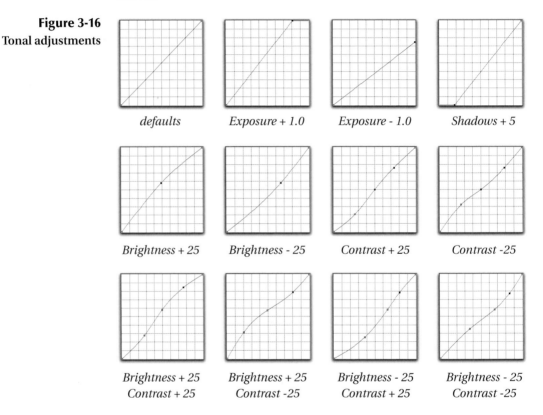

defaults   Exposure + 1.0   Exposure - 1.0   Shadows + 5

Brightness + 25   Brightness - 25   Contrast + 25   Contrast -25

Brightness + 25   Brightness + 25   Brightness - 25   Brightness - 25
Contrast + 25   Contrast -25   Contrast + 25   Contrast -25

If you use significant negative Exposure adjustments, the logic of the tonal controls changes somewhat, because extended highlight recovery tries to undo some of the highlight compression applied by the Brightness slider, but the same general principles still apply.

▶   **Exposure.** The Exposure slider controls the mapping of the tonal values in the image to those in your designated working space, but it's first and foremost a white-clipping adjustment. Remember—half of the captured data is in the brightest stop, so Exposure is a highly critical adjustment!

Large increases in exposure value (more than about 0.75 of a stop) may increase shadow noise and possibly even make some posterization visible in the shadows, simply because large positive exposure values stretch the relatively few bits devoted to describing the shadows further up the tone scale. If you deliberately underexpose to hold highlight detail, your shadows won't be as good as they could be.

The Exposure control also allows you to recover highlight information from overexposed images. For the technical details behind highlight recovery, see the sidebar "How Much Highlight Detail Can I Recover?" in Chapter 2, *How Camera Raw Works*; for a practical hands-on look at highlight recovery, see the second image in the continuation of Figure 3-35 on page 86, later in this chapter.

When the Exposure field is selected, the up and down arrows change the exposure in increments of 0.05 of a stop. Adding Shift changes the exposure in increments of 0.5 of a stop.

▶ **Shadows.** The Shadows slider is the black clipping control. It works very like the black input slider in Photoshop's Levels, letting you darken the shadows to set the black level. But the Shadows control operates on the linear-gamma data, so small moves tend to make big changes compared to using the black input slider in Levels, at least in the current version (2.2) of Camera Raw. Hence caution is required—I usually leave a little headroom so that I can fine-tune the black clipping in Photoshop on the converted image. One planned enhancement to Camera Raw is to make the Shadows slider a little gentler, but it will remain first and foremost a black-clipping tool.

When the Shadows field is selected, the up and down arrow keys change the shadows in increments of 1. Adding Shift changes the shadows in increments of 10.

Tip: Use the Clipping Display in Exposure and Shadows. For years, I've relied on the threshold clipping display in Levels to show me exactly what's being clipped in each channel as I adjust the black and white input sliders. Camera Raw offers the same feature for the Exposure and Shadows sliders (I wish it offered it for Saturation, too). Hold down the Option key as you move the Exposure or Shadows slider and you'll see the clipping display. White pixels indicate highlight clipping, black pixels indicate shadow clipping, and colored pixels indicate clipping in one or two channels. See Figure 3-17.

Figure 3-17
Camera Raw
clipping display

Exposure clipping display   *Shadows clipping display*

▶ **Brightness.** Unlike its image-destroying counterpart in Photoshop, Camera Raw's Brightness control is a non-linear adjustment that works very much like the gray input slider in Levels. It lets you redistribute the midtone values without clipping the highlights or shadows.

The up and down arrow keys change the brightness in increments of 1. Adding Shift changes the brightness in increments of 10.

▶ **Contrast.** The Contrast slider applies an S-curve to the data, while leaving the extreme shadows and highlights alone. Increasing the Contrast value from the default setting of +25 lightens values above the midtones and darkens values below the midtones, while reducing the Contrast value from the default does the reverse.

The up and down arrow keys change the contrast in increments of 1. Adding Shift changes the contrast in increments of 10.

Saturation. The Saturation slider acts like a gentler version of the Saturation slider in Photoshop's Hue/Saturation command. It offers somewhat finer adjustments than Hue/Saturation; but a Hue/Saturation Adjustment Layer allows you to fine-tune by varying the layer opacity, so as with Shadows, Brightness, and Contrast, it's pretty much a wash whether you make the adjustments in Camera Raw or in Photoshop. The up and down arrow keys change the saturation in increments of 1. Adding Shift changes the saturation in increments of 10.

Figure 3-18 shows a normally exposed image as shot, and a typical set of adjustments that we might make in Camera Raw's Adjust tab. I'll look at the fairly complex interaction of the Exposure, Shadows, Brightness, and Contrast controls on more difficult exposures a little later in this chapter.

Figure 3-18
Basic Camera
Raw adjustments

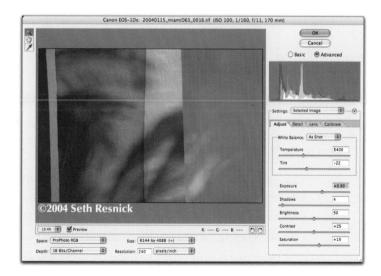

The image as shot, above. It fits comfortably into the camera's dynamic range, so it's easy to increase contrast by adjusting the endpoints with Exposure and Shadows. A Saturation boost completes the adjustments, shown below.

The Detail Tab

The sliders in the Detail tab let you apply global sharpening and reduce noise in both luminance and color (see Figure 3-19). To use these controls effectively, you need to zoom the preview to at least 100%—often 200% or higher is more effective. The up and down arrow keys move the sliders in increments of 1. Adding Shift moves the sliders in increments of 10.

Most cameras need some amount of color noise reduction regardless of ISO speed. Each camera vendor makes its own compromise between image softness and color artifacting—if an image detail falls on only a red, only a green, or only a blue pixel, the demosaicing algorithm has to make some guesses to figure out what color the resulting image pixel should really be, and sometimes single-pixel color artifacts result. Color noise reduction can also eliminate rainbow artifacts in highlights and green-magenta splotches in neutral grays.

The need for luminance noise reduction tends to be more dependent on ISO speed and the image content.

Figure 3-19
The Detail tab

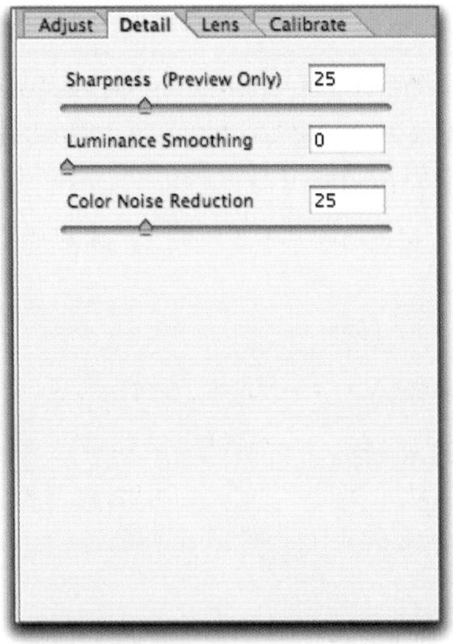

Sharpness. The Sharpness slider lets you apply a variant of Unsharp Mask to the preview image or to both the preview and the converted image, depending on how you set Camera Raw Preferences (see "The Camera Raw Menu," earlier in this chapter). Unlike Unsharp Mask, Camera Raw's Sharpness only offers a single control—the Threshold value is calculated automatically based on the camera model, ISO, and exposure compensation values reported in the image's metadata.

I find the Sharpness control a bit of a blunt instrument, and for images that will receive more than cursory attention, I either set the slider to zero or, more likely, set the Preference so that Sharpness only applies to the preview. If, on the other hand, I'm simply trying to get a bunch of images processed for approval, trying to make them good rather than great, I'll apply a quick sharpen here, knowing that I can reprocess the "hero" shots from the raw file with no sharpening once I know which ones they are.

Luminance Smoothing. The Luminance Smoothing slider lets you control grayscale noise that makes the image appear grainy—it's typically a problem when shooting at high ISO speeds. The default setting is zero, which provides no smoothing; but many cameras benefit from a modest amount—say 5 or so—of luminance smoothing even at slow speeds, so you may want to experiment to find a good default for your camera. At very high settings, the Luminance smoothing slider produces images that look like they've been hit with the Median filter, so always check the entire image at 100% view or above before committing to a setting.

Color Noise Reduction. Color noise manifests itself as random speckles of color rather than gray, and again it's a bigger problem on some cameras than on others. I usually leave this control at its default setting of 25 unless I see a need to increase (or, much more rarely, reduce) it.

The Lens Tab

The controls in the Lens tab let you address two problems that occasionally show up in digital captures, one much more common than the other (see Figure 3-20). The up and down arrow keys move the sliders in increments of 1. Adding Shift moves the sliders in increments of 10.

Chromatic aberration. Chromatic aberration is a phenomenon where the lens fails to focus the red, green, and blue wavelengths of the light to exactly the same spot, causing red and cyan color fringes along high-contrast edges. In severe cases, you may also see some blue and yellow fringing. It typically happens with wide-angle shots, especially with the wide end of zoom lenses. Vignetting, which is much less common, happens when the lens fails to illuminate the entire area of the sensor evenly, and shows up as darkening in the corners of the image.

Figure 3-20
The Lens tab

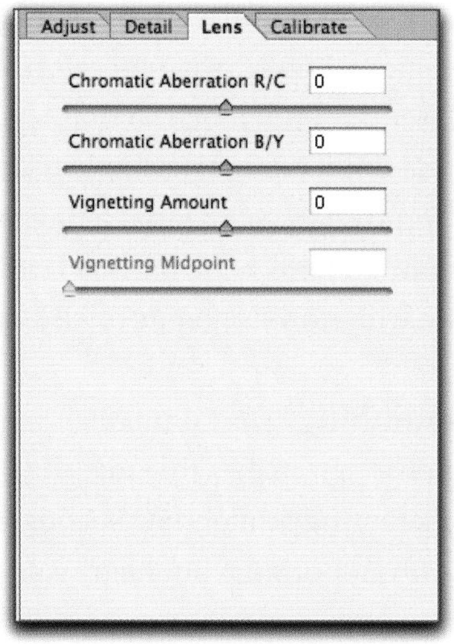

Some pundits claim that chromatic aberration in digital captures is caused by the microlenses some camera vendors place in front of each element in the array, but I'm skeptical—I've seen it happen on cameras without microlenses, using wide-angle lenses that don't display chromatic aberration when shooting film. I believe it's simply because digital capture is more demanding on lenses—film scatters the incoming light due to grain and to the presence of the multiple layers in the emulsion, so it's somewhat more forgiving than digital sensors. Whatever the reason, it's entirely likely that you'll encounter chromatic aberration in some wide-angle shots.

▶ **Chromatic Aberration R/C.** This slider lets you reduce or eliminate red/cyan fringes by adjusting the size of the red channel relative to the green channel. While the red/cyan fringes are usually the most visually obvious, chromatic aberration usually has a blue/yellow component too.

▶ **Chromatic Aberration B/Y.** This slider lets you reduce or eliminate blue/yellow fringes by adjusting the size of the blue channel relative to the green channel.

Figure 3-21 shows before-and-after versions of a chromatic aberration correction. As with the controls in the Detail tab, I always zoom the preview to 100% or more when making corrections with the chromatic aberration sliders.

Figure 3-21
Chromatic aberration
correction

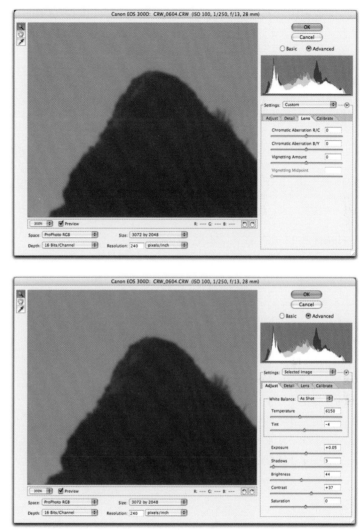

*Uncorrected image
viewed at 300% zoom*

*Image after chromatic
aberration correction*

Vignetting. Vignetting, where the lens fails to illuminate the entire sensor area, darkening the corners, is a less-common problem with digital capture because the sensor area is usually smaller than the film for which the lens was designed. But if you do encounter it, the vignetting sliders can help compensate.

▶ **Vignetting Amount.** This slider controls the amount of lightening or darkening (negative amounts darken, positive amounts lighten) applied to the corners of the image.

▶ **Vignetting Midpoint.** This slider controls the area to which the Vignetting Amount adjustment gets applied. Smaller values reduce the area, larger ones increase it.

The Calibrate Tab

This set of controls lets you fine-tune the behavior of the built-in camera profiles to tweak for any variations between *your* camera and the one that was used to build camera Raw's built-in profiles for the camera model (see Figure 3-22). The up and down arrow keys move the sliders in increments of 1. Adding Shift moves the sliders in increments of 10.

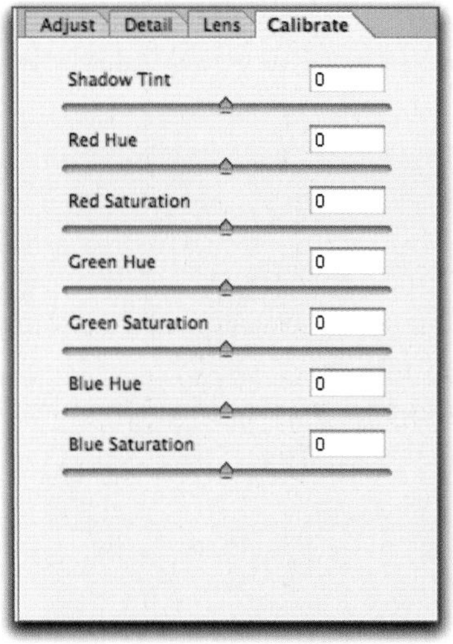

Figure 3-22
The Calibrate tab

I find that an effective way to use it is to shoot a 24-patch Macbeth Color Checker and then compare it with a Lab version of the target, converted to your chosen RGB working space. You can download a Lab image of the Color Checker, made from averaged measurements of several physical targets, at www.colorremedies.com/realworldcolor/downloads.html.

If you're shooting under controlled lighting, do a custom white balance in the camera before capturing the target. In all cases, make sure that the target is evenly lit, and avoid having anything significantly brighter than the target's white patch in the scene—using shiny metal clips to hold the target in place is a Bad Idea!

Start by adjusting the controls in the Adjust panel to get approximately the same luminance values for the black and white patches as are in the

Lab file, and use the tonal controls to get an approximate visual match to the gray patches in the Lab image. It's better to concentrate on getting a good visual match rather than trying obsessively to match the numbers exactly, but if you want to build a calibration setting for a specific lighting setup, it's worthwhile to look at the numbers as well as the visual match.

If you want to go by the numbers, convert the Lab image of the Color Checker to the RGB space you've chosen in the workflow settings' Space menu, and type the RGB values for each patch on text layers. That way, you can compare the RGB numbers in the Color Checker image with those supplied by Camera Raw's RGB readout—see Figure 3-23.

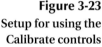

Figure 3-23
Setup for using the
Calibrate controls

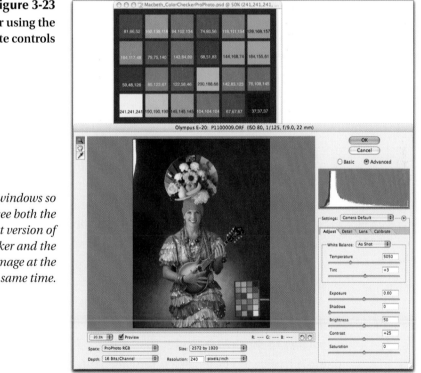

Arrange your windows so that you can see both the color-correct version of the Color Checker and the calibration image at the same time.

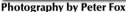
Photography by Peter Fox

Don't try to achieve an exact numeric match for every patch—that's a fast route to the funny farm! Instead, try to nail the relative overall hue and saturation relationships, using the numbers as a guide. Two handy shortcuts let you keep the cursor on the image to read the RGB values while you adjust the controls. The Tab key selects the next field. The up and down arrows increase and decrease the values in the selected field by 1, while adding Shift changes the increment to 10.

Tonal adjustments. Before touching the Calibrate controls, use the tonal controls in the Adjust tab to create a reasonable contrast match to the Color Checker image. I suggest the following step-by-step procedure, always comparing the patches in the raw image to those in the Color Checker image.

▶   Use the Exposure control to match the white patch.

▶   Click the White Balance tool on the second-lightest gray patch (Row 4, Column 2 of the target).

▶   Use the Brightness control to match the mid-gray patches (R4C3 and R4C4).

▶   Use the Contrast control to fine-tune the darkest patches (R4C5 and R4C6) and the second-to-lightest patch (R4C2). In some cases, you may need to use the Shadows slider to get the darkest patches where you want them.

Often, you'll find that you need to bring the Brightness and Contrast values down to the point where the image looks extremely flat. Don't worry—this is normal, and the goal is simply to get the overall contrast to a point where you can achieve reasonable color matches. Once you've tweaked the color response in the Calibrate tab, you'll find that you have a great deal of freedom to tweak the tonality without affecting hue and saturation. But if you don't match the overall contrast of the target, your color tweaks will be wildly off, and they'll produce unpredictable color shifts as you tweak the tonal values.

The final adjustment you'll want to make before turning your attention to the Calibrate tab is to the Saturation slider. Examine the red, green, and blue patches in the Color Checker (R3C1, R3C2, R3C3, respectively), and note the Red value for the red patch, the Green value for the green patch, and the Blue value for the blue patch; then adjust the Saturation control to get the values in the capture to match the values you just noted in the Color Checker image as closely as possible—there will likely be an element of compromise here, so just get as close as you can. This is the one step where it's easier to go by the numbers than to proceed visually. See Figure 3-24.

Figure 3-24
Adjust tab preparation
for the Calibrate
adjustments

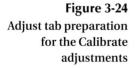

*Zoom in so that you can
easily sample the color
values from the Color
Checker patches, and then
use the Adjust controls
to match the overall
contrast of the target to
the reference image.*

Calibrate adjustments. The Calibrate tab offers a Shadow Tint control and separate Hue and Saturation controls for Red, Green, and Blue.

▶ **Shadow Tint.** This slider controls the green-red balance in the shadows. Negative values add green, positive values add red. Check the darkest patch on the target. If it's significantly non-neutral, use the Shadow Tint control to get the R, G, and B values to match as closely as possible— normally, there shouldn't be more than one level of difference between them.

▶ **Red, Green, and Blue Hue.** These sliders work like the Hue sliders in Photoshop's Hue/Saturation command. Negative values move the hue angle counterclockwise, positive values move it clockwise.

▶ **Red, Green, and Blue Saturation.** These sliders work like gentler versions of the Saturation slider in Photoshop's Hue/Saturation command. Negative values reduce the saturation, positive values increase it.

The key point to wrap your head around in using the Hue and Saturation adjustments is this: The Red Hue and Red Saturation sliders don't adjust the red value, they adjust the blue and green; the Green Hue and Saturation sliders adjust red and blue; and the Blue Hue and Saturation sliders adjust red and green. That's why you need to adjust the global Saturation control in the Adjust tab first!

Concentrate on the red (R3C1), green (R3C2), and blue (R3C3) patches in the target. Positive adjustments to the Red Hue slider increase green and decrease blue, negative ones decrease green and increase blue. Positive adjustments to the Red Saturation slider decrease green and blue equally, negative ones increase green and blue equally. Adjust the Red Hue and Saturation while checking the red patch, the Green Hue and Saturation while adjusting the green patch, and the Blue Hue and Saturation while adjusting the blue patch. See Figure 3-25.

Figure 3-25
Calibrate adjustments

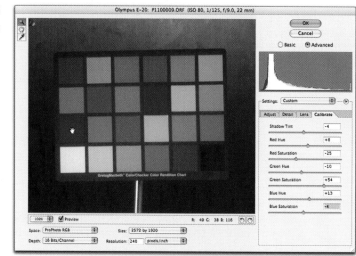

Concentrate on the red, green, and blue patches. It's unlikely that you'll achieve an exact numeric match, but you should be able to nail the relative hue and saturation relationships.

The calibrated image

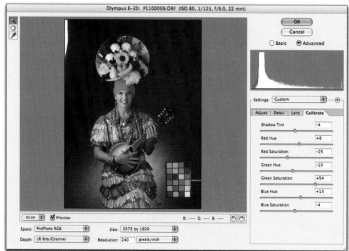

Photography by Peter Fox

You'll quickly notice that everything you do here affects everything else! You may have to go through two or three rounds of tweaking the sliders, and possibly revisit the tweaks you made in the Adjust tab. But if you persevere, you'll find that five to ten minutes work can get you a very close visual match.

An exact numeric match is unlikely, but you can get close. The important things to nail are the relative hue and saturation of the red, green, and blue patches—when you get these right, the rest of the color pretty much falls into place. You may want to create separate calibrations for tungsten and for strobe or daylight—many cameras respond significantly differently to tungsten and to daylight (or daylight-like) sources.

Once you've dialed in your camera's response, you can save the Calibrate settings (along with any other settings you'd like to make defaults) as a new Camera Default for that camera, using the Save Camera Default command on the Camera Raw menu.

It may be tempting to use the Calibrate controls as color-correction tools, and within limits you can do so; but if you see a need to do so, it's usually a sign that the calibration for your camera leaves something to be desired. That said, the Calibrate controls offer some interesting creative possibilities that I'll demonstrate later in this chapter.

Figure 3-26 shows images from several cameras before and after applying custom calibration settings. They demonstrate the effectiveness of the feature in dialing in the performance of very different cameras. Here are a few pointers in getting the most from the Calibrate tab.

▶ In the initial contrast edits, it's unlikely that you'll be able to maintain the tonal separation of the white patch from the second and third gray patches. Use the white patch to set the initial Exposure adjustment, then concentrate on the other gray patches to make the Brightness, Contrast, and Shadows edits.

▶ When you go to make the Saturation edit in the Adjust tab, you'll typically find that the red value of the red patch is higher and the blue value of the blue patch is lower than the aim points. Set the master Saturation to match the green value on the green patch.

▶ In the Calibrate tab, I suggest editing the Shadow Tint using the black patch, then the Green Hue and Saturation, followed by Blue Hue and Saturation, leaving Red Hue and Saturation for last.

Figure 3-26
Before and after calibration

The top row shows images at camera default settings, the bottom row shows the same images after applying Calibrate adjustments.

Canon EOS 1Ds   *Nikon D1H*   *Nikon D100*

Photography by Peter Fox

Hands-On Camera Raw

Knowing what each control does in Camera Raw is only half the battle. The other half is in knowing how the various controls interact, and when (and in what order) to use them. So with these goals in mind, let's look at a simple scenario, processing individual images, one at a time, in Camera Raw.

It's useful to split the work into three phases, even though the third phase is where most of the work gets done, because if you mess up the first phase, you won't get the results you wanted, and if you skip the second phase you may miss critical issues in the image when you execute phase three. The three phases are:

▶ Setting up Camera Raw—Preferences and workflow settings

▶ Evaluating the image

▶ Editing the image

Let's look at these in turn.

Camera Raw Setup

The first order of business is to set up Camera Raw to make it work the way you want it to. To do that, you must open a raw image, because until you actually launch Camera Raw you can't do anything with it. Size the Camera Raw window by dragging the handle at the lower-right corner so that you can see a decent-sized image preview, with the controls conveniently placed. If most of your images are verticals, you may prefer a narrower Camera Raw window than if you mostly shoot horizontals. I like to size the Camera Raw window to fill the entire screen.

Preferences. Next, make sure that Camera Raw's Preferences are set to behave the way you want them to. There's no right or wrong answer to how the Preferences should be set other than that they should produce the behavior you want. You can open Camera Raw's Preferences either by choosing Preferences from the Camera Raw menu (Camera Raw must be set to Advanced mode) or on the Mac only, by choosing Camera Raw Preferences from the Photoshop menu (the command only appears when Camera Raw is open; see Figure 3-27).

Figure 3-27
Camera Raw
Preferences command

*Choose Camera Raw
Preferences either from
the Photoshop menu
when Camera Raw is
open, or from the
Camera Raw menu
in Advanced mode.*

©2004 Seth Resnick

Camera Raw's Preferences are pretty straightforward. You only have two settings to worry about—where to save settings and how to apply sharpening.

▶ **Save image settings in:** controls where your image settings get saved, with two choices; "Camera Raw database" or "Sidecar ".xmp files." Each has its advantages and disadvantages.

When you save settings in the Camera Raw database, they're indexed by file content rather than name, so even if you rename the raw file, Camera Raw will associate the correct settings with the image. But if you move the image to a different computer, the settings won't be available because they're stored in the Camera Raw database on the first computer.

When you save settings as sidecar .xmp files, they're saved as separate files, in the same folder as the image, and with the same name as the image except that they take a .xmp extension instead of the extension that identifies raw files (.CRW, .NEF, and so on). The File Browser has a preference setting that automatically keeps the sidecar files with the images as long as you use the File Browser to move or copy them. You can run Batch Rename, and the sidecar files will get renamed along with the images; but if you move or copy the images outside the File Browser, it's up to you to make sure that the sidecar files go with them.

If you only use a single computer and never send your raw files to any-one else, it may make sense to store all the Camera Raw settings in the Camera Raw database, but I find that sidecar files offer more flexibility at the cost of slightly more complex file management. If you want to archive your settings along with the images when you burn them to CD or DVD, sidecar files are the only way to go.

Tip: If You Used the Wrong Setting… If you inadvertently saved your settings in the Camera Raw database when you wanted sidecars, or vice versa, the only way to get what you wanted is to change the preference setting in Camera Raw and then open each image in Camera Raw and click Update (hold down Option) to make the OK button change to the Update button. Root canal therapy sans anesthesia compares favorably with doing this to a folder of several hundred images, so instead, create an action that simply opens the files and closes them without saving, and then let it run overnight. (This technique is also handy if you're a belt-and-suspenders type who wants the settings saved in both locations.) I'll discuss writing actions like this in Chapter 7, *Exploiting Automation.*

▶ **Apply sharpening to:** controls whether sharpening applied by the Sharpness slider in the Detail tab is applied to the image preview only or to the converted image. (If you choose Preview Images Only, a label to that effect appears beside the Sharpness slider.)

I usually sharpen the image post-conversion in Photoshop, but it's often useful to apply some sharpening to the preview to aid in making decisions about contrast. So I normally leave Camera Raw's preference set to Preview Images Only. (Note that the sharpening is applied not only to Camera Raw's image preview, but also to the previews and thumbnails displayed by the File Browser.)

However, if I need to process a lot of images quickly, I'll use Camera Raw's sharpening and change the preference to apply sharpening to All Images—that way, the sharpening I set with the Sharpness slider is applied to the converted image as well as to the preview.

If either of the preferences are set incorrectly, you'll need to redo all of your work once you've set them the way you want, so always make sure that they're set the way you think they are—it will save time in the long run.

Workflow settings. The workflow settings govern the color space, bit depth, size, and resolution of the converted image. They're called "workflow settings" because you'll typically change them to produce different types of output. For example, when you want to create JPEGs for online viewing or review, it would make sense to choose sRGB as the color space, 8-bit for bit depth, the smallest size for your camera for size, and 72 ppi for resolution. But to produce images for large prints, you'd probably switch to a wider color space, use 16-it for bit depth to accommodate further editing in Photoshop, the largest size supported for your camera, and 240 ppi for resolution.

The workflow settings are recordable in actions, so once you've learned your way around, you can easily incorporate the workflow settings you want in batch processes—I'll discuss building actions for batch processes in Chapter 7, *Exploiting Automation.*

Four different menus make up the workflow settings (see Figure 3-28).

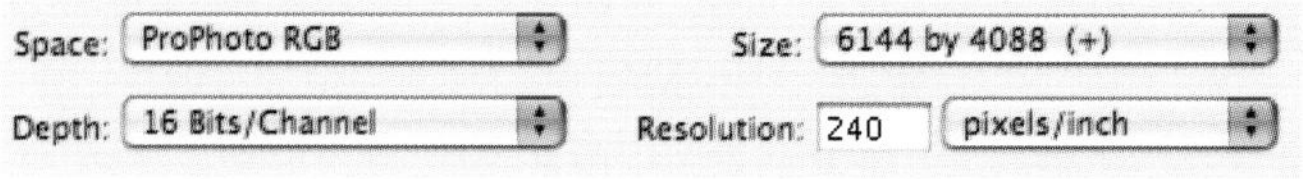

Figure 3-28
Camera Raw
workflow settings

Space: ProPhoto RGB   Size: 6144 by 4088 (+)

Depth: 16 Bits/Channel   Resolution: 240   pixels/inch

▶ **Space** dictates the color space of the converted image. The choices are Adobe RGB, Colormatch RGB, ProPhoto RGB, and sRGB. If you use one of these spaces as your Photoshop RGB working space, choose that space here, unless you're producing imagery for the Web, in which case you should choose sRGB.

A huge number of words have already been expended on the subject of RGB working spaces, and I don't want to add to them here—if you want to read some of mine, www.creativepro.com:80/story/feature/8582.html is a good place to start. The one practical recommendation I'll make regarding choice of working space is, use Camera Raw's histogram to detect colors being clipped by the chosen output space. If a space clips colors, look to see if they're important to you. If they are, choose a wider space. See "Evaluating Images," later in this chapter.

Tip: When You Need a Different Output Space... If none of the four spaces supported by Camera Raw suits your workflow, use ProPhoto RGB as the space in Camera Raw, set the bit depth to 16-bit, then use Photoshop's Convert to Profile command to convert the images into your working space of choice, using Relative Colorimetric rendering. ProPhoto RGB is large enough that it makes any color clipping extremely unlikely, so the intermediate conversion won't introduce any significant loss.

▶ **Depth** lets you choose whether to produce an 8-bit/channel image or a 16-bit/channel one. Unless I'm creating JPEGs for Web or email use, I always convert to 16-bit/channel images, because they allow a great deal more editing headroom than 8-bit/channel ones. The inevitable trade-off is that the files are twice as large.

If you plan on doing minimal editing in Photoshop, converting to 8-bit/channel may save you some time, particularly if you run Photoshop on older, slower machines. Everyone has their own pain point! See the sidebar "The High-Bit Advantage" for more on 16-bit/channel images.

▶ **Size** lets you choose one of several output sizes. The specific sizes vary from camera to camera, but they always include the camera's native resolution as well as higher and lower ones.

With cameras that produce non-square pixels, there's a clear advantage to using Camera Raw to go one size up from native—for the details, see "Size" in Chapter 2, *How Camera Raw Works*—but for the majority of cameras, the difference is much less clear-cut and is as much about workflow convenience as it is about image quality. See the sidebar "When to Resample" for further discussion.

▶ **Resolution** lets you set a default resolution for the image. This is purely a workflow convenience—you can always change it later using Photoshop's Image Size command. If you need 240-ppi images for inkjet printing or 72-ppi images for Web use, set that resolution here to save yourself a trip to the Image Size dialog box later.

You can't load and save workflow settings as you can image settings, but you *can* record workflow settings in actions that you can then use for batch processing. The workflow settings are sticky per camera model, so always check to make sure that they're set the way you need them.

The High-Bit Advantage

Any camera that shoots raw captures at least 10 bits per pixel, offering a possible 1,024 tonal values, while most capture 12 bits for 4,096 levels, and a few capture 14 bits, for 16,384 possible tonal values. An 8-bit/channel image allows only 256 possible tonal values in each channel, so when you convert a raw image to an 8-bit/channel file, you're throwing away a great deal of potentially useful data.

The downsides of 16-bit/channel images are that they take up twice as much storage space (on disk and in RAM) as 8-bit/channel ones, and an ever-shrinking list of Photoshop features don't work in 16-bit/channel mode. The advantage is that they offer massively more editing headroom.

If you're preparing images for the Web or you need to use a Photoshop feature such as Liquify that only works in 8-bit/channel mode, by all means go ahead and process the raw images to 8-bit channel files. In just about every other scenario, I recommend processing to a 16-bit/channel file. Even if you think the image will require little or no editing in Photoshop, it's likely that at some point the image will have to undergo a color space conversion for output, and making that conversion on a 16-bit/channel image can often avoid problems such as banding in skies or posterization in shadows that suddenly appear after an 8-bit/channel conversion.

Evaluating Images

Before starting to edit a raw image, it's always a good idea to do a quick evaluation. Is the image over- or underexposed? Does the subject matter fall within the camera's dynamic range, or do you have to sacrifice highlights or shadows? Camera Raw offers three features that help you evaluate the raw image and answer these questions.

► **The histogram** lets you judge overall exposure and detect any clipping to black, white, or a fully saturated primary.

► **The image preview** shows you exactly how the converted image will appear in Photoshop, and the clipping display, available when you adjust the Exposure and Shadows sliders, lets you see exactly which pixels, if any, are being clipped.

► **The RGB readout** lets you sample the RGB values from specific spots in the image.

If an image is too dark or too light, you need to decide whether to fix it by adjusting Exposure or Brightness. If it's too flat, you need to decide whether to increase the Contrast value or add snap to the shadows with the Shadows control. For decisions like these, Camera Raw's histogram is a useful guide.

When to Resample

A good deal of controversy surrounds the question of whether to upsample in Camera Raw or post-conversion in Photoshop. Be very wary of absolute answers—in most cases, the differences are quite subtle and very likely camera-dependent. (And it's also quite likely they're photographer-dependent, too!) That said, I'll give half an absolute answer: if you need a smaller-than-native file, it's a no-brainer to choose the size closest to your needs in Camera Raw. The controversy really revolves around upsizing.

With the exception of images captured on non-square-pixel cameras, the differences between upsampling in Camera Raw and upsampling in Photoshop using Bicubic Sharper are quite subtle (though I prefer to use Bicubic Smoother for upsampling). If you factor in the other variables, and in particular the huge variable of how and when you sharpen the image, the question of when to resample becomes even more complex. I personally prefer to convert raw images at the camera's native resolution and do as much work as possible before upsampling, because the work goes faster on a smaller file than on a larger one. But others whose judgment I respect prefer to upsample in Camera Raw.

Ultimately, it's a question you'll have to answer for yourself. You may even find that some types of imagery respond better to one method, while others respond better to another. If you're disinclined to devote a lot of time to testing, another entirely rational strategy is to punt on the whole question and simply do whatever is most convenient in your workflow.

The histogram. Camera Raw's histogram is simply a bar chart that shows the relative populations of pixels at different levels. The colors in the histogram show what's going on in each channel.

White in the histogram means that this level has pixels from all three channels. Red, green, and blue mean that this level has pixels from these individual channels. Cyan means that this level has pixels from the green and blue channels, magenta means this level has pixels from the red and blue channels, while yellow means that this level has pixels from the red and green channels. (If it's easier, you can think of cyan as "no red," magenta as "no green," and yellow as "no blue.")

Spikes at either end of the histogram indicate clipping—white pixels mean that all three channels are being clipped, colored ones indicate clipping in one or two channels—see Figure 3-29.

Figure 3-29
Clipping and the histogram

Tonal clipping to black and white   *Saturation clipping to yellow and red*

The histogram can help you determine whether or not the captured scene fits within the camera's dynamic range. If there's no clipping at either the highlight or the shadow end, it clearly does. If there's clipping at both ends, it probably doesn't. If there's clipping at only one end, you may be able to rescue highlight or shadow detail (if you want to) by adjusting the Exposure slider.

The histogram also shows clipping in individual channels. Typically, clipping in one or two channels indicates one of two conditions.

▶   The RGB space selected in the Space menu is too small to hold the captured color. In that case, try switching to a larger space if the color is important.

▶   You've pushed the saturation so far that you've driven one or more channels into clipping. Again, this isn't necessarily a problem. To see exactly what's being clipped, you can use the Exposure or Shadows slider's clipping display, which I'll discuss next.

Image preview. The main function of the image preview is, of course, to show you how the converted image will appear. After looking at the histogram, I usually use the white balance tool to do a quick click-balance by clicking on an area of detail white (though I'll probably fine-tune it later with the Temperature and Tint controls). However, if the histogram tells me I need to use Camera Raw's extended highlight recovery, I'll wait until I've set endpoints before attempting a white balance.

The image preview also offers a couple of indispensable tricks in the form of the highlight clipping display and shadow clipping display offered by using the Option key in conjunction with the Exposure and Shadows sliders, respectively. Hold down the Option key, and then hold down the mouse button on either slider to see the clipping display. The display updates dynamically as you move the slider, so it's also very useful for editing.

▶   **Exposure clipping display.** Holding down the Option key as you move the Exposure slider turns the image Preview into a highlight clipping display—see Figure 3-30.

Figure 3-30
Highlight clipping display

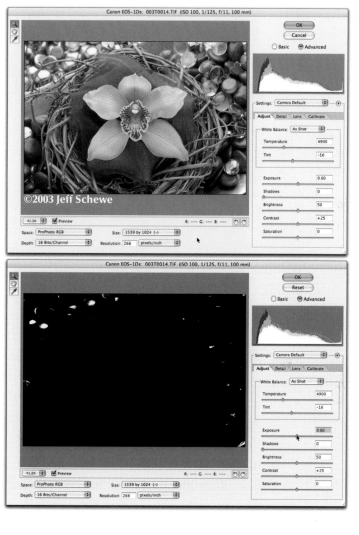

*The image at
Camera Default*

*Hold down the Option
key, then hold down the
mouse button on the
Exposure slider to see
highlight clipping. Note
that the clipping display
confirms the highlight
clipping indicated by the
histogram.*

Unclipped pixels display as black. The other colors show you which channels are being clipped to level 255. Red pixels indicate red channel clipping, green pixels indicate green channel clipping, blue pixels indicate blue channel clipping. Yellow pixels indicate clipping in both red and green channels, magenta pixels indicate clipping in the red and blue channels, and cyan pixels indicate clipping in the green and blue channels. White pixels indicate that all three channels are clipped.

▶ **Shadows clipping display.** Holding down the Option key as you move the Shadows slider turns the image preview into a shadow clipping display—see Figure 3-31.

Figure 3-31
Shadow clipping display

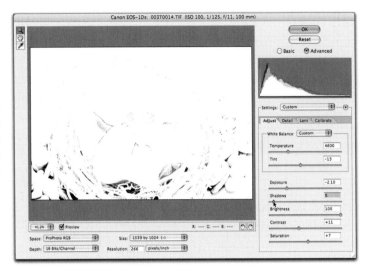

*Hold down the Option
key, then hold down the
mouse button on the
Shadows slider to see the
shadow clipping display.*

Unclipped pixels display as white. The other colors show you which channels are being clipped to level 0. Cyan pixels indicate red channel clipping, magenta pixels indicate green channel clipping, yellow pixels indicate blue channel clipping. Red pixels indicate clipping in both green and blue channels, green pixels indicate clipping in the red and blue channels, and blue pixels indicate clipping in the red and green channels. Black pixels indicate that all three channels are clipped.

While the histogram shows you whether or not clipping is taking place, the clipping displays show you *which* pixels are being clipped. If you want to evaluate clipping on single pixels, you'll need to zoom in to 100% view. Camera Raw does its best to show you clipping at lower zoom percentages, but it's only completely accurate at 100% or higher zoom levels.

RGB readout. The RGB readout lets you sample the RGB values of the pixel under the cursor. The readout always reports the average of a five-by-five sample of screen pixels. You can't sample individual pixels, though you can get close at a 400% zoom level. To sample fewer pixels, zoom in, and to sample more pixels, zoom out.

The RGB readout helps you distinguish between, for example, a yellow cast and a green one, or a magenta cast and a red one. Sample an area that should be close to neutral. If the blue value is lower than red and green, it's a yellow cast; if the green value is higher than red and blue, it's a green cast.

Figure 3-32 shows the evaluation process for several different images, with a variety of exposures. In the next section, I'll proceed with editing these images.

Figure 3-32
Evaluating images

A quick examination of the histogram indicates that the image is slightly overexposed.

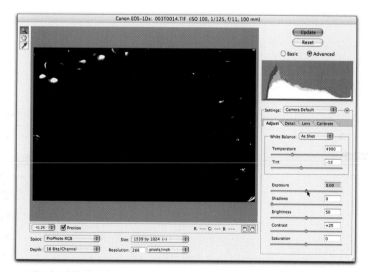

The highlight clipping display confirms that the highlights are clipped. There's no significant shadow clipping, so I may be able to rescue some highlight detail without clipping shadows.

Figure 3-32
Evaluating images,
continued

The histogram shows some highlight clipping in the blue channel only, and no shadow clipping. The white balance seems excessively cold.

The highlight clipping display confirms what we learned from the histogram. The clipping is in areas with no detail and doesn't represent a problem—in fact, the Exposure value can probably stand to be increased.

The image falls entirely within the dynamic range of the camera, with no clipping, but it's flat. I can't make any decisions about the white balance until I tweak the contrast.

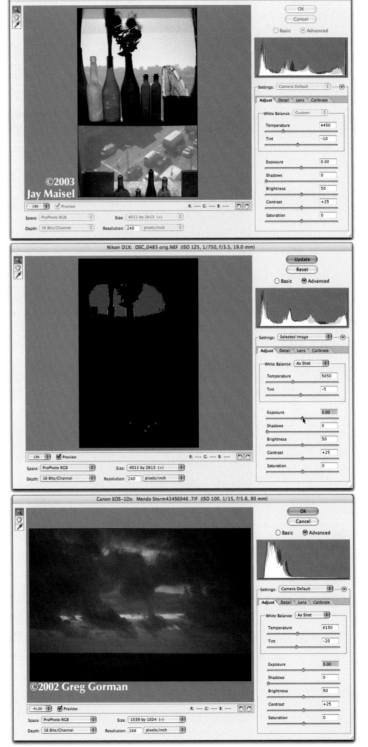

The histogram merely confirms what the image preview makes obvious— the image is significantly overexposed.

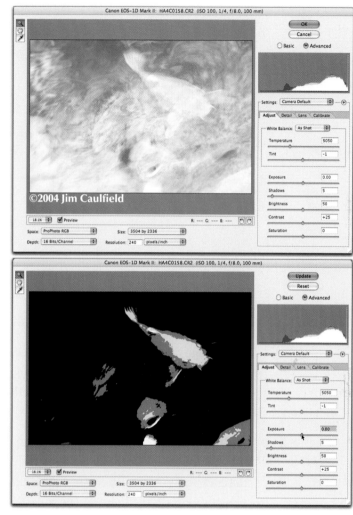

The highlight clipping display shows that there's significant highlight clipping in the red and green channels, but relatively few pixels are completely blown out to white. The image may be rescuable.

Editing Images

At last, we come to the heart of the matter—editing raw images! The controls in Camera Raw are presented in a fairly logical order. I always start with the controls in the Adjust tab, followed by those in the Detail tab, and then, if necessary, those in the Lens tab. Normally, I don't make adjustments to individual images in the Calibrate tab, reserving it for fine-tuning the response of specific cameras; but on occasion, it can be a handy creative tool, too.

Using the Adjust tab controls. The Adjust tab contains the controls that let you set the overall contrast and color balance for the image—see Figure 3-33. A simple rule of thumb that has served me well over the years is to fix the biggest problem first. In the case of raw images, this always boils down to starting with either the Exposure or the White Balance controls.

Figure 3-33
The Adjust tab

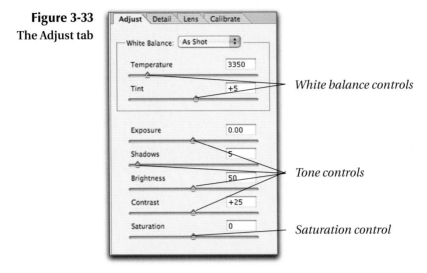

White balance controls

Tone controls

Saturation control

If the image needs a major (more than 0.25-stop up or down) exposure adjustment, it's better to do that before setting the white balance, because the exposure adjustment will probably affect the white balance. If the image needs little or no exposure adjustment, set white balance first.

▶ **White Balance.** The Temperature control adjusts the color of *the light for which Camera Raw is compensating* in Kelvins. So as you increase the color temperature, the color balance moves towards yellow to compensate for the bluer light, and as you decrease the color temperature, the image heads toward blue to compensate for the yellower light.

The Tint control adjusts the red-to-green color balance—positive values head toward red, negative ones head toward green.

It's often easiest to start by doing a rough click-balance with the white balance tool by clicking on an area of detail white in the image. Don't click on a specular highlight unless you're going for psychedelic results! Then you can fine-tune using the Temperature and Tint sliders—see Figure 3-34.

Figure 3-34
Setting white balance

A quick click-balance with the white balance tool on the bright sky area warms the image a hair too much, producing Temperature at 5700 and Tint at -3. Fine-tuning to Temperature 5650, Tint -5, produces this result.

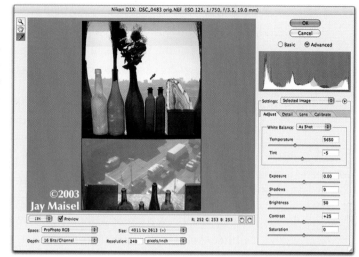

It's pointless to attempt setting white balance on this image until the exposure issues are fixed. Click-balancing produces a variety of unpredictable results, none of which are particularly useful!

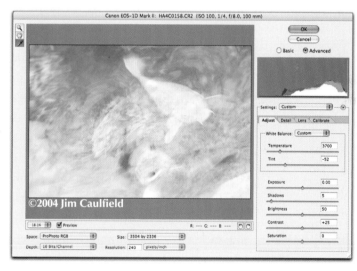

The White Balance controls are designed to reconstruct the actual white balance of the scene, but they're also amenable to creative use. You can warm or cool an image with more control and less image degradation than you can in Photoshop. Figure 3-39, later in this chapter, shows two examples.

▶ **Exposure.** Along with the White Balance controls, the Exposure slider is possibly the most critical tool in Camera Raw—if you don't take advantage of the White Balance and Exposure tools to optimize your captures, you're essentially negating the benefits of shooting raw!

At positive values, the effects of the Exposure slider closely mimic increasing the exposure using the on-camera controls. At negative settings, its behavior depends on whether or not the image contains any completely clipped pixels—that is, pixels that are blown out to solid white in all three channels. If the image contains no completely blown pixels, the Exposure slider works very much like reducing the exposure in camera. Otherwise, Camera Raw leaves completely white pixels as white, rather than turning them gray, and stretches the highlight range to recover as much detail as possible. The amount of recoverable highlight detail varies from camera to camera—see the sidebar "How Much Highlight Detail Can I Recover?" in Chapter 2, *How Camera Raw Works*, for more details.

The Exposure slider affects the entire tonal range, but it's essentially a tool for setting the white point. This is a much more critical operation with digital captures than it is with film scans due to the linear-gamma nature of digital raw, which uses half of the captured bits to describe the brightest f-stop (see the sidebar "Exposure and Linear Gamma" in Chapter 1, *Digital Camera Raw*). Use the Exposure slider to make sure that diffuse highlights still contain detail (the RGB readout is useful for checking pixel values, while the highlight clipping display aids in adjusting the Exposure slider), without worrying overmuch about what it does to the midtones and shadows. See Figure 3-35.

▶ **Brightness and Contrast.** While the Shadows slider is presented before the Brightness and Contrast sliders in Camera Raw's user interface, it's almost always better to use the Brightness and Contrast controls to shape the overall tonality of the image and reserve the Shadows slider for fine-tuning the black point afterward. Small changes to the Shadows value often produce big changes in the image due to the linear nature of the raw image—raw captures have far fewer bits describing the shadows than they do describing the highlights.

Figure 3-35
Setting Exposure

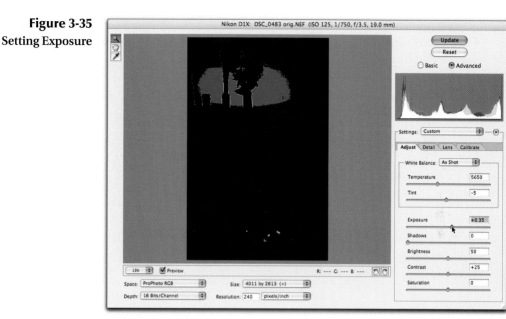

*The highlight clipping display reveals that I can increase the Exposure value
by 0.35 without losing any important detail.*

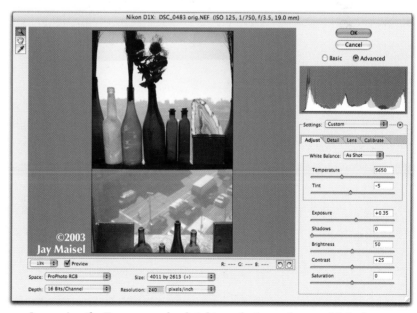

*Increasing the Exposure value brightens the image by one-third of a stop
without blowing out any important highlight detail.*

Figure 3-35
Setting Exposure,
continued

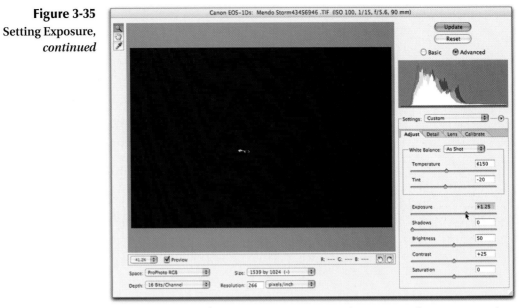

Using the highlight clipping display as a guide, I increase the Exposure value until I just start to see some clipping in one or two channels, in the brightest part of the sky.

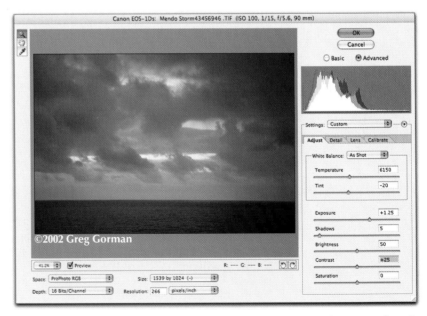

Opening up the image with the Exposure slider brings it to the point where I can start making reasonable decisions about contrast and white balance.

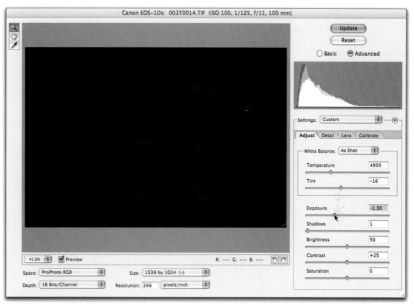

*Using the highlight clipping display as a guide, I reduce the Exposure value
to eliminate almost all the highlight clipping, leaving a few small specular
highlights.*

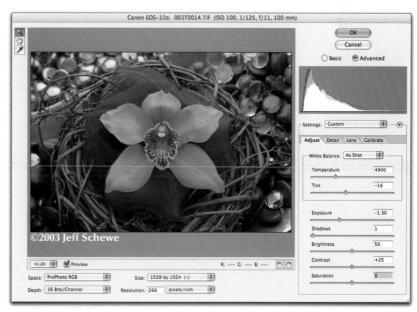

*This leaves the image rather dark, so I'll fix it later with the Brightness and
Contrast controls.*

Figure 3-35
Setting Exposure,
continued

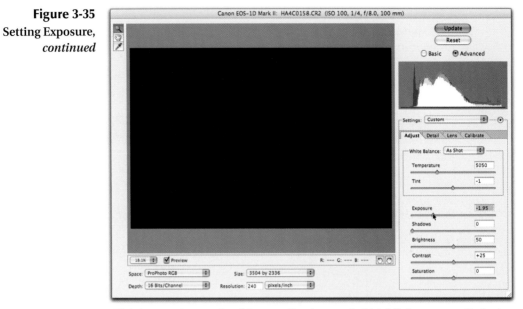

This is a good example of Camera Raw's extended highlight recovery. Reducing the Exposure value by almost two stops eliminates all the highlight clipping.

Recovering the highlight detail makes it clear that there is, in fact, an image here! By fixing the biggest problem first, I can now start to make reasonable decisions about contrast and white balance.

The Brightness control adjusts midtone brightness without affecting the endpoints of the tonal range, so it's generally the next adjustment you want to make. The Contrast control, at positive settings, brightens values above the midpoint set by Brightness and darkens values below that midpoint. At negative settings, it darkens values above the midpoint and brightens those below, but in both cases it leaves the endpoints alone. Due to the linear capture, Contrast has a more obvious effect on the darker three-quarter-tones than it does on the brighter values. See Figure 3-36.

Figure 3-36
Setting Brightness
and Contrast

Slight Contrast and
Saturation tweaks
complete the editing
process for this image.

A significant Contrast
boost leaves this image
ready for White Balance
adjustment.

Figure 3-36
Setting Brightness
and Contrast, *continued*

This image allows many different white balance treatments—this is the one preferred by the artist.

A major Brightness move and a smaller Contrast move restore the midtones that were darkened by the Exposure move I made to bring down the highlights. I also added some saturation.

Reducing Brightness and increasing Contrast gets this image ready for a White Balance adjustment.

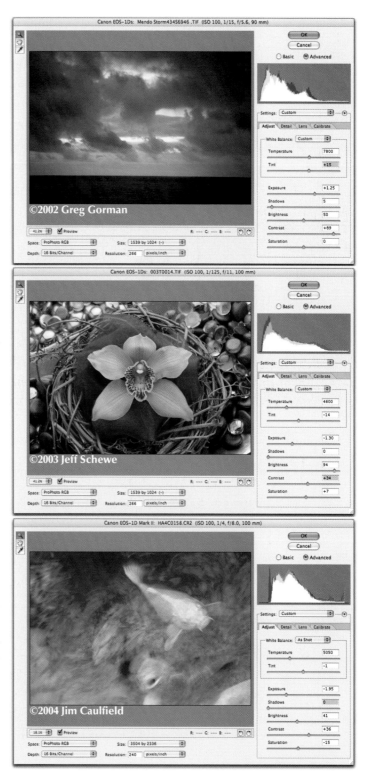

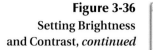

Tip: Don't Be Afraid to Reduce Contrast. Many photographers are hesitant to reduce the value of a slider labeled "Contrast," but if you're looking to brighten the dark three-quarter-tones without affecting the midtones, reducing the Contrast value will do a better job than increasing the Brightness value. If you're worried about the image going flat, rest assured that you can put plenty of punch back into the shadows using the Shadows slider.

▶ **Shadows.** The Shadows control sets the black point. If you use the shadow clipping display obtained by holding down the Option key as you move the Shadows slider, you'll typically see big clumps of pixels being clipped with each change in the Shadows value. If you want to make big changes to the black point, you can make a Shadows adjustment immediately after adjusting Exposure and before tweaking Brightness and Contrast. But in most situations, it's best to make the other tonal moves first and reserve Shadows for fine-tuning the black point. See Figure 3-37.

Tip: Dealing With Important Shadow Detail. If your image contains important detail in the deep shadows, either set the Shadows slider at zero or leave some headroom. Once the image has been converted to a gamma-corrected space in Photoshop, you'll have much finer control over the shadow behavior.

Figure 3-37
Setting Shadows

Shadow clipping at
Shadows value of 5

Shadow clipping at
Shadows value of 6

The final image

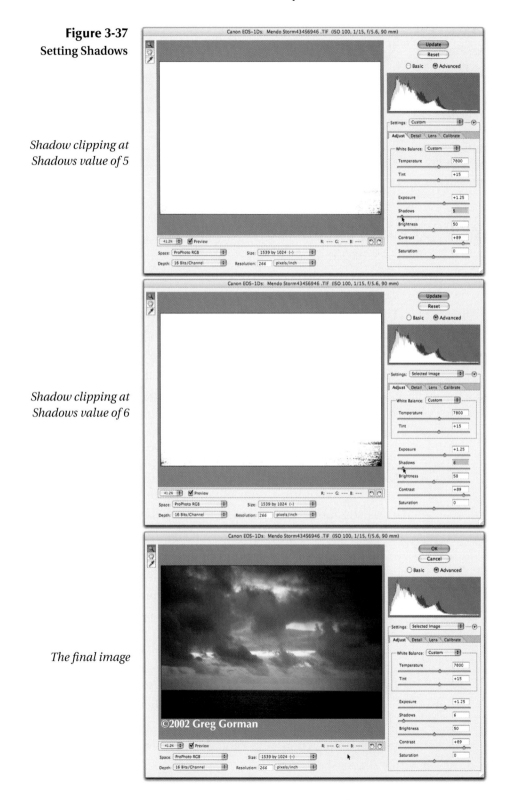

Figure 3-37
Setting Shadows,
continued

Shadow clipping at
Shadows value of 0

Shadow clipping at
Shadows value of 2

The final image

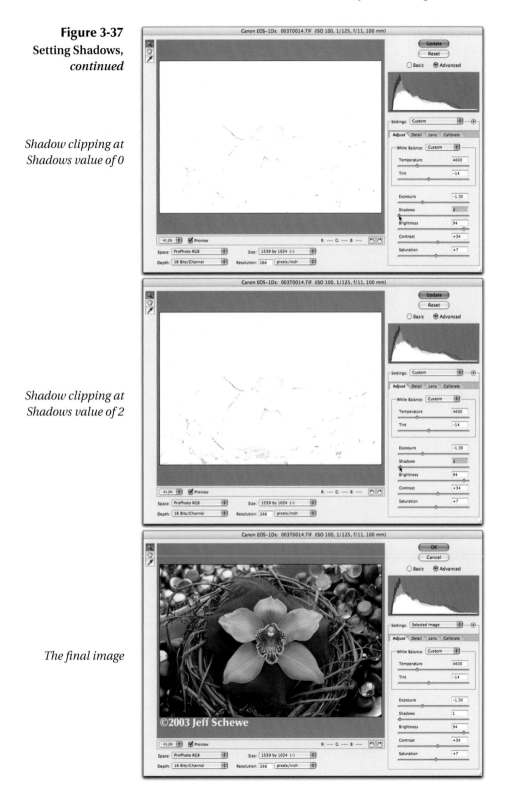

Figure 3-37
Setting Shadows,
continued

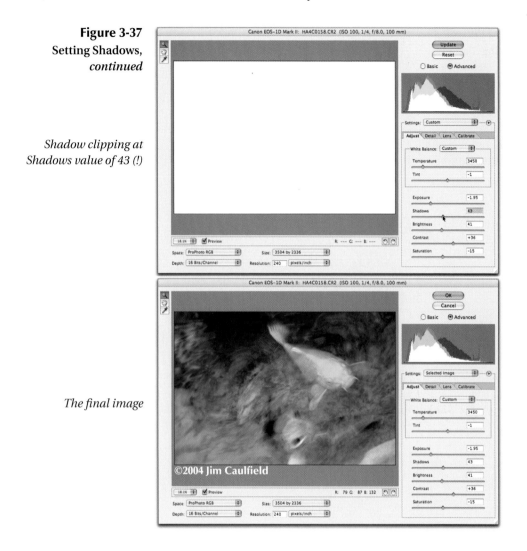

Shadow clipping at
Shadows value of 43 (!)

The final image

▶ **Saturation.** The Saturation control works similarly to the master Saturation slider in Photoshop's Hue/Saturation command. I typically make small moves with the Saturation slider, preferring to fine-tune selective color ranges on the converted image in Photoshop. Due to the linear nature of raw captures, Camera Raw's Saturation control has a stronger effect on the quarter-tones than on other parts of the tonal range. If that's what you need for a particular image, use it; otherwise save the saturation moves for Photoshop.

Last but not least, don't overlook the creative possibilities Camera Raw offers. Figure 3-38 shows some very different treatments of the same image.

Figure 3-38
Creative Camera Raw

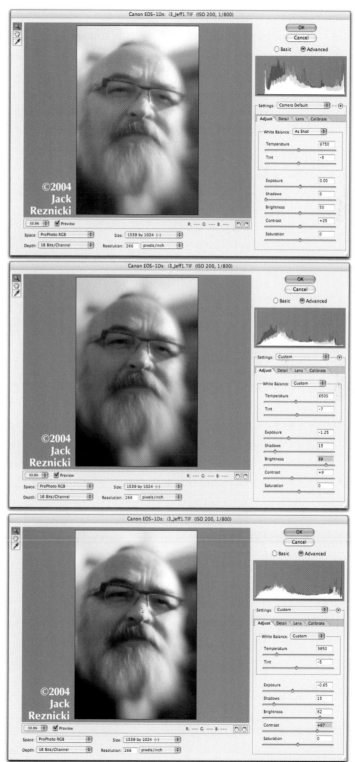

The image at camera
default settings

These two very different
interpretations should
give you some idea of the
creative flexibility
offered by Camera Raw.

The "digital Holga" is
available from
www.lensbabies.com.

The White Balance tools are also amenable to creative use. Figure 3-39 shows two examples. At default settings, Camera Raw's white balance attempts to reproduce the white balance of the actual scene, but the tools

Figure 3-39
Creative white balance

The image with white balance as shot

The image with a much colder white balance. Note that in addition to lowering the Temperature value, the Tint value has also been increased.

also allow you to apply radical warming or cooling effects in a way that Photoshop just can't achieve.

Figure 3-39
Creative white balance,
continued

The image with white balance as shot

The image with a much warmer white balance. In this case, the required Tint adjustment is much smaller.

Once you've made all the adjustments in the Adjust panel, it's time to move on to the Detail panel. The reason for making all the tonal adjustments first is that they can change the noise signature of the image significantly, so until you've made these adjustments, you won't have a good idea of what needs to be done in terms of noise reduction.

The Detail tab. The Detail tab contains three controls, Sharpness, Luminance Smoothing, and Color Noise Reduction—see Figure 3-40. Their effect is only visible when you zoom in to 100% view or higher, but it's usually useful to zoom to a higher percentage when working the Luminance Smoothing and Color Noise Reduction controls to really see what's happening.

Figure 3-40
The Detail tab

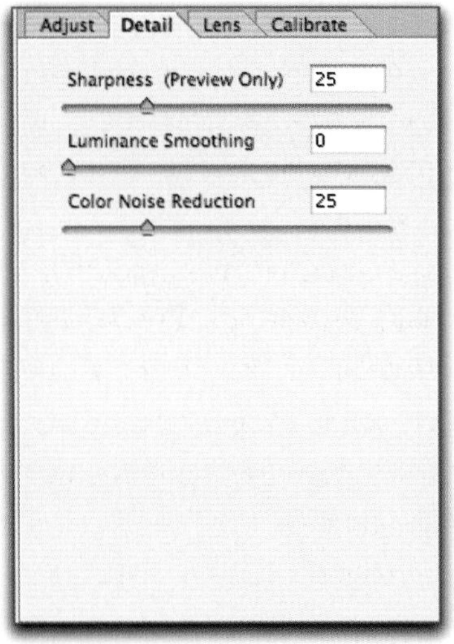

▶ **Sharpness.** The Sharpness slider lets you apply sharpening either to the preview image only or to both the preview and the converted image—see "Preferences," earlier in this chapter.

I usually apply sharpening to the preview image only—it's easier to make decisions about contrast on a reasonably sharp image than on a very soft one, so I set the Sharpness slider to a default of 25 and incorporate that in my Camera Default settings (see "Saving Settings," later in this chapter). The value isn't set in stone—you may want to choose a higher or lower value based on your camera, your display type and resolution, and your personal taste. The goal is simply to make the preview image reasonably sharp to aid editing decisions. Then I apply more controllable sharpening to the converted image in Photoshop.

However, if I'm converting a large number of images to JPEGs for review or transmission, and time is of the essence, I'll temporarily switch my Camera Raw Preferences to apply sharpening to the converted image.

▶ **Luminance Smoothing.** Luminance noise shows up as random speckled variations in tone that are usually more prominent at higher ISO speeds than at lower ones. The noise tends to be concentrated in the darker tones; it's much easier to see if you apply some sharpening to the preview image using the Sharpness slider and zoom in as far as you can go.

If you see luminance noise, simply raise the value of the Luminance Smoothing slider until it goes away. (Unlike many aspects of Camera Raw, this one isn't complicated!) Luminance smoothing does soften the image somewhat, so don't apply more than you need. The default value is zero, but depending on your camera and your shooting style, you may want to increase this value slightly (6-10) and save it as a new camera default if you don't want to check each individual image. Higher ISO speeds, long exposures, or underexposing to hold highlights all tend to increase the luminance noise, so it's worth spending some time analyzing your images to determine a good default value for the Luminance Smoothing slider.

▶ **Color Noise Reduction.** Color noise usually shows up as random magenta and green splotches in dark areas, but with some cameras it can also manifest itself as colored speckles around highlights.

As with luminance noise, raise the Color Noise Reduction slider value until the color noise disappears—see Figure 3-41. The order in which you apply Luminance Smoothing and Color Noise Reduction isn't critical—I tend to fix the worse of the two problems first. Color Noise Reduction has much less impact on image sharpness than does Luminance Smoothing, so it's fairly safe to leave it at the default value of 25 if you don't want to check each individual image.

Figure 3-41
Color Noise Reduction

To check for color noise,
zoom all the way into a
dark area of the image.

At 400% view, with the
Color Noise Reduction
slider set to zero, the color
noise is clearly visible.

Increase the value of the
Color Noise Reduction
slider until the color noise
is no longer visible.

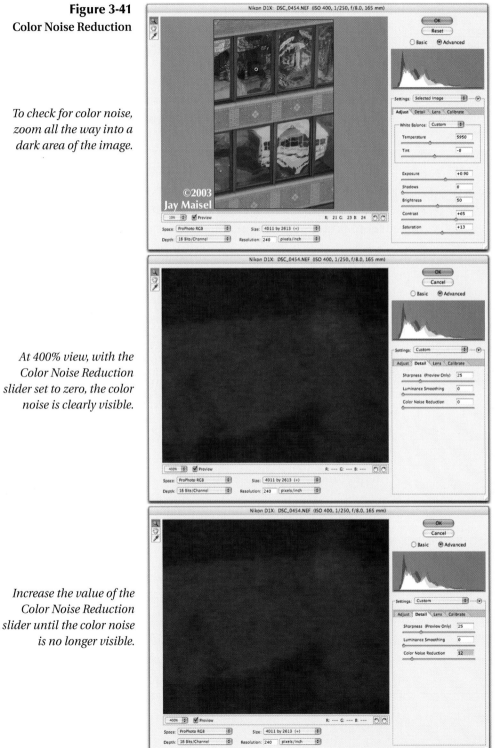

Tip: Pan for Before-and-Afters. The easiest way to judge the effect of your noise reduction settings, for both luminance and color noise, is to pan the image using the hand tool (press the Spacebar to get the hand tool temporarily). As you pan, the new image areas that come into view don't have the noise reduction applied until you release the mouse button, so you can easily see a quick before-and-after.

Most cameras exhibit some degree of color noise at all speeds. Luminance noise tends to be more common at high speeds, but both types of noise vary considerably from one camera model to another. The built-in defaults are a reasonable starting point, but you'll almost certainly want to tweak them and save as your own Camera Default settings. You may even want to save separate settings for different ISO speeds—see "Saving Settings," later in this chapter.

The Lens tab. The controls in the Lens tab let you address two problems, one common, the other pretty rare. If you use zoom lenses, you'll almost certainly run into chromatic aberration—color fringing along high-contrast edges caused by the inability of the lens to bring all the wavelengths of light to focus at the same plane—at some point in your work. Digital capture is extremely demanding on lenses, and it's not at all unusual for a lens that performs superbly on film to show some chromatic aberration on digital captures, particularly at the wide end of the range. Vignetting, where the corners are darkened because the lens fails to illuminate the sensor evenly, is rarer, but you may encounter it at very wide apertures. The controls in the Lens tab let you address both problems—see Figure 3-42.

Figure 3-42
The Lens tab

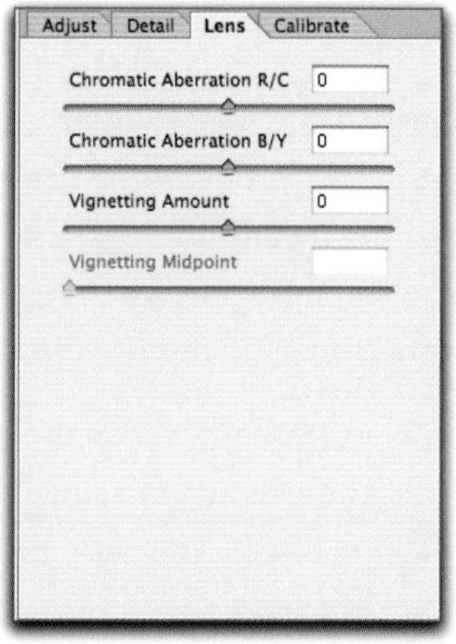

▶ **Chromatic Aberration controls.** Camera Raw offers two Chromatic Aberration sliders, one to address red/cyan fringing (Chromatic Aberration R/C), the other to address blue/yellow fringing (Chromatic Aberration B/Y). They work by adjusting the size of the red and blue channel, respectively, in relation to the green channel.

The adjustments have remarkably little impact on the rest of the image. Mathematical comparisons of the non-edge pixels may reveal a one- or two-level difference in one channel in a few areas; but I've yet to see a difference that could be detected visually, so don't be afraid to use these controls to eliminate color fringes. Two tips may help you do so.

Tip: Turn Off Sharpening. To see the color fringes clearly and to judge the optimum settings for the sliders, turn off any sharpening you've applied with the Sharpness slider in the Detail tab. The color fringes are usually most prominent along high-contrast edges, and sharpening applies a halo to such edges that makes it harder to see exactly where the color fringes start and end.

Tip: Option-Drag the Sliders to Hide the Other Channel. Red/cyan fringing is usually much easier to see than blue/yellow fringing, but chromatic aberration is almost always a combination of both. Holding down the Option key as you drag either of the Chromatic Aberration sliders hides the channel that isn't being affected by the adjustment, making it much easier to apply exactly the right amount of correction to both channels.

Figure 3-43 shows a typical example of chromatic aberration, along with the necessary fixes.

▶ **Vignetting controls.** Camera Raw offers two controls for addressing vignetting. Vignetting Amount controls the degree of darkening (negative values) or lightening (positive values) applied to the image. Vignetting Midpoint, which is enabled only when Vignetting Amount is set to a non-zero value, controls how far the correction extends from the corners.

Thus far, the only example I've seen of vignetting on digital captures has been with tilt/shift lenses, and since this vignetting is asymmetrical, the controls don't help. They are, however, handy for burning in the corners of the image!

Figure 3-43
Chromatic Aberration
corrections

To check for chromatic aberration, turn off any sharpening, then zoom into an area with high-contrast edges.

In this case, there's slight color-fringing along the high-contrast edges of the car.

Start with the Chromatic Aberration R/C slider. Option-dragging the slider hides the blue channel so that you only see the red/cyan fringe. Adjust the slider until the color fringe disappears, then repeat with the Chromatic Aberration B/Y slider.

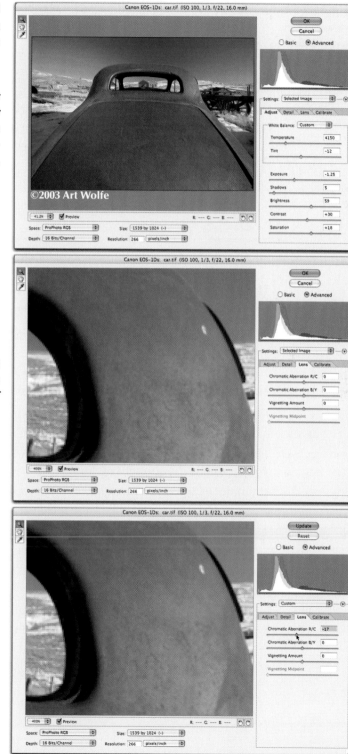

Figure 3-43
Chromatic Aberration
corrections, *continued*

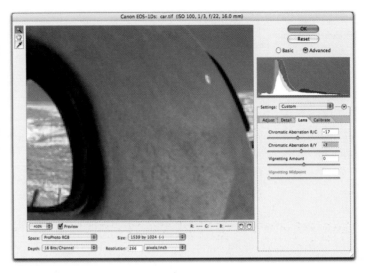

*These settings eliminate
the color fringe.*

The Calibrate tab. I've already covered the intended use of the Calibrate tab controls—fine-tuning the color rendering for a specific camera—in detail earlier in this chapter. Here I'll look at some creative uses of the controls.

One non-obvious use of the Calibrate tab, which I must credit to Adobe evangelist, raconteur, bon vivant and demomeister Russell Brown, is in color-to-grayscale conversions. Start by reducing the Saturation control in the Adjust tab to –100, and then move to the Calibrate tab. The Hue sliders control the panchromatic response, while the Saturation controls let you modulate the strength of the Hue controls' effect. Figure 3-44 shows examples of different black and white conversions, along with the settings that produced them. Note that the ideal values will vary from camera to camera, but the ones shown here should get you in the ballpark.

These conversions approximate the use of traditional color filters, but you aren't limited to this approach—you can create intermediate settings or make image-specific conversions.

If you're going for natural color, it's probably a bad idea to use the Calibrate controls as selective color correction tools—selective color corrections are better left for Photoshop—but you can certainly use them for creative color effects like the one in Figure 3-45!

Figure 3-44
Color to grayscale

Starting with the color image, reduce the Saturation slider in the Adjust tab to zero to get a grayscale image, and then adjust the Calibrate controls to vary the panchromatic response.

©2002 Jeff Schewe   *Color image*

©2002 Jeff Schewe   *Orange contrast*

©2002 Jeff Schewe   *Deep red contrast*

©2002 Jeff Schewe   *Green contrast*

©2002 Jeff Schewe   *Blue contrast*

Figure 3-45
Creative color
with Calibrate

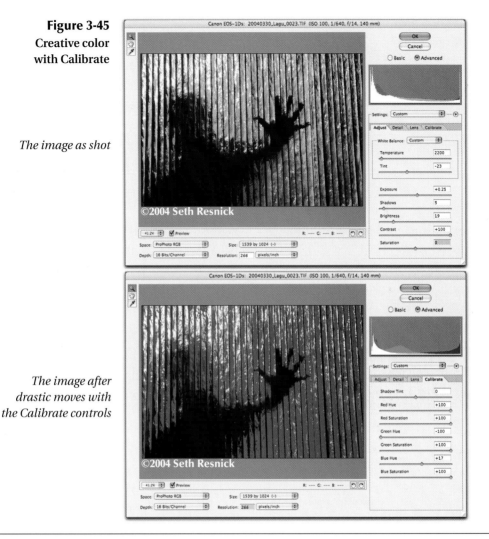

The image as shot

The image after
drastic moves with
the Calibrate controls

Saving Settings

If you had to adjust every slider on every image, you might reasonably conclude that Camera Raw was an instrument of torture rather than a productivity tool. Fortunately, Camera Raw offers great flexibility in saving and applying settings (and, as you'll learn in the next chapter, the File Browser lets you apply Camera Raw settings to one or more images without even opening Camera Raw).

Depending on how you set Camera Raw's "Save image settings in:" Preference, settings get saved either in the Camera Raw Database, or as individual sidecar .xmp files—see "The Camera Raw Menu," earlier in this chapter.

The Camera Raw database (file name is Adobe Camera Raw Database) lives in the Application Data folder as Document and Settings/ *user name*/ Application Data/Adobe/Camera Raw on Windows systems, and in the user's Preferences folder as Users/ *user name*/Library/Preferences on Mac OS.

Camera Raw Database

If you want to do absolutely no file management, and you work on only one computer, the advantage of saving settings in the Camera Raw database is that they're indexed by file content rather than name. You can rename your raw images and move them anywhere on your computer, and Camera Raw will still associate the correct settings with each image.

The significant downside is that you rely on a single file on a single computer to hold all your image settings. If you move the images to a different machine, or even just burn them on a CD, the settings won't travel with the images. So while settings saved in the Camera Raw database are easy to handle in terms of file management on a single machine, they're very inflexible. This inflexibility leads me to always save my settings as sidecar .xmp files.

Sidecar XMP Files

Adobe's XMP (Extensible Metadata Platform) is an open, documented, W3C-compliant standard for saving metadata (literally, data about data), including all the EXIF data generated by the camera; IPTC information such as captioning, keywording, and copyright notices; and, last but not least, all the settings you used in Camera Raw on a given image.

When you elect to save image settings as .xmp sidecar files, they're saved in a small file with the same name as the image and a .xmp extension. The sidecar file is automatically saved in the same folder as the image, which is usually what you want.

As you'll learn in the next chapter, Photoshop's File Browser offers features that automatically keep the sidecar files with the raw images as long as you use the File Browser to copy or move them. If you use some other software to move or copy your images, it's up to you to keep the sidecar files with the images. Since they're always saved in the same folder as the images, and the file names match those of the images, this isn't hard to do.

But whichever method you use, Camera Raw doesn't limit you to saving only the entire group of settings for a specific image. Much of the power and flexibility of Camera Raw comes from its ability to save subsets of settings in addition to complete sets of image settings.

Save Settings Subset

When you edit an image, you generally want to save all the settings that apply to that image so that the settings get applied each time you open the raw file. But it's also useful to save and recall subsets of settings to speed editing, hence the Save Settings Subset command on the Camera Raw menu.

For example, if you create Calibrate settings, either for color calibration or for black-and-white conversions, it's useful to have them available at all times. You may also wish to save Exposure or White Balance settings, or noise reduction settings for different ISO speeds, so that you can simply choose them from the Settings menu instead of manipulating sliders. The Save Settings Subset command lets you choose exactly which settings you want to save—see Figure 3-46.

Figure 3-46
Save Settings Subset

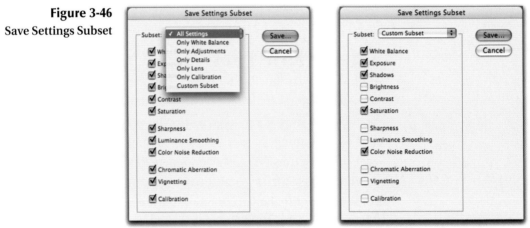

The Subset menu lets you choose groups of settings quickly.

The checkboxes let you create custom subsets of settings.

To make settings subsets constantly available, save them in the Camera Raw Presets folder (that's the Camera Raw folder inside the Presets folder inside the Adobe Photoshop CS folder). Saving the settings in the Presets folder is useful for two reasons.

▶ I always know where to find them.

▶ Each saved setting is represented by a separate file, so when my Settings menu becomes unmanageably long, I can easily prune it by going into the Camera Raw Presets folder and trashing the files I no longer need rather than laboriously selecting each setting and then choosing Delete Current Setting from the Camera Raw menu.

Saving settings in separate sidecar files makes it easy to share them with others or to create multiple settings files for a single image. For example, you may want to create one setting for highlights and another for shadows, and then combine both versions in Photoshop to increase the apparent dynamic range, as shown in Figure 3-47.

Figure 3-47
Combining multiple
exposures

Here I process the image twice, with one set of settings for the shadows and another for the highlights. Then I combine the two exposures in Photoshop.

Figure 3-47
Combining multiple
exposures, *continued*

*The exposures combined
in Photoshop*

©2002 Jeff Schewe

If you consistently find yourself making the same setting over and over again, it's probably a good candidate for a preset. But if you save too many settings as presets, your Settings menu becomes unmanageably long. The bottom line is that we each need to arrive at our own ideal trade-off between the convenience of presets and the length of the Settings menu.

Beyond Camera Raw

If Camera Raw were the only place to apply Camera Raw settings, the ability to save presets would be a minor convenience. But as I mentioned at the beginning of this chapter, you don't have to open and edit every single image in Camera Raw. Instead, you can select multiple images in Photoshop's File Browser and apply Camera Raw settings there.

In this chapter, I focused on editing one image at a time in Camera Raw. In the next chapter, we'll look at the various vital roles the File Browser plays in building an efficient workflow, one of which is to apply Camera Raw settings to dozens or hundreds of images, quickly and efficiently.

The File Browser

Your Digital Light Table

When the File Browser first appeared in Photoshop 7, I thought of it as a nice alternative to the File menu's Open command when dealing with a folder full of files, because it let me see thumbnails and previews of the images, allowing me to identify the ones I wanted quickly. But in Photoshop CS, the File Browser is a mission-critical tool for anyone who shoots raw.

You can make your initial selects from a shoot using the File Browser as a digital light table. When you want to convert your images, you can apply Camera Raw settings through the File Browser. You can also use the File Browser to add and edit metadata—one of the first things I do to a new folder of raw images is to add my copyright notice to each image. And while I admit to being less assiduous than I really should be, I'm also using the File Browser to add keywords to images so that I can find them easily several years hence. See the sidebar "All About Metadata," later in this chapter.

If you've considered the File Browser as just an Open dialog box on steroids, let me introduce you to the bigger picture. The File Browser is really a mini-application in its own right, and it's surprisingly deep. So in this chapter I'll introduce you to its various parts, explain what they do, and show you how to use them to handle your images efficiently.

Opening the File Browser

When I work on single-monitor systems, I usually keep the File Browser closed unless I'm actually using it. On dual-monitor Macs, I keep the File Browser open on the second monitor. Unfortunately, Windows operating systems prevent you from doing this—dual-monitor support is one of the few remaining areas where the Mac offers a significant advantage in Photoshop work.

To open the File Browser, do any of the following (see Figure 4-1):

▶ Choose File>Browse, or press Command-Shift-O.

▶ Choose Window>File Browser.

▶ Click the File Browser button in the Options bar (it's the icon that looks like a magnifying glass over an open folder).

Figure 4-1
Opening the File Browser

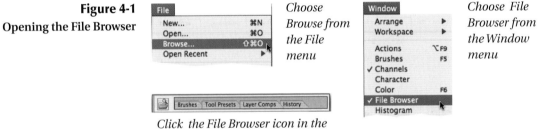

Choose Browse from the File menu

Choose File Browser from the Window menu

Click the File Browser icon in the Options bar.

Anatomy of the File Browser

The File Browser has evolved from being a somewhat oddly behaved palette in Photoshop 7 to being a mini-application in its own right in Photoshop CS, so the first thing you need to do is to acquaint yourself with its various parts (see Figure 4-2).

The File Browser window contains six different areas, two of which, the menu and toolbar, and the main window containing the thumbnails, are always visible. The four remaining components are resizable palettes that you can rearrange, resize, or combine just as you can other Photoshop palettes.

The main window holds thumbnails, which you can display at four different sizes. The Folders palette lets you quickly browse through folders and also lets you move or copy files by dragging or Option-dragging

Figure 4-2
The File Browser

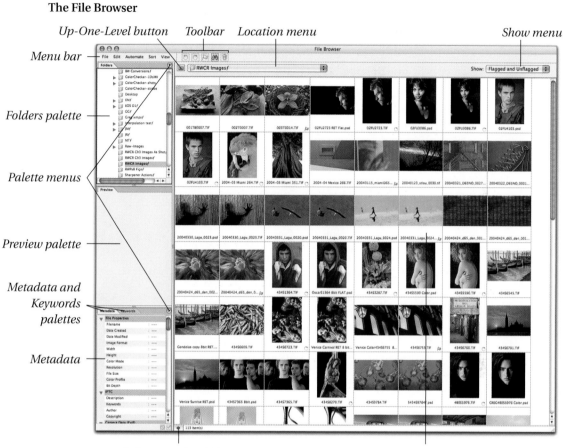

Up-One-Level button   *Toolbar*   *Location menu*   *Show menu*

Menu bar

Folders palette

Palette menus

Preview palette

Metadata and Keywords palettes

Metadata

Palette toggle (click to collapse palettes)   *Main window*

their thumbnails to a Folder icon in the Folders palette. The Preview palette shows a preview of the selected image. The Metadata palette shows the metadata associated with the selected image—you can control which fields are displayed. The Keywords palette lets you create keywords and sets of keywords, assign them to images, and perform searches.

File Browser Menu Bar

As befits a mini-application, the File Browser has its own menu bar. Rather than giving a blow-by-blow description of every single menu command, I'll give you an overview of the menus, along with details about the commands I find particularly useful and/or interesting.

The File menu. The File menu deals with the usual tasks of opening and closing files, but it also lets you work with the File Browser's cache for the current folder. The cache holds the thumbnails and previews, as well as any flagging or ranking information you apply to the images (see "Selecting and Sorting," later in this chapter). When you burn a CD or copy the folder to removable media, you can export the cache using the Export Cache command, so that when Photoshop opens the folder on the CD, you don't have to wait for the cached information to get rebuilt. See Figure 4-3.

Figure 4-3
The File Browser
File menu

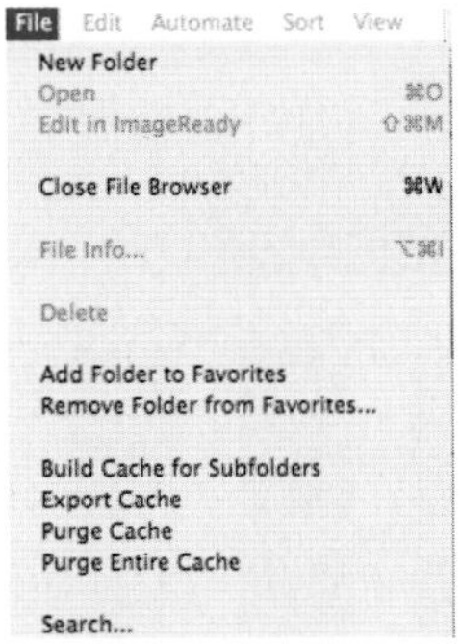

In a dire emergency, you can use the Purge Cache command to free up hard disk space—depending on just what's in the cache, you may recover anything from about 2 to about 8 megabytes—but you'll lose all the cached information, so make sure that the emergency is indeed dire.

The File Info command offers a way to edit an image's IPTC metadata without first opening the image, which is handy when you just want to add copyright or captioning information to a huge file. It also allows you to save metadata templates for IPTC info, which you can use to apply metadata quickly to multiple files—see Figure 4-4.

The Edit menu. The Edit menu generally offers somewhat slower ways to do things you can accomplish faster by other means, such as selecting, deleting, rotating, and flagging images, or applying metadata templates, but three commands are of particular interest.

Rank lets you apply a ranking to multiple images simultaneously by selecting them in the File Browser, choosing Rank from the Edit menu, and then entering a rank in the dialog box. Photoshop's online help shows ranks like "Good" and "Bad"; but using a single number or, if you really need more than 10 ranks, a single letter, makes it much easier to sort images by rank (see "Selecting and Sorting," later in this chapter).

Figure 4-4
Save Metadata Template

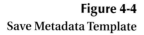

Metadata Display Options lets you specify which metadata fields appear in the metadata palette and gives you the option to automatically hide fields that are empty for the current image. If you don't have a GPS-enabled camera, for example, you may as well hide all the GPS fields—see Figure 4-5.

Figure 4-5
Metadata Display Options

These fields will be displayed.

These fields will be hidden.

Empty fields will be hidden.

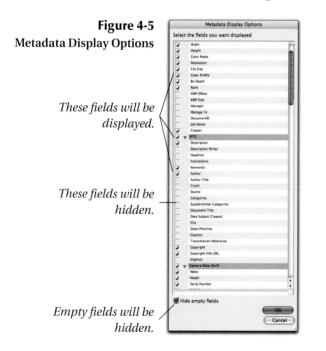

All About Metadata

Metadata (which literally means "data about data") isn't a new thing. Photoshop's File Info dialog box has allowed you to add metadata such as captions, copyright info, and routing or handling instructions, for years. But digital capture brings a much richer set of metadata to the table.

Most current cameras adhere to the EXIF (Exchangeable Image File Format) standard, which supplies with each image a great deal of information on how it was captured, including the camera model, the specific camera body, shutter speed, aperture, focal length, flash setting, and of course the date and time.

IPTC (International Press Telecommunications Council) metadata has long been supported by Photoshop's File Info feature, allowing copyright notices and the like. Other types of metadata supported by Photoshop CS include GPS information from GPS-enabled cameras (it's immensely cool that my good

friend Stephen Johnson's stunning landscape images include GPS metadata that will allow people to identify where they were shot 10 or 100 years from now, and note how the landscape has changed). You can apply Camera Raw settings as metadata to instruct Photoshop how you want the image to be processed, without actually doing the conversion. You can even record every Photoshop operation applied to the image as metadata using the History Log feature.

Adobe has been assiduous in promoting XMP (eXtensible Metadata Platform), an open, extensible, W3C-compliant standard for storing and exchanging metadata—all the Creative Suite applications use XMP, and because XMP is extensible, it's relatively easy to update existing metadata schemes to be XMP-compliant. However, it will probably take some time before all the other applications that use metadata, such as third-party digital raw converters, get

updated to handle XMP. But let's be very clear: XMP is not some proprietary Adobe initiative. It's an open, XML-based standard. So if you find that another application is failing to read XMP metadata, contact the publisher and tell them you need them to get with the program!

Right now, unless you're a programmer or a very serious scripting wonk, there may not be a great deal you can do with much of the metadata, at least, not automatically; but it likely won't be too long before you start seeing things like camera-specific sharpening routines that vary their noise reduction with ISO value and exposure time, to give just one example. The more information you have about an image, the better your chances of being able to do useful things to it automatically; and the more things you can do automatically, the more time you can spend doing those things that only a human can do, like exercising creative judgment.

Preferences opens the File Browser Preferences (it's the same dialog box you get from Photoshop's Preferences>File Browser command—see Figure 4-6).

▶ If you're primarily concerned with processing raw digital captures, you can set the limit under Do Not Process Files Larger Than to a value a little bigger than your raw files so that the File Browser doesn't spend time churning away on those layered 16-bit monster images.

Figure 4-6
File Browser Preferences

▶ The Custom Thumbnail Size field lets you set a custom size for thumbnails, up to 1,024 pixels wide. I usually set the Custom Thumbnail Size to make the largest thumbnails that will let me see two thumbnails side by side on my display.

▶ Allow Background Processing lets the File Browser keep working—generating thumbnails and previews, and reading metadata—while you do something else. If that something else is answering email or surfing the Web, by all means use this feature, but be warned that even if you have a really fast machine, allowing the File Browser to do background processing makes both it and Photoshop very unresponsive until the processing is finished. So I usually leave this option turned off.

▶ High Quality Previews, on the other hand, is an option I always leave turned on—I find the ability to view large previews invaluable in making initial selects, and when it's turned off, large previews get very pixellated.

▶ I *always* leave Keep Sidecar Files with Master Files checked. That way, whenever I move image files using the File Browser, the sidecar files containing the metadata always travel with them.

The Automate menu. The Automate menu offers many of the options found on Photoshop's File>Automate menu, with two important additions—Batch Rename and Apply Camera Raw Settings.

▶ **Batch Rename** lets you replace the less-than-useful names digital cameras typically assign to images—CRW_0403.CRW, for example—with ones that are more meaningful to you (see Figure 4-7). I always archive my raw captures preserving the original file names and folder structure from the camera storage media; then I make duplicates and use Batch Rename to rename them, but I admit that there may be an element of superstition in doing so.

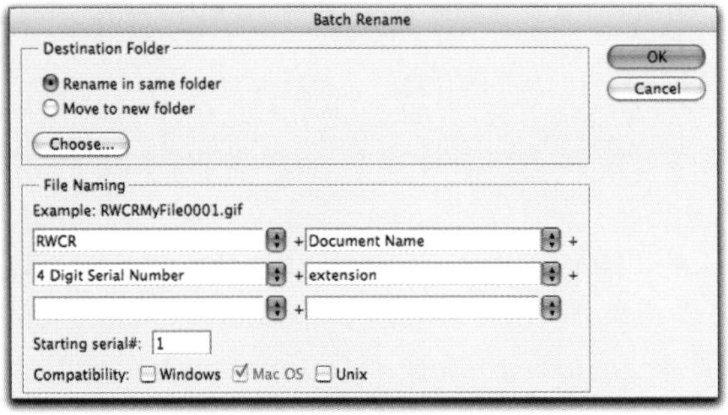

Figure 4-7
Batch Rename

Tip: Don't Forget the Extension. If your raw captures are accompanied by sidecar thumbnail and .xmp (metadata) files, you *must* include the extension in the new file names; otherwise the Batch Rename will fail.

▶ **Apply Camera Raw Settings** is one of the most important commands in the File Browser's menus. It lets you quickly apply saved Camera Raw settings, or settings from the previous image, to multiple files selected in the File Browser, without opening them or going through the Camera Raw interface (see Figure 4-8).

In its Advanced mode, Apply Camera Raw Settings offers a great deal of flexibility by letting you choose subsets of settings to apply, so you can, for example, keep each image's white balance unchanged and just adjust the exposure, or any other permutation you find useful.

The Sort menu. The Sort menu lets you control the order in which images are displayed. The Custom option appears when you reorder the images by dragging them, just as you would on a light table.

Figure 4-8
Apply Camera Raw
Settings

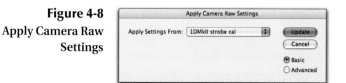

*In Basic mode, Apply
Camera Raw Settings lets
you load and apply saved
settings. In Advanced
mode, you can apply
subsets of settings or
create new ones, which
are then applied to
the selected images.*

The View menu. The View menu lets you control whether or not the browser displays things other than image files, the size of the thumbnails (including the custom size you specify in the File Browser's Preferences), and whether to show Flagged, Unflagged, or Flagged and Unflagged images (see "Selecting and Sorting," later in this chapter).

File Browser Toolbar

The toolbar is a great deal simpler than the menu bar, with only five simple tools—see Figure 4-9. The rotate counterclockwise and rotate clockwise tools (keyboard shortcuts are Command-[and Command-], respectively) are pretty self-explanatory. The flag tool (Command-') provides a simple mechanism for making "yes/no" binary selections—clicking the flag tool toggles the flag for all selected images. The search tool (which lacks a keyboard shortcut) lets you perform fairly detailed searches on files in the current folder (including subfolders) using file information, EXIF, or other metadata as criteria. The trash tool (keyboard shortcut is Delete) moves selected images to the Trash, but doesn't actually delete them.

Figure 4-9
File Browser Toolbar

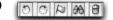

File Browser Main Window

The main window is devoted to displaying thumbnails. You can control the size of the thumbnails using the commands from the File Browser's View menu and the sort order using the commands from the File Browser's Sort menu.

At the top of the main window, the Up One Level button lets you navigate upward through the folder hierarchy, and the Location menu shows the current folder, its parent folder, all mounted volumes, the number of recent folders you specified in the File Browser's Preferences, and any folders you add to your Favorite Folders list using the File Browser's File>Add Folder to Favorites command.

The Show menu lets you choose whether to display thumbnails for Flagged files, for Unflagged files, or for both Flagged and Unflagged files (see "Selecting and Sorting," later in this chapter). At the lower left, the Toggle Expanded View button lets you hide or show the palettes—when they're hidden, the main window expands to fill the entire area with thumbnails—see Figure 4-2, earlier in this chapter.

The Folders Palette

The Folders palette displays the volume and folder hierarchy, allowing you to navigate to different folders—see Figure 4-10. It also displays two items that aren't really folders but act as folders inside the File Browser. The Favorite Folders folder holds any folders you designate as favorites, and the Search Results folder holds the results of any searches you perform with the search tool. Neither of these folders actually exists outside of the File Browser—they're "virtual" folders.

The palette menu contains but one command, Refresh.

Figure 4-10
Folders palette

The Folders palette lets you browse quickly through your directory structure.

The Preview Palette

The Preview palette displays a preview for the selected image. Like the other palettes, you can collapse it by double-clicking on its tab and resize it by dragging its size controls, but it has no menu and no secrets.

The Metadata Palette

The Metadata palette displays the metadata associated with the currently-selected image or images (when you have more than one image selected, many of the fields read "Multiple Values Exist"). See Figure 4-11.

Figure 4-11
Metadata palette

*The Metadata palette lets
you see the metadata
associated with the
selected image. The
fields with a pencil
icon are editable.*

The only metadata fields that are editable in Photoshop are the IPTC fields—they appear in the palette with a pencil icon next to the title. To edit these fields, select the images or images whose metadata you wish to edit, and then either click the pencil icon or click directly in the text area to enter the new metadata. The only IPTC field that isn't editable here is the Keywords field—to edit keywords, you need to use the Keywords palette.

The Metadata palette menu lets you launch a search (it's the same as clicking on the search tool), increase or decrease the font size used in the palette, and append or replace metadata from templates (see Figure 4-12)—saved templates appear in the menu. I find it's a lot easier to add a copyright notice, for example, from a template than it is to type the notice manually for all selected images, but either method works.

Figure 4-12
Metadata palette menu

Saved metadata templates

Metadata Display Options has the same functionality as the identically named command in the File Browser's Edit menu—use whichever one is the more convenient. It's definitely worth taking the few minutes needed to decide which fields you want to display (see Figure 4-5)—very few Photoshop users need to see them all!

The Keywords Palette

The Keywords palette lets you create keywords (which you can group into categories called *keyword sets*), and apply them to a selected image or images. The keywords get written into the Keywords field of the IPTC metadata, so they're visible in the Metadata palette—you just can't edit or apply them there.

Keyword sets appear as folders—the triangle to the left lets you expand and collapse them. When they're expanded, you can see the list of keywords in the set (see Figure 4-13). To apply a keyword to selected images, click in the column at the left of the palette—a checkmark appears, indicating that the selected images contain this keyword. To apply all the keywords in a set, click to the left of the set name rather than beside the individual keyword.

Figure 4-13
Keywords palette

Icons at the bottom of the palette let you create a new keyword set or keyword, or delete an existing keyword set or keyword. Note that deleting keywords removes them only from the list, not from any files that contain them. You can also move keywords to a different category by dragging them.

The palette menu mostly replicates the functions of the control buttons, but the Rename command provides the sole path for renaming keywords or categories.

Configuring the File Browser

The default layout of the File Browser lets you see where all the bits and pieces are, but it's definitely less than optimal for doing any real work. Fortunately, one of the File Browser's great strengths is its configurability. You can resize the palette area and the individual palettes by dragging the size controls, and display different-sized thumbnails using the commands on the File Browser's View menu. I typically use at least four different File Browser layouts for different tasks—see Figure 4-14.

Of course, if I had to resize everything manually every time I wanted to change the layout, I'd be a distinctly unhappy camper. Fortunately, Photoshop's Workspace feature applies to File browser layouts, so I save each of my layouts as a workspace. To do so, I arrange the File Browser's elements the way I want them for a particular task, then choose Save Workspace from the Workspace submenu on Photoshop's Window menu so that I can recall each layout quickly.

I create each workspace with all the other palettes hidden, so the File Browser can use all the available desktop real estate—that way I don't have to waste time hitting Tab to hide the palettes. You can, if you wish, take things a step further by recording actions that let you switch between the different File Browser layouts using keystrokes—I'll describe doing so in detail in Chapter 7, *Exploiting Automation*.

File Browser Navigation

Like any decent mini-application that resides inside Photoshop, the File Browser is well equipped with keyboard shortcuts (which is just as well, because the new keyboard-shortcut customization features in Photoshop CS don't extend to the File Browser).

In the Folders panel, the up and down arrow keys move up and down one folder at a time. Adding the Command key moves up one level in the hierarchy.

Figure 4-14   File Browser layouts

The standard File Browser layout lets you see all the File browser elements, but it isn't particularly well suited to any specific task.

I use the all-thumbails view to sort images visually, as I would on a light table.

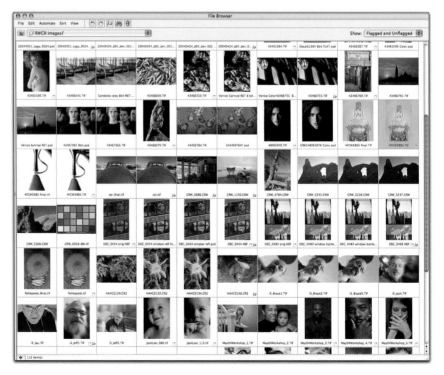

Figure 4-14   File Browser layouts, *continued*

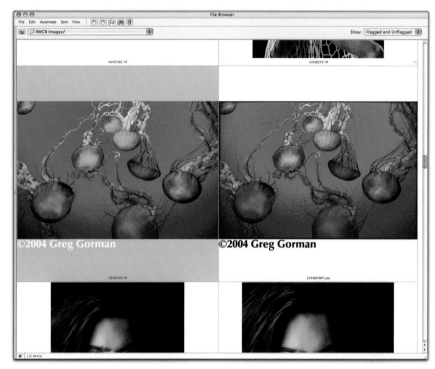

I use the Custom Thumbnail feature to make large thumbnails that let me compare two images at a time.

When I make initial selects using the Flag feature, I make the preview as large as possible and use the keyboard shortcuts to advance through the images and to apply the flag.

In the main window, the up, down, left, and right arrows move the selection to the next thumbnail in their respective directions. Adding Shift extends the selection to include the next thumbnail in that direction. (You can't, however, make discontiguous selections from the keyboard—you have to Command-click the thumbnails to add discontiguous images to the selection.) Home selects the first thumbnail, End selects the last one. Command-A selects all thumbnails, Command-Shift-A selects all Flagged thumbnails, and Command-D deselects all thumbnails.

Working in the File Browser

Camera Raw is a wonderful raw converter, and the File Browser is maturing into a more-than-competent image manager, but what really makes Photoshop CS a compelling solution for a raw digital workflow is the integration between the two. As soon as the File Browser encounters a folder of raw files, Camera Raw kicks in automatically, generating thumbnails and generous-size previews that allow you to make good judgments about each image without actually converting it, so that you can quickly make your initial selects.

Note that the high-quality previews are based on Camera Raw's default settings for your camera. If you find that they're consistently off, it's a sign that you need to change your Camera Default settings—see "Saving Settings" in Chapter 3, *Using Camera Raw*.

Then, when you've decided which images you want to work with, the File Browser lets you apply conversion settings from Camera Raw by writing them to the image's metadata, again without doing an actual conversion, using the Apply Camera Raw Settings command.

When I do conversions other than quick one-offs, I almost always do so as batch processes, incorporating other actions—I might set up one batch to produce high-res JPEGs for client approval, another to produce low-res JPEGs for emailing, and still another to prepare images for serious editing, with adjustment layers already added so that much of the grunt work is already done for me. Then, when the computer is busy doing my work for me, I go off and lead my glamorous life....

So let's look at the many ways in which Camera Raw and the File Browser can work together to help you to be more efficient and more productive.

Selecting and Sorting

One of the biggest bottlenecks in a raw digital workflow is in making your initial selects from a day's shoot. The File Browser helps in getting past this bottleneck with the Flag and Rank features.

I start by copying the files from the camera media to my hard drive—I've learned from bitter experience to avoid opening images directly from the camera media in all but the direst emergency. Then I point the File Browser at the folder full of raw images and wait the few minutes while it builds the thumbnails and previews and reads the metadata.

Next, I enter my copyright notice on all the images by pressing Command-A to Select All and either using a metadata template from the Metadata palette menu or clicking in the copyright field in the IPTC section of the Metadata palette and typing in the notice manually—see Figure 4-15.

Figure 4-15
Entering a
copyright notice

The easiest way to add copyright notices is to save a metadata template that you can apply quickly to the selected images.

You can also select the images and type the copyright notice into the Copyright field in the Metadata palette.

Yes/No sorting. For simple binary sorts, I set the File Browser to show a large preview, and then I use the arrow keys to advance from one image to the next. For the keepers, I press Command-' (apostrophe) to apply the Flag attribute. The rest I simply bypass (though I may rotate images that need it by pressing Command-[or Command-] to rotate them left or right, respectively).

When I've gone through all the images, I choose Flagged Files from the main window's Show menu, so that I can start processing the keepers without being distracted by the rejects—see Figure 4-16. (Of course, later on I'll probably choose Unflagged Files from the Show menu so that I can take a more nuanced look at the rejects.)

Figure 4-16
Show flagged

Using the keyboard shortcuts to advance from image to image and to apply the flag, I look at each image with a large preview, flag the keepers, and do nothing with the rejects.

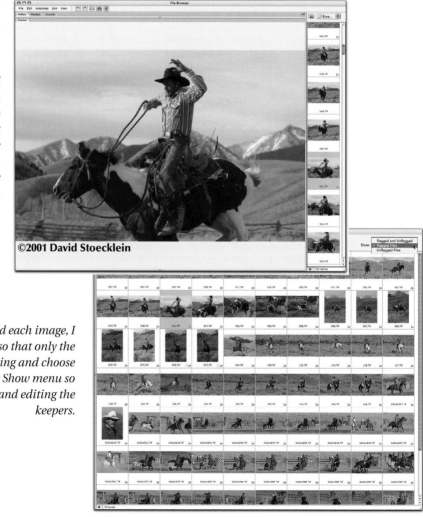

Once I've examined each image, I collapse the palettes so that only the thumbnails are showing and choose Flagged Files from the Show menu so that I can start sorting and editing the keepers.

Sorting by rank. If a yes/no/maybe approach appeals to you more than a straight binary choice, you can use the Rank feature instead of the Flag. If you want to use ranking, it's usually a good idea to choose Show Rank from the File Browser's View menu so that you can actually see what you're doing. Press Option-Enter to highlight the Rank field; then type a for yes, b for maybe, c for no, and hit Enter again to confirm the entry—see Figure 4-17. However, you can add ranking to images and search by rank, even when the Rank field is hidden—it's just a bit more mysterious that way! The keyboard shortcuts won't work when the Rank field is hidden, but you can choose Rank from the File Browser's Edit menu and then type the rank into the dialog box that appears.

Figure 4-17
Ranking images

To rank images with the Rank field visible, press Option-Enter, or click on the Rank field to select it, and then type the rank and press Enter to confirm it.

To rank images with the Rank field hidden, choose Rank from the File Browser Edit menu and then type the rank in the ensuing dialog box.

If you want go quickly through all the images, assigning a rank, you can rank the first image and then press Tab to advance to the next image with the Rank field already highlighted, ready for input. When you're done, you can either choose Rank from the Sort menu to sort by rank or use Search to find just the yesses, just the nos, or just the maybes—see Figure 4-18.

Figure 4-18
Search and sort by rank

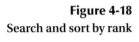

To sort by rank, choose Rank from the Sort menu (you can change the order by selecting or deselecting Ascending Order).

To search by rank, click the Search tool, then enter the desired rank under Criteria.

You can also select multiple images and apply the same rank to all of them, but to do so you need to select the images, then choose Rank from the File Browser's Edit menu—if you try to use the Option-Enter shortcut, it simply highlights the Rank field for the first selected thumbnail and deselects the rest.

Ranking, of course, isn't limited to three levels. You can enter up to 16 characters in the Rank field (if you *really* think you can keep track of 1E+16 possible levels of excellence—or, for the math-challenged, 9,999,999,999,999,999 possible ranks). For most of us, using either single digits from 0–9 or single letters from a–z provides more than enough flexibility.

Sequencing. Last but not least, if you're the type who thinks in terms of sequences of images rather than single images, you can drag the thumbnails into the order you want, just as you did with film on a light table—see Figure 4-19. Once you've sequenced the images, you can use Batch Rename to rename the files, including a numbering scheme that reflects your custom sort order.

Figure 4-19
Custom sort order

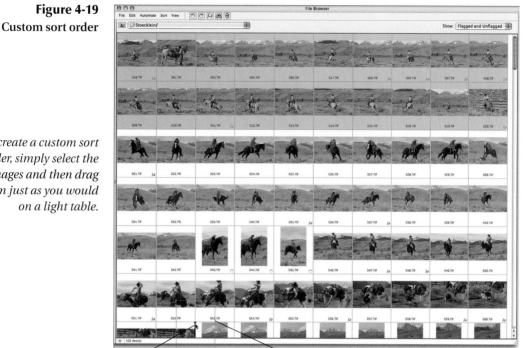

*To create a custom sort
order, simply select the
images and then drag
them just as you would
on a light table.*

Insertion point   Image outline

Applying Camera Raw Settings

The slowest possible way to process raw images in Photoshop CS is to open them one by one, make adjustments in Camera Raw, click OK to open the image in Photoshop, and then save it. Unless you're working for an hourly rate, I don't recommend this as a workflow.

Instead, I usually apply Camera Raw settings to each image as metadata using the Apply Camera Raw Settings command from the Edit menu—see Figure 4-20. Then I either open all the images at once or run a batch process so that I don't have to wait for Camera Raw to process each image individually. Much of the time, the goal is simply to deal with a lot of images and try to make them all good. When I've whittled the workload down to the few that I'll try to make perfect, I may revisit each one in Camera Raw and apply carefully customized settings to make them perfect, but even then I'll almost certainly run a batch process to convert them and prepare them for final editing in Photoshop.

Figure 4-20
Apply Camera Raw
Settings

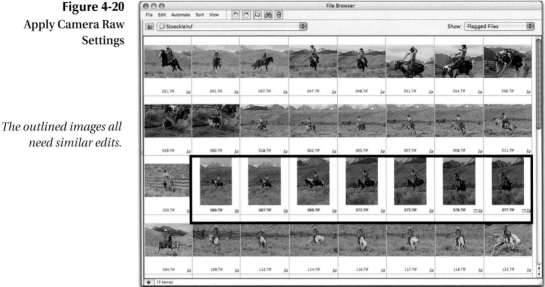

*The outlined images all
need similar edits.*

*I open the first image in
Camera Raw and make
some quick edits. At this
stage in the process, I'm
aiming for improvement
rather than perfection—
doing a rough edit to the
images at this stage will
aid in making final
selections later, to
which more polished
edits will apply.*

Applying one image's settings to others. The simplest way to process a bunch of similar images is to edit one in Camera Raw and then apply those edits to the others. With a contiguous series of images, I edit the first one, then select both the edited image and the other similar candidates—I just go to the last image in the series and Shift-click. Then I choose Apply

Figure 4-20
Apply Camera Raw
Settings, *continued*

I select all the images that need the same edit, and choose Apply Camera Raw Settings from the File Browser's Edit menu. Then I simply choose First Selected Image from the Settings menu, and click Update.

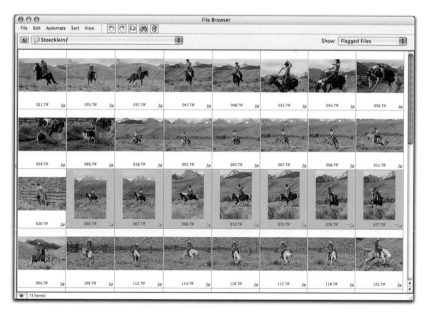

The edits I made to the first image are applied to all the other images in the selection. Later, I may return to each image and fine-tune the individual settings, but this is a very quick way to apply ballpark edits to lots of images.

Camera Raw Settings from the File Browser's Edit menu and choose First Selected Image from Camera Raw's Settings menu.

With noncontiguous images, I again edit the first one in Camera Raw. Then I select the other images by Command-clicking, choose Apply Camera Raw Settings from the File Browser's Edit menu, and choose Previous Conversion from Camera Raw's Settings menu.

Working with saved settings subsets. Often, I need to apply more individualized settings to each image, so one of the first things I did when I first started working with Camera Raw was to save subsets of settings that I could apply to images. In addition to creating Calibrate settings, I've created saved settings for exposure adjustments in 0.25-stop increments, and Brightness and Contrast adjustments in increments of 10 units—see Figure 4-21. I've played with saving White Balance adjustments, but thus far I've found them less useful because I usually need to adjust the Temperature and Tint controls interactively. But I almost invariably shoot with available light. If you shoot in the studio under controlled lighting, you may find it worthwhile to save White Balance settings too. See "Saving Settings" in Chapter 3, *Using Camera Raw*.

Figure 4-21
Working with
saved settings

These settings are all saved as presets in Camera Raw's Presets folder. Each one updates a single parameter, Exposure, Brightness, or Contrast.

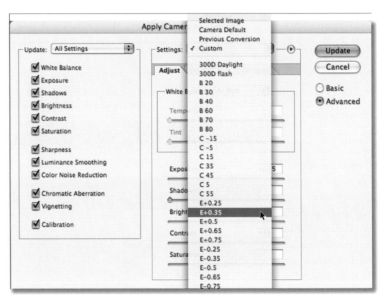

Obviously there's a trade-off between the number of settings you save and the ease with which you can find and apply them. If you create hundreds of subsets, your Camera Raw Settings menu will become very long and unmanageable. After you've spent some time applying settings from the File Browser, it should be apparent which settings are really useful to you and exactly what trade-off *you* need to make between the number of saved settings and the usability of the Camera Raw Settings menu.

The key to being productive when applying subsets is to apply them to all the images that need them simultaneously, which boils down to selecting images that all need the same (or very similar) treatment. For example, I may look for all the images that need a +0.25-stop exposure boost, then for the ones that need a half-stop, and so on. The image thumbnails and previews update to reflect the new settings, so checking the preview at a reasonably large size gives me a good idea of their effect.

Opening images. Once you've applied settings to an image or images, you can open them and bypass the Camera Raw dialog box by Shift-double-clicking. (If you're opening multiple images, Shift-double-click on the last one; otherwise you'll just change the selection.) Add Option if you also want to close the File Browser.

Camera Raw then processes the images using their assigned settings and opens the converted images in Photoshop. However, if I'm dealing with more than a handful of images, I almost invariably run a batch process instead, by choosing Batch from the File Browser's Automate menu—see Figure 4-22.

Figure 4-22
Batch dialog box

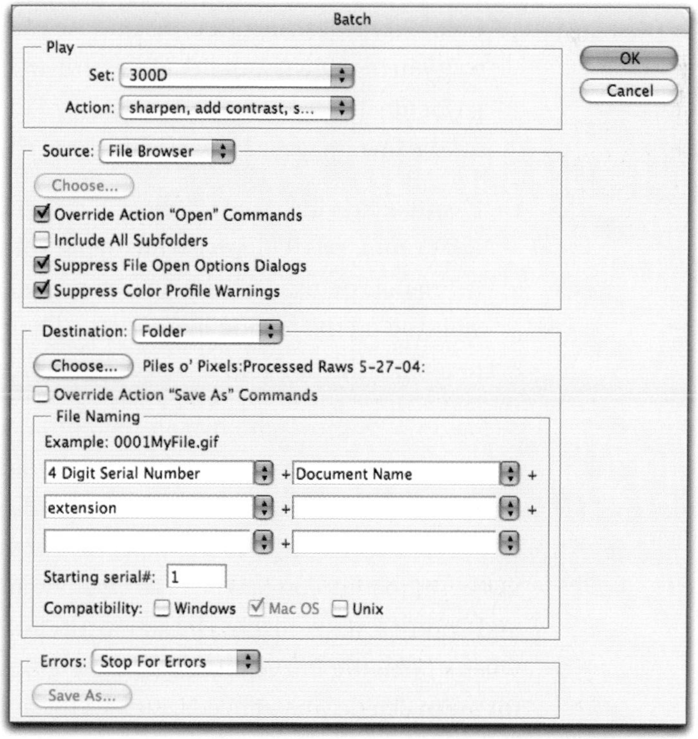

This batch process converts the selected images using each image's individual settings. It then calls an action that sharpens, adds an adjust-ment layer, and saves the layered file as a TIFF, adding a four-digit serial number to the original document name.

Using Batch. The Batch feature lets you process images with Camera Raw and, optionally, rename and save them to a different location, while also applying an action. Including an action in the batch allows for tremendous flexibility in automating different tasks. For example, I use one action to batch the creation of 1,024-pixel JPEGs and another to save 16-bit/channel TIFFs with adjustment layers included ready for editing, using Zip compression to save storage space. Actions like these save me hours of repetitive grunt work, which is after all what computers are supposed to do.

There are, however, a few stumbling blocks that can trip you up when you first try to implement this kind of automation.

▶ If you want the batch process to save the images in a specific format, you need to record the saving steps as part of the action you'll call for the batch.

▶ If you want to bypass the Camera Raw interface when you run the batch, you must check Suppress File Open Options Dialogs in the Batch dialog box (see Figure 4-22). It's probably a good idea to check Suppress Color Profile Warnings too, just in case your working space isn't set the way you thought it was. (It's always frustrating to start a batch process, go for lunch, then come back to find that the Profile Mismatch warning for the first image is sitting on the screen waiting for input.)

▶ If your action included a save, you must check Override Action "Save As" Commands. Otherwise the batch will try to save each file under the name you used for the save when you recorded the action, and it will stop on the second image when Photoshop asks you if you want to replace the previous image of the same name.

Figure 4-23 shows the two aforementioned actions, one for creating JPEGs that are converted to sRGB after the sharpening and resizing have been carried out on the 16-bit/channel ProPhoto RGB file, and another that prepares images for final editing in Photoshop by adding adjustment layers set to Multiply, Screen, and Overlay, and named Darken, Lighten, and Contrast, respectively. The action turns off the layers' visibility so that when I open the image, I see it with no adjustments—that way it's easy for me to decide what it needs, turn on the appropriate layers, and tweak their opacities to get the desired effect. I'll look at actions, batch processing, and other automation features in much more detail in Chapter 7, *Exploiting Automation*.

Figure 4-23
Useful actions

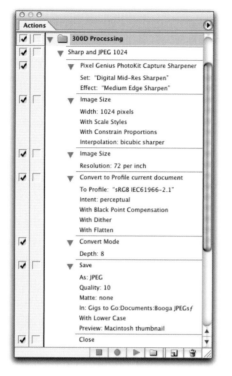

This action, when included in a batch, opens the raw image and converts it to a 16-bit/channel RGB image using the assigned Camera Raw settings. It then applies Pixel Genius's PhotoKit Capture Sharpener, downsizes the image to 1,024-pixel width, sets the resolution to 72 ppi, converts the image to sRGB, downsamples to 8 bits/channel, and saves the result as a JPEG with a quality of 10.

This action, when included in a batch, opens the raw image and converts it to a 16-bit/channel RGB image using the assigned Camera Raw settings. It then adds a Curves adjustment layer (with no curve adjustment applied) set to Multiply, renames the layer as "Darken," and hides it. It adds two more such layers, one set to Screen and named "Lighten," another set to Overlay and named "Contrast."

Finally, it saves the image as a 16-bit/channel TIFF, with ZIP compression applied to both the image and the layers. When I open the file, it's ready for editing without my having to do the grunt work of adding the layers and setting the blending modes.

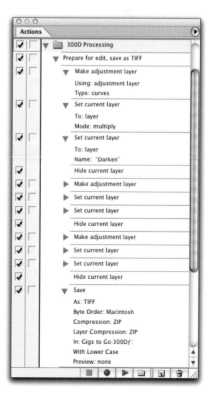

It's Smart to Be Lazy

Any way you slice it, shooting digital virtually guarantees that you'll spend more time in front of the computer and less time behind the lens. But the power of automation is there to let you make sure that when you *are* sitting in front of the computer, you're doing so because your critical judgment is required.

Digital capture involves processing masses of data—the files themselves may be smaller than film scans, but you'll almost certainly have to deal with a lot more of them. One of the great things about computers is that once you've figured out how to make the computer do something, you can make it do that something over and over again. So if you find yourself doing the same things to images over and over again, you can save yourself a great deal of work by teaching Photoshop how to do them for you. That way, you can concentrate on the exciting stuff. I'll look at automation in detail in Chapter 7, *Exploiting Automation*. But first, I'll take a step back and look at the bigger picture as I build a workflow from start to finish in the next chapter, *It's All About the Workflow*.

It's All About the Workflow

That's Flow, Not Slow

In the previous two chapters, I've shown you how to drive Camera Raw and the File Browser in detail (some might say excruciating detail). But knowing what buttons to push to get the desired result just means you know how to do the work. To turn that understanding into a practical workflow, you need to understand and optimize each part of the process. So in this chapter, I'll look at some important details, but I'll put them in the context of the big picture.

There are four basic stages in a raw workflow. You may revisit some of them—going back and looking at the initial rejects, or processing the images to different kinds of output file—but everything you do falls into one of four stages.

▶ You start by copying the raw images to the computer.

▶ You point the File Browser at the newly copied images and let it cache the thumbnails, previews, and metadata.

▶ You work with the images in the File Browser, selecting, sorting, applying metadata, and editing with Camera Raw.

▶ You process the raw images to output files.

In this chapter, I'll look at all four stages of the workflow, but the major emphasis is on the work you do in the File Browser, because the File Browser really is command central for an efficient raw workflow.

The File Browser

The File Browser lets you make your initial selects, add copyright and keyword metadata, sort your images in the order you want, rename them to reflect that order, and apply Camera Raw settings that get the most out of the capture.

By far the most efficient way to convert the raw files to output files is to do so as a batch, using the selected images in the File Browser as a source. Once you've completed your work in the File Browser, it's trivial to produce different versions of your images for different purposes—low-res JPEGs for web or email, higher-res JPEGs or Web photo galleries for client review, or 16-bit high-res images delivered into Photoshop for final polishing prior to final delivery.

But you need to do the work in the File Browser first, and since it forms the basis for just about everything else you do, it's important to understand just how that work gets saved and store by Photoshop. So let me state, very clearly, what information each of these key components stores.

▶ Image thumbnails, previews, flagging, ranking, rotation, and sort order are stored in the File Browser cache.

▶ All the other information about your images—keywords, and everything that appears in the Metadata palette—is stored in the sidecar .xmp file, with the possible exception of Camera Raw settings. You can choose whether to store these in the sidecar .xmp or in the Camera Raw database. I recommend storing them in the sidecar .xmp files for reasons that will become apparent later in this chapter.

Understanding how to handle the File Browser cache and the sidecar .xmp files is key to building an efficient workflow. Without this understanding, you're liable to wind up cursing as you redo work you thought you'd already completed. So I'll be referring to the cache and the .xmp files throughout the chapter.

The first order of business, though, is to transfer your raw images safely to the computer so that you can begin working with them. So I'll start by looking at the very first stage of the workflow—getting your images off the camera storage media and onto your hard drive—because mistakes made there can wreck your entire day's shoot.

Storing and Transferring Raw Images

The workflow starts with your in-camera storage media, typically but not invariably Compact Flash Type I or II. Transferring your images from the camera to the computer is one of the most critical, yet often one of the least examined, stages of your workflow. The following ground rules have stood me in good stead for several years—I've had my share of equipment problems, but thus far, I've yet to lose a single image.

- ▶ Don't use the camera as a card reader. Most cameras will let you connect them to the computer and download your images, but doing so is a bad idea for at least two reasons. Cameras are typically very slow as card readers, and when the camera is being used as a card reader, you can't shoot with it.

- ▶ Never open images directly from the camera media.

- ▶ Don't rely on just one copy of the images—always copy them to two separate drives before you start working.

- ▶ Don't erase your images from the camera media until you've verified the copies—see "Verifying Images," later in this chapter.

- ▶ Always format the cards in the camera in which they will be shot, never in the computer.

Following these rules may take a little additional time up front, but they will save you time in the long run.

Camera Media and Speed

All CF cards are not created equal, but vendor designations like 4x, 24x, 40x, Ultra, and Write Accelerated aren't terribly reliable guides as to the performance you'll get with your personal setup.

There are two distinctly different aspects to CF card speed.

▶ Your burst shooting rate is dictated by the speed with which the CF card writes images in the camera.

▶ Your image offloading speed is dictated by the speed with which images can be read from the CF card onto your computer's hard disk.

In either case, the bottleneck may be the CF Card, or it may be the hardware used to write to it (your camera) or read from it (your card reader).

Compact Flash write speed. Most of today's high-speed CF cards can write data as fast as the camera can send it. However, older cameras may not be able to deliver the data fast enough to justify the premium prices the fastest cards command.

One good source of comparative data on different cameras' write speeds to different cards can be found on Rob Galbraith's web site, www. robgalbraith.com—look for the CF Database link on the front page. Note that the database no longer gets updated for some older cameras, so if the notes say something to the effect of "this camera will benefit from the fastest card available," look in the table to check which card that actually was and when that page was last updated.

Compact Flash read speed. The card reader and even the operating system can play an equal role in determining read speed to that of the card itself. Card readers almost invariably use one of three interfaces: USB 1.1, USB 2.0, or FireWire.

Almost any card available today can max out the speed of a USB 1.1 reader. In theory, USB 2.0 is faster than FireWire, but in practice, as the EPA says, "your mileage may vary"—I've generally found FireWire to be both faster and more reliable than USB 2.0, particularly with fast cards such as the SanDisk Ultra II and Extreme and the Lexar 40x product lines.

Mac OS X users should take note that OS X versions prior to Panther (OS 10.3) were very slow at reading 2GB and larger cards that use FAT-32 formatting. Panther fixed the problem.

Microdrives. In addition to solid-state Compact Flash cards, microdrives—miniature hard disks in Compact Flash form factor—are also available. Microdrives were introduced when solid-state CF cards were still quite limited in both speed and capacity.

Today, solid-state CF cards have outstripped microdrives in both capacity and speed, and they also have enormous advantages in durability. Like all hard drives, microdrives use moving parts machined to very fine tolerances, so they don't respond well to impacts—it's easy to destroy both the data and the drive itself by dropping it. Solid-state CF cards are a great deal more robust—while I don't recommend abusing them in any way, I have one that survived being run over by a Ford Explorer!

Basically, microdrives seemed like a good idea at the time, but you're much better off using today's fast solid-state CF cards—you can keep the microdrives around for emergencies.

Secure Digital (SD) cards. If microdrives are the wave of the past, Secure Digital (SD) cards are the wave of the future, though at the time of this writing only a couple of cameras support them. The main impetus behind the development of SD is the built-in encryption, which is inviting for the music and movie industries, since it will let them distribute copyrighted material digitally.

For camera use, SD is simply too new for me to be able to say much about it, other than that it's currently a little slower than the fastest CF cards and the capacities are still lower than the largest CF cards. Both of these statements are subject to change. All the recommendations for handling and using CF cards apply equally to SD.

Formatting Camera Media

Always format your camera media, whether CF card, microdrive, or SD card, in the camera in which it will be used! Your computer may appear to let you format the card while it's loaded in the card reader, but it's quite likely that it will either do so incorrectly or offer you a set of options from which it's easy to make the wrong choice.

Formatting CF cards on Windows systems can, at least in theory, be done correctly, but the only time I'd recommend doing so is if you've used software supplied by the card vendor to perform data recovery or diagnostics *and* the software recommends formatting. Formatting CF cards under any flavor of the Mac OS is a recipe for disaster. Formatting cards in the camera in which they will be used is always safe and guarantees that the format will be the one your camera can use.

Tip: When Disaster Strikes. If you wind up with a card that's unreadable but contains data you want to recover (it's rare, but it can be caused by doing things like pulling the card out of the reader without first ejecting it in software), *do not* format it! Doing so will guarantee that any data that was still on the card will be permanently consigned to the bitbucket. Major CF card vendors such as SanDisk and Lexar include data-recovery software with the cards (which for my money is sufficient reason to stick with those brands). Before attempting anything else, try the recovery software. If that fails, and the data is truly irreplaceable, several companies offer data recovery from CF cards, usually at a fairly hefty price—a Google search for "Compact Flash Data Recovery" will turn up all the major players.

Camera Card Capacities

Bigger isn't always better, and in the case of CF cards, large capacities often come at premium prices. A 4GB card will generally cost more than twice as much as a 2GB one, and so on.

Using two smaller cards rather than one big one offers an immediate workflow advantage. When the first card is full, you can switch to the second one to continue shooting while the first card is being copied to the computer. By the time the second card is full, the first one will have finished copying, and you can format it in the camera and continue shooting.

Acquiring Images

I always copy images onto a hard drive before attempting to open them. (Actually, I always copy the images onto two different hard drives. I may be paranoid, but I've yet to lose a digital capture.)

It's possible to connect the camera to your computer and actually open the images while they're still on the CF card. It's likewise possible to put the CF card in a card reader and open the images directly from the CF card. But "possible" doesn't mean it's a good idea! It's possible to run a Porsche on kerosene or to perform brain surgery with a rusty Phillips screwdriver, and I consider either one about as advisable as opening images directly from the camera media.

I always copy to two hard drives for the simple reason that hard drives break, usually at the least convenient moment they could possibly choose to do so. If you simply can't take the time to make two copies, consider setting up a mirrored (not striped) RAID array. Mirrored RAID arrays copy the data to two drives simultaneously, so unless both drives fail simultaneously (which is extremely unlikely), you'll always have a copy of the data.

You can even kill two birds with a single stone by using a casing that allows hot-swapping of the drives, and use the drive mechanisms themselves, suitably boxed, to archive the data—hard disks are much faster than CD-R or DVD-R; will almost certainly last at least as long, particularly if they're simply being stored; and can cost less than a dollar per gigabyte—see the next section, "Archiving Images."

However you choose to accomplish the task, my overriding recommendation is that you wait until the copy from camera media to hard drive is complete before you try to do anything at all to the images.

Archiving Images

I've heard of photographers who don't bother to archive their raw images once they've processed them to gamma-corrected color ones. That seems about as sensible to me as throwing out all your negatives because you've made prints that you like! Given the huge amount of processing that goes into converting a digital raw capture and the fact that the techniques for doing said conversions are only likely to get better, it seems extraordinarily short-sighted at best not to archive your raw captures.

The issues then become when, in what form, and on what media you archive them.

When to archive. I confess that there may be an element of superstition in this, but I like to archive my raw captures preserving the original file names and folder structures created in the camera, before doing any editing of the images or the metadata. When I first copy the raw images to the computer, I always copy them to two different drives. One copy becomes my working copy, the other serves first as a short-term backup and then as a long-term archive.

Once I've done my selecting, sorting, ranking, and renaming, and I've applied initial Camera Raw edits, I archive this too. Yes, it makes for a heavy storage requirement, but storage space is relatively inexpensive, time is expensive, and images are irreplaceable.

What to archive. You should archive anything you want yourself or someone else to be able to retrieve at some unspecified time in the future. It's really that simple.

Don't confuse archives and backups. Backups are usually automated, incremental copies that reflect the current state of your system. Archives are long-term storage, designed to remain undisturbed unless and until the data is required. An archive isn't a substitute for backups, and backing up isn't a substitute for archiving!

Archive media. Strictly speaking, there's no such thing as an archival medium for digital storage—any of the even slightly convenient solutions available for recording ones and zeroes will degrade over time. Archives must be maintained!

There are really two problems in archival storage. The obvious one is the integrity of the storage medium. The less obvious but equally critical one is the availability of devices that can read the storage medium. There's probably still magnetic tape from 1970s mainframes that has good data on it, but good luck finding a drive that can read it.

Any archiving strategy must include periodic refreshing of the data onto new media, preferably taking advantage of improvements in technology. I've migrated most of my early-90s CD-ROMs onto either DVD-Rs or to large-capacity hard disks, and unless something better comes along I'll probably refresh that data onto the larger, faster, cheaper hard disks that will be available in three or four years.

Burnable CDs and DVDs, both read-only and rewritable, differ from commercially pressed CDs and DVDs in an important way. In the commercially manufactured disks, the data is stamped on a foil layer made of metal. (It's about the same thickness as the foil in a cigarette pack, but it's metal nonetheless.) Burnable CDs and DVDs use a photosensitive dye layer to record the data—the dye changes color when the laser writes to it. Photographers should be well aware of the fragility of dyes…. So use whatever storage medium you find convenient, but recognize that it *will* fail, and plan accordingly.

Loading Images in the File Browser

Once you've copied the raw files to your hard disk, the next thing to do is to point the File Browser at the folder containing the raw images. The File Browser is command central for dealing with hundreds of images. You'll use it to make your initial selects, to apply and edit metadata including Camera Raw settings, and to control the processing of the raw images into a deliverable form.

But before you start doing any of these things, give the File Browser a few minutes to generate the thumbnails and previews and to read the image metadata. Doing so serves two purposes.

▶ Editing, and in particular the display of previews, goes much faster once the File Browser has generated and cached the thumbnails and previews. I've heard several complaints to the effect that the File Browser is agonizingly slow for editing, but when pressed, it always seems that those who complain fail to wait the couple of minutes to let the File Browser get itself organized, with the result that it is indeed agonizingly slow.

▶ If there's a problem with any of the raw files, it will almost certainly show up in the File Browser, so you can deal with it *before* you reformat the camera media and lose the original data.

If you don't let the File Browser build its cache before you start working, you'll be fighting every inch of the way, so let it take the short time it needs to cache the images before trying to do anything else—see "Feeding the Cache," later in this chapter, for more detail on the process.

Key Preference Settings

Four key preference settings will help your work go smoothly, one set in Camera Raw, the others in the File Browser. My advice is to set 'em and forget 'em, because it's extremely unlikely that you'll ever want to change them. Just remember to check them in the event that you're forced to do a clean installation of either your OS or Photoshop, because either one may trash the preferences.

Camera Raw Preferences. Open a raw image to launch Camera Raw. Make sure that the Advanced radio button is set, then choose Preferences from the Camera Raw menu and make sure that your Camera Raw Preferences are set to "Save image settings in sidecar ".xmp" files"—see Figure 5-1.

Figure 5-1
Save image settings

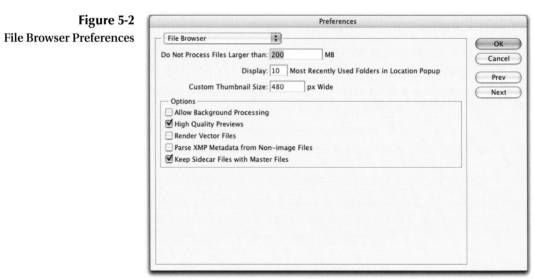

File Browser Preferences. The first two of these settings are mandatory for a reliable workflow. The third is merely strongly encouraged—see Figure 5-2.

Figure 5-2
File Browser Preferences

▶ **Keep Sidecar files with Master Files.** This option *must* be checked. When it is, the File Browser automatically moves or copies the sidecar files whenever you move or copy images using the File Browser, so your metadata travels with the image. If it isn't, you'll have a merry old time trying to find where your keywording and metadata have gone.

▶ **High Quality Previews.** You want these. When this option is unchecked, the previews are soft and heavily pixellated, and they don't show accurate color. The high-quality previews let you see a large enough preview to judge things like facial expression and focus, and they're indispensable when you're making selects or sorts.

▶ **Allow Background Processing.** I strongly recommend keeping this turned off if you're in anything resembling a hurry. When it's checked, it lets the File Browser continue to cache thumbnails and previews while you do something else. Even on a fast machine, it severely degrades the foreground performance, and the File Browser takes far less time to build its cache when it's running in the foreground than it does as a background process.

Feeding the Cache

The File Browser's cache holds the thumbnails, previews, sort order, and flagging information for each folder at which you point it. The File Browser's File menu has several commands that let you work with the cache, which I'll look at a little later, but the first order of business is to let the File Browser build it.

When you point the File Browser at a folder of raw images for the first time, it goes to work. The first thing you'll see is a message that reads "Getting directory file list" for a brand-new folder, or "Updating directory file list" if the File Browser has already seen the folder but the contents have changed—see Figure 5-3.

Figure 5-3
Getting directory file list

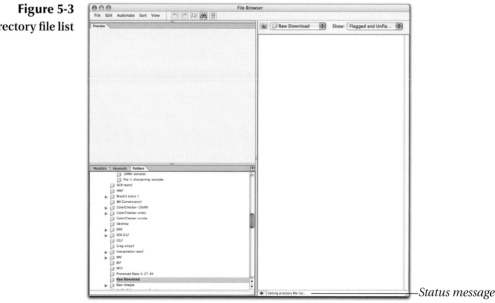

—*Status message*

Even with several hundred images, the "Getting directory file list" message flashes by so quickly that if you blink, you may miss it. The second message that appears is "Getting *filename* thumbnail," and this one takes a little longer, since it's extracting the camera-created thumbnail from the raw images—see Figure 5-3.

Figure 5-3
Getting thumbnails

All images ©2001
David Stoecklein

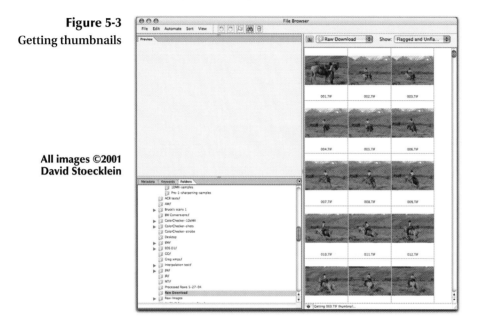

Next, the File Browser reads the metadata for each image. Some of the metadata, such as the EXIF metadata, is generated in the camera, while other metadata, such as the File Properties metadata, is generated on the fly by the File Browser. Again, the File Browser displays a status message to let you know what it's doing—see Figure 5-4.

The last phase of the initial cache-building process is also probably the most crucial—generating previews. In this phase, the File Browser also uses Camera Raw to build higher-quality thumbnails than the ones that appear initially. (They're downsampled versions of the result you'd get if you processed the raw file using the current Camera Default settings for the camera that shot the images in Camera Raw.) If you look closely, you can see the thumbnails updating. The status message reads "Generating filename preview"—see Figure 5-5.

Figure 5-4
Getting metadata

All images ©2001
David Stoecklein

Figure 5-5
Generating previews

All images ©2001
David Stoecklein

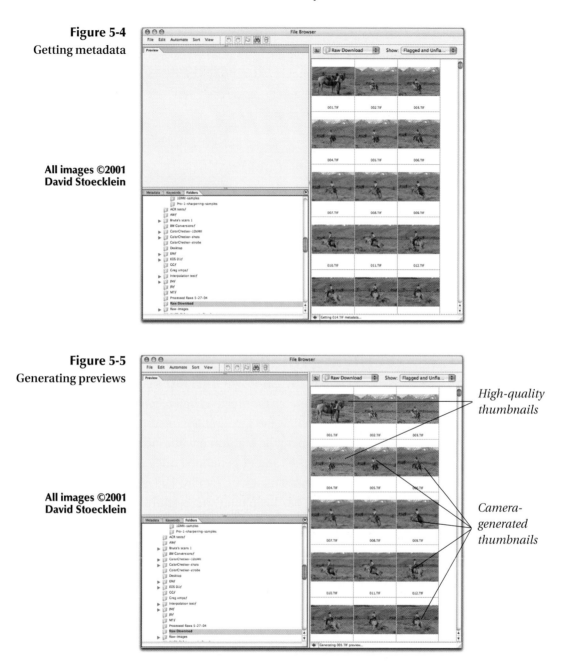

High-quality
thumbnails

Camera-
generated
thumbnails

Once the File Browser has completed the process of generating the previews, it displays a message that states the number of images in the folder, indicating that it's ready for you to start working. Large previews appear almost instantaneously when you advance from one image to another, allowing you to see each image in sufficient detail to apply a yes/no flag or a more nuanced rank. See Figure 5-6.

Figure 5-6
The cached images

All images ©2001
David Stoecklein

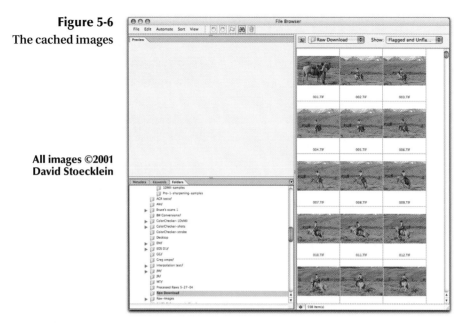

Verifying Images

A second important reason why it's always a good idea to wait until the File Browser has generated the previews before reformatting the camera media is that if Camera Raw has any problem reading the images, the problems will only show up on the high-quality thumbnail and preview. The initial thumbnails are the camera-generated ones, and they don't indicate that the raw file has been read successfully. The high-quality ones *do* indicate that the raw file has been read successfully, so wait until you see them before erasing the raw image files from the camera media.

If you do see a problem at this stage, check the second copy (if you made one) or go back to the camera media—you haven't reformatted it yet, right? It's fairly rare for the data to get corrupted in the camera (though it does sometimes happen), so the first suspect should be the card reader.

If you have only one reader available, try copying the problem images one by one. If you have a second reader available, try copying the files using the second reader. If this copy fails, try running the rescue software provided by the card vendor. If none of these suggestions work, your options are to reshoot, to accept the loss and move on, or to resort to an expensive data-recovery service.

Interrupting the Cache

In an emergency—if you need to see and start working with a specific image right now—you can force the File Browser to read all the data and build the preview for that image by selecting it in the File Browser. The File Browser will give preference to that image, and generate a preview quickly.

You can also scroll the File Browser window to give preference to a series of images—the File Browser always builds previews for those images whose thumbnails are currently visible in the main window. But there's no such thing as a free lunch. When you open an image in Camera Raw, the File Browser will stop processing the rest of the images (unless you have its Preferences set to allow background processing, in which case your foreground performance will suffer). And when you bring the File Browser back to the foreground, it will resume building the cache.

Tip: Download to Your Fastest Drive. The cache-building process is largely dependent on disk speed, so the faster the drive to which you download the raw images, the faster the File Browser will build the cache. Consider dedicating a partition on your fastest drive, the same size as your camera media, for downloading and caching your raw images.

Caching Multiple Folders

Some cameras create subfolders on the camera media with 100 images in each. If you use larger-capacity cards, you may have three or four image folders. The fastest way to deal with multiple folders is to copy all the image folders to a single enclosing folder. Then, when the copy is complete, point the File Browser at the enclosing folder and choose Build Cache for Subfolders from the File Browser's File menu. Contrary to what the online help says, Build Cache for Subfolders simply does that—it builds a cache for each subfolder in the enclosing folder, reading the thumbnails and metadata and generating previews for all the images contained in the subfolders. It displays a progress bar so you'll know when it's done.

Wait until the File Browser has finished building its cache before you try to do anything to the images. The typical tasks you perform in the File Browser include renaming, sorting, flagging or ranking, applying rotation, entering keywords and IPTC metadata, and applying Camera Raw settings.

Working with the Images

The absolute order in which you perform tasks like selecting, sorting, re-naming, keywording, and so on, isn't critical, so the order in which I'll discuss them is, I freely admit, arbitrary. But in those cases where the result of one task depends on the prior completion of another, I'll point that out. I do, however, offer one golden rule.

Start with the operations required by the largest number of images, and complete these before you start handling individual images on a case-by-case basis. For example, the first thing I always do with a folder full of new raw images is to enter my copyright notice—see Figure 5-7.

Figure 5-7
Entering a
copyright notice

To enter a copyright notice for all images, select all the thumbnails, then click to highlight the Copyright field in the Metadata panel and enter your copyright notice, or…

…if you've saved a metadata template, simply choose it from the Metadata palette menu.

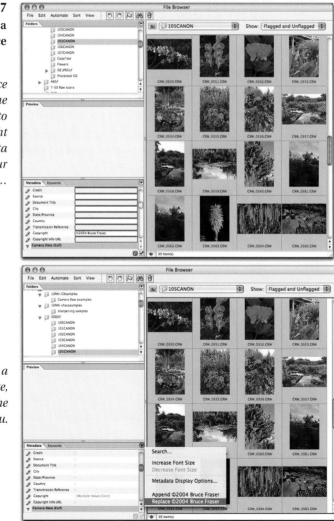

Similarly, if you know that you want to add the same keyword or keywords to all the images in a shoot, do it now (see "Applying Keywords and Metadata," later in this chapter). But if you don't care about copyrighting or keywording your rejects, you can make your initial selects first.

Selecting and Editing

Some photographers like to do a rough application of Camera Raw settings on all the images before they start making selects by flagging or ranking. Then they look at a large preview for each image and apply a flag or rank accordingly. Others may take a quick scan of the thumbnails and weed out any obvious junk before proceeding. Still others may want to do keywording and metadata editing before they start making selects. The File Browser can accommodate all these different styles.

So start out by loading a File Browser configuration that works for the task you want to start with—if you need to refresh your memory on configuring the File Browser's layout for different tasks and saving those layouts as workspaces, see "Configuring the File Browser" in Chapter 4, *The File Browser*.

Selecting by thumbnail. If the large or custom thumbnail view lets you see enough detail to make initial selects, choose an all-thumbnail view, then click-select the keepers or the rejects, whichever is easier. Shift-clicking selects all contiguous files between the last-selected image and the one on which you click, Command-clicking selects discontiguous images one at a time. See Figure 5-8.

Figure 5-8
Picking selects
by thumbnail

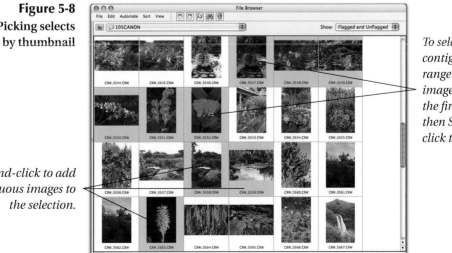

To select a contiguous range of images, click the first and then Shift-click the last.

Command-click to add discontiguous images to the selection.

Once you've made your selection, you can apply a flag or rank—see "Flagging" and "Ranking," later in this chapter.

Selecting by preview. To see more detail, you can look at each image's preview to make flagging or ranking decisions. Choose a layout that lets you see the largest preview possible, with a single column of thumbnails. The up and down arrow keys let you navigate from one thumbnail to the next and display the corresponding preview—see Figure 5-9.

Figure 5-9
Picking selects
by preview

Make the Preview palette
as large as possible.

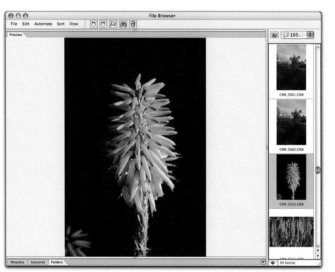

Use the up
and down
arrow keys
to move from
one image to
the next.

You can apply flags or ranks as you go—see the following sections, "Flagging," and "Ranking."

Flagging. To toggle the flag as an attribute for one or more selected images, click the Flag icon in the File Browser's toolbar, or press Command-' (single quote). (Or, if you're being paid by the hour, choose Flag from the File Browser's Edit menu.)

If the selection contains both flagged and unflagged images, the first application of the Flag command flags the unflagged images and preserves flagging for the flagged ones. When all the selected images have the same attribute (all flagged, or all unflagged), the command acts as a toggle, flagging unflagged images or removing the flag from flagged ones.

Once you've applied the flag, you can segregate the flagged and unflagged images in any of the following four ways—see Figure 5-10.

Figure 5-10
Working with
the Flag attribute

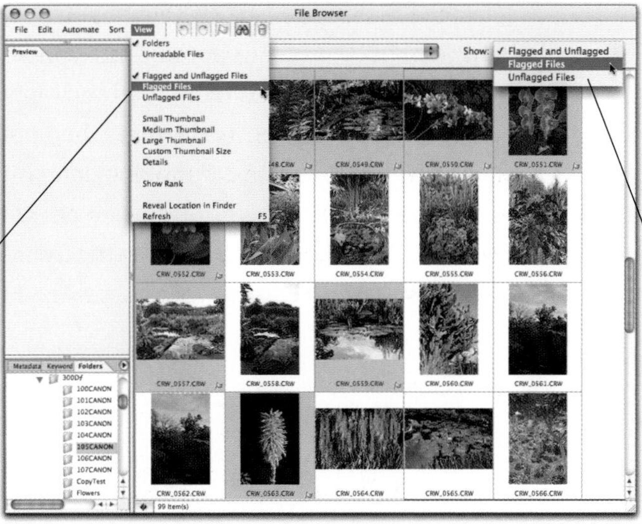

Choose Flagged Files
from the File Browser's
View menu.

Choose
Flagged Files
from the File
Browser's
Show menu.

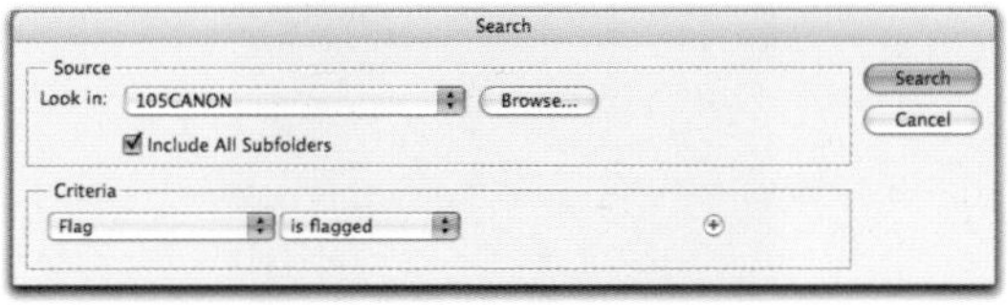

Click the search tool,
then enter Flag is
Flagged as your Criteria,
optionally including
subfolders.

▶ Choose Flagged Files or Unflagged Files from the File Browser's Show or View menus.

▶ Press Command-Shift-A to select all flagged files.

▶ Choose Flag from the File Browser's Sort menu to change the sort order to display all flagged files before the unflagged ones.

▶ Click the search tool in the File Browser's toolbar, or choose Search from the Metadata palette menu; then, in the Search dialog box, choose Flag from the Criteria menu and "is flagged" or "is unflagged" from the accompanying popup. The search results then appear in the "virtual" Search Results folder, and the File Browser points to the Search Results folder. (This is the only option for searching multiple folders—point the File Browser at the enclosing folder and check Include All Subfolders.)

Flagging is great for making quick, yes/no, binary decisions—keep or reject—but for more nuanced choices, you need to use the Rank feature.

Ranking. To rank images one by one using the large preview, first make sure that Show Rank is checked in the File Browser's View menu. Then select the first image and highlight its Rank field either by clicking in the Rank field or by pressing Option-Enter, and enter the desired rank.

To advance to the next thumbnail and highlight its Rank field as a single operation, press Tab, enter the rank, then press Tab again to confirm the entry, advance to the next thumbnail, and highlight its Rank field.

To apply a rank to multiple selected images, choose Rank from the File Browser's Edit menu and then enter the desired rank in the ensuing dialog box. See Figure 5-11.

Figure 5-11
Ranking images

Click in the first image's Rank field and enter a rank, then press Tab to confirm the entry and advance to the next image with the Rank field selected.

To display the images in order of rank, choose Rank from the File browser's Sort menu. To display only images with a specific rank, click the Search tool in the File Browser's toolbar, or choose Search from the Metadata palette menu; then in the Search dialog box, choose Rank from the Criteria menu and make the appropriate choices in the accompanying popups. The search results then appear in the "virtual" Search Results folder, and the File Browser points to the Search Results folder. See Figure 5-12.

Figure 5-12
Working with rank

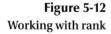

The Search tool offers flexible methods for searching by rank, including the option to search subfolders.

Applying Camera Raw settings. There are basically three ways to approach the task of applying rough Camera Raw edits to multiple images. Remember, at this stage in the workflow, you're simply aiming for good, not perfect. (Perfect comes later, when you've whittled the images down to the selects you'll actually deliver.)

To work efficiently, look for and select images that require approximately the same edit. Once you've done so, you can apply the edits in any of the following three ways—you can mix and match techniques as required.

▶ **Edit by example.** Select the first of the images that need the same edit, and double-click its thumbnail to open it in Camera Raw. Make your edits— white balance, exposure, whatever the image needs—and then dismiss the Camera Raw dialog box by Option-clicking the OK button (when you hold down Option, the button changes from "OK" to "Update").

Extend the selection to include all the other images needing that same edit, choose Apply Camera Raw Settings from the File Browser's Automate menu, and choose First Selected Image from the Settings menu in the Apply Camera Raw Settings dialog box. Then click Update to dismiss the dialog box and apply the settings to the selected images.

Or, edit the first image, then select the other images needing the same edit, choose Apply Camera Raw Settings from the File Browser's Automate menu, and choose Previous Conversion from the Settings menu in the Apply Camera Raw Settings dialog box. See Figure 5-13.

Figure 5-13
Edit by example

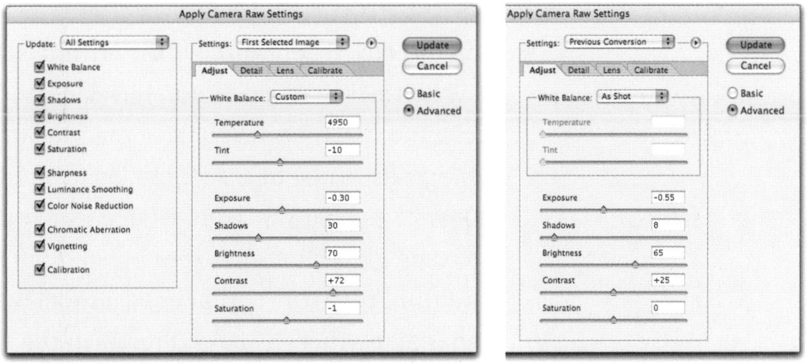

Include the edited image in the selection and choose First Selected Image from the Settings menu, or…

choose Previous Conversion from the Settings menu.

▶ **Edit by presets.** If you've saved presets for Camera Raw—see "Saving Settings" in Chapter 3, *Using Camera Raw*, if you need a refresher—you can apply them to selected images by choosing Apply Camera Raw Settings from the File Browser's Automate menu and then loading settings or settings subsets by choosing them from the Settings menu in the Apply Camera Raw Settings dialog box. See Figure 5-14.

Figure 5-14
Edit by presets

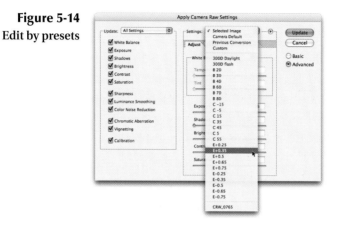

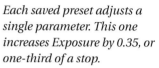

Each saved preset adjusts a single parameter. This one increases Exposure by 0.35, or one-third of a stop.

Saving Settings Subsets as presets is particularly powerful, because you can simply choose them in succession. Each one affects only the parameters recorded when you saved it, so you can load a preset for white balance, followed by one for Exposure, for Brightness, for Contrast, for Calibrate settings, and so on. Once you're done, click Update to dismiss the dialog box and apply the settings to the selected images.

▶ **Edit directly.** When you click the Advanced button in the Apply Camera Raw Settings dialog box, you have access to all of Camera Raw's controls. You don't, however, have the preview, the clipping displays, the histogram, or the RGB readout, so to some extent you're flying blind. But once you become comfortable working in Camera Raw and the File Browser, it's fairly easy to spot images that need the Exposure bumped up a third of a stop, or that need a small Brightness or Contrast tweak, and making those tweaks directly in the Apply Camera Raw Settings dialog box is quick and easy. See Figure 5-15.

Once you've made your initial selects, you may want to revisit images individually and fine-tune the Camera Raw settings.

Figure 5-15
Edit directly

You can adjust all the Camera Raw controls directly in the Apply Camera Raw Settings dialog box.

Sorting and Renaming

By default, the File Browser sorts images by file name, so new raw images appear in the order in which they were shot, because the camera applies consecutive numbering to each image. You can vary the sort order by choosing any of the options on the File Browser's Sort menu—see Figure 5-16.

Figure 5-16
Sort options

The File Browser's Sort menu offers a variety of automatic sorting options. If you sort by dragging thumbnails in the File Browser, the sort order appears as Custom.

You can also create a custom sort order by dragging the thumbnails, just as you would with chromes on a light table. When you do so, the Custom item on the Sort menu is checked.

The File Browser will remember this sort order inside the folder in which it was created. It will even remember the sort order if you use the File Browser to move the images to a new empty folder. But if you're combining images from several folders into a different folder, you are in effect creating a new sort order, and it may well not be the one you wanted. So a simple way to preserve that order is to use the Batch Rename command to rename the images including a numbering scheme that reflects your custom sort order.

Or you may wish to batch rename your raw images using some other scheme entirely. For example, my friend and colleague Seth Resnick, who has put more sheer ingenuity into building his workflow than anyone else

I know, uses a sophisticated naming scheme that, to the initiated, at least, conveys a great deal of information at a glance.

For example, he might rename a raw file called 4F3S0266.tif to 20040521STKSR3_0001.tif. This decodes as follows. 20040521 defines the date on which the image was shot (May 21st, 2004), so the files are automatically sorted by date order. STK indicates that the image was shot for stock, and SR indicates that it was shot by Seth Resnick. The number 3 indicates that it belonged to the third assignment or collection of images of the day, while the 0001 indicates that it was the first image in the collection. The .tif is the file extension that defines the file type. Figure 5-17 shows how to set up the Batch Rename dialog box to accomplish this renaming—to perform a batch rename, select the images you want renamed and then choose Batch Rename from the File Browser's Automate menu.

Figure 5-17
Batch Rename

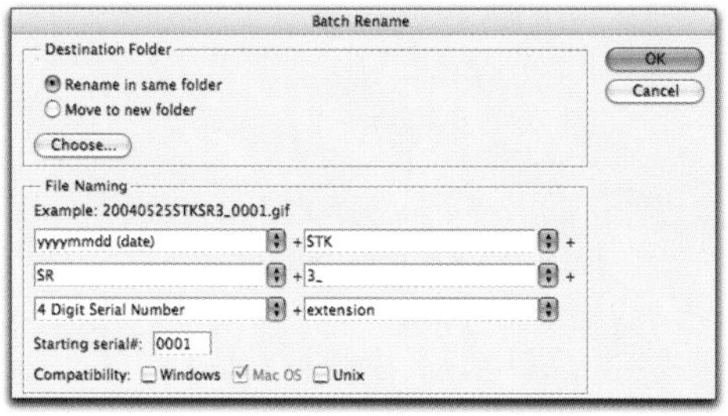

Tip: Always Include the Extension as the Last Item. Remember, each image is accompanied by a sidecar .xmp file that differs in name from the raw file only by the extension. If you include the extension as the last element, and you have your File Browser Preferences set to Keep Sidecar Files with Master Files, the sidecar files will get renamed correctly along with the raw files. If you fail to do so, the batch rename will fail with a message saying "file already exists."

Tip: Process JPEGs Separately. The Batch Rename command is smart enough to handle sidecar .xmp files, but if you shoot raw and JPEG, and you have three files whose names are distinguished only by their extension rather than two, you need to do a little more work. First, use the search tool to search for all the JPEGs, and run the batch rename on them. Then use the search tool again to find all the raws and run the same batch rename. You'll wind up with correctly named raws, JPEGs, and sidecar .xmp files for each image.

Tip: Be Careful with Length and Special Characters. To remain compatible with today's operating systems, your file names should be no longer than 31 characters, including the extension. Some antediluvian systems may limit you to an 8.3 (eight characters plus a three-character extension) file name, but those are fortunately getting rarer with each passing moment. For cross-platform compatibility, limit yourself to the lower 128 characters of the ASCII character set and avoid characters that have a reserved use in the operating system such as \ /:*?<> or |. If you limit yourself to lowercase and uppercase alphabetic characters, numerals, underscores, and hyphens, and only use the period immediately before the extension, you'll be safe.

Batch Rename offers you the choice of renaming the images in the same folder or moving them to a different folder. Either way, Photoshop is smart enough to keep track of the cached thumbnails, previews, rotation, flagging, or ranking. Batch Rename doesn't, however, offer the option to copy the files to a new folder. If you want to keep a copy that preserves the original file names, the easiest way to do so is to address the issue up front, and copy the folder before you start working in the File Browser.

Applying Keywords and Metadata

The key to being efficient with keywords and metadata is the same as that for being efficient with applying Camera Raw edits. Look for and select images that need the same treatment, and deal with them all at once.

IPTC metadata. The only metadata that is editable in the File Browser (or anywhere else in Photoshop, for that matter) is the IPTC metadata. For recurring metadata such as copyright notices, metadata templates provide a very convenient way to make the edits. You can create and save metadata templates from the File Info dialog box—to open it, select a single image to which you want to apply the metadata, then choose File Info from the File Browser's File menu.

The editable metadata is spread across three different File Info panels—see Figure 5-18. You need to save separate templates for each panel.

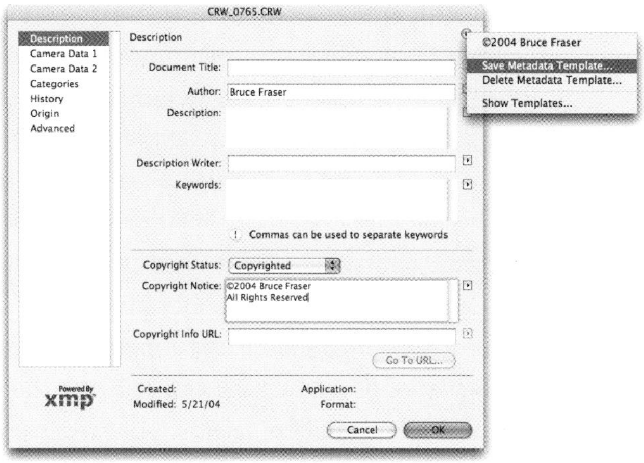

Figure 5-18
Saving metadata
templates

Alternatively, you can select multiple images and then edit the metadata directly in the Metadata palette. Click in the first field you want to edit, and type in your entry. Then press Tab to advance to the next field. Continue until you've entered all the metadata shared by the selected images, and then click the checkmark icon at the lower-right of the palette, or press Enter or Return, to confirm the entries—see Figure 5-19.

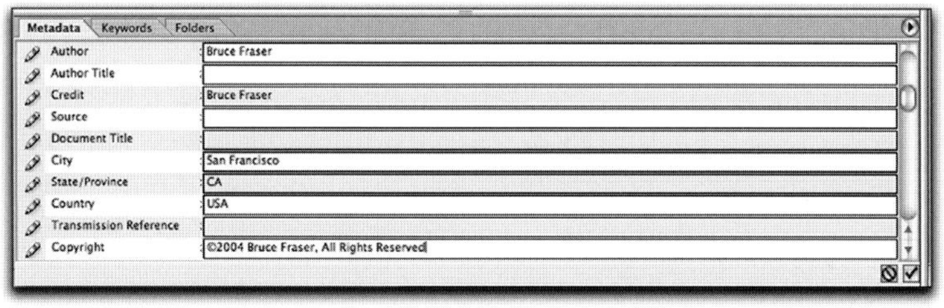

Figure 5-19
Entering metadata

Keywords. Keywords show up in the IPTC section of the Metadata palette, but you can't enter or edit them there—you have to use the Keywords palette. The Keywords palette contains individual keywords grouped into sets (represented by the folder icons). The default keywords and sets are pretty useless unless you know a lot of people called Julius and Michael, but you can easily replace them with ones that are more useful for your purposes.

To apply a keyword, select one or more images and then click in the column to the left of the keyword. A check mark appears in the column, and the File Browser writes the keyword to each file's .xmp sidecar file. To remove a keyword, select the images and then uncheck the checkmark.

Deleting a keyword from the Keywords palette doesn't delete the keyword from any images to which it has been applied, it only deletes it from the palette. So I find that it makes sense to keep only keywords I know I'll use a lot stored in the palette. For keywords that apply only to the current session, I create them in a set called Temp and delete them when I'm done, to keep the palette manageable.

Keyword sets let you organize keywords, but they also offer a very useful functionality—they let you apply all the keywords in the set to selected images by clicking next to the set name rather than the keyword names. This is the only way to apply multiple keywords to a set simultaneously. When you click next to a keyword to apply it, the File Browser insists on writing the keyword to all the selected images before it will let you apply the next one. Hence the following tip.

Tip: Sets Are Not Set in Stone. I keep an empty set called Temp (though it could as easily be called Fred or whatever other name tickles your fancy) purely for the purpose of applying multiple keywords. When I want to apply multiple keywords to a set of images, I drag any existing keywords I want to use into the Temp set and create any new ones I want to apply inside the Temp set. Then I click beside the Temp set icon to apply all the keywords it currently contains to all the selected images—see Figure 5-20.

Figure 5-20
Applying multiple keywords

You can drag keywords into a set and add any one-off keywords to the set, and then click beside the set name to apply all the keywords simultaneously to all selected images.

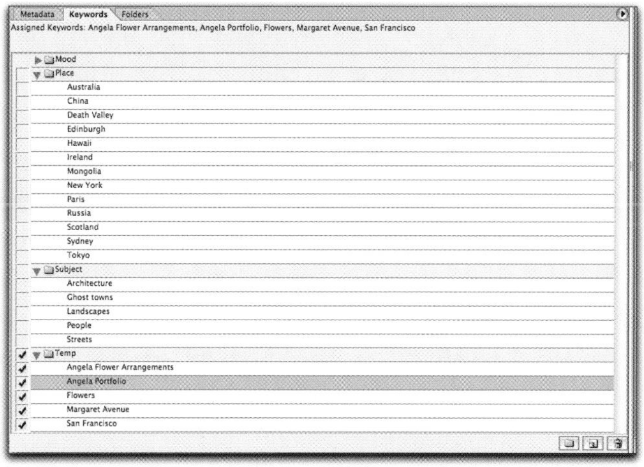

All the work you do in the File Browser is aimed at setting things up to produce converted versions of your chosen raw images, with the correct Camera Raw settings to get the tone and color you want, and including all the metadata you've entered. So let's look at this last stage of the workflow, actually converting your raw images.

Processing Images

When it comes to efficiency in converting raw images, actions are the key. I almost always convert raw images in batches using actions rather than simply opening them in Photoshop. But before I look at the various automated options, I'll list the methods for opening raw images manually from the File Browser.

▶ Press Return (Mac) or Enter (Windows), double-click, or press Command-O, to open the selected image or images in the Camera Raw dialog box. If you select multiple images, the first one will open in Camera Raw. Then when you click OK to convert the image or Update to write the settings to the image's metadata, the second image will appear in Camera Raw, and so on.

▶ Press Shift-Return (Mac) or Shift-Enter (Windows), Shift-double-click the last selected image of a contiguous selection, or hold down the Shift key while choosing Open from the File Browser's File menu, to open the selected image or images in Photoshop while bypassing the Camera Raw dialog box. The images are converted using the current Camera Raw settings in each image's metadata or, if no settings have been specified, using the Camera Default settings for the camera model on which the images were shot. (Command-Shift-O doesn't work, it just brings the File Browser to the foreground; and Shift-double-clicking with a discontiguous selection will turn the selection into a contiguous one and then open all the newly-selected images as well as the ones you wanted.)

▶ Press Option-Return (Mac) or Option-Enter (Windows), Option-double-click, or hold down Option while choosing Open from the File Browser's File menu to open the selected image or images in the Camera Raw dialog box while closing the File Browser.

▶ Press Shift-Option-Return (Mac) or Shift-Option-Enter (Windows), Shift-Option-double-click the last selected image of a contiguous selection, or hold down Shift and Option while choosing Open from the File Browser's File menu to open the selected image or images directly in Photoshop, bypassing the Camera Raw dialog box and closing the File Browser.

Automated conversions

These shortcuts are handy when you're dealing with a handful or so of images, but for industrial-strength operations, the options on the File Browser's Automate menu are much more useful. I'll discuss these in much greater detail in Chapter 7, *Exploiting Automation*, but for now I'll give you the 30,000-foot overview.

Batch. This is the Big Daddy of all the automation features, and is capable of doing just about anything that Photoshop can be made to do. The basic idea, though, is that it will take selected images in the File Browser as its source and open them in Photoshop using the Camera Raw settings for each image. Then it runs an action on the images in Photoshop, and either leaves them open in Photoshop, saves them in a destination folder (and optionally, renames them in the process), or, a potential big hurt-me button, saves and closes the files in place.

Most raw files are read-only in that Photoshop can't write the raw formats, but some cameras create their raw files as TIFF. If you have one of these cameras, avoid Save and Close like the plague, because it will overwrite your raw originals with the processed versions!

PDF Presentation. This option lets you create a slideshow in PDF format or a multi-page PDF with one image per page. For the slide show, you can specify how long each image stays on screen and choose a transition, but you can't add captions or copyright notices. It's quick and easy, but limited.

Contact Sheet II. This option lets you build a contact sheet. You can specify a page size, select how many images appear per page, choose whether to preserve rotation or orient all images the same way for best fit, and choose whether or not to include file names as captions, with the choice of font and size.

Picture Package. This option lets you produce a package of each image, with multiple copies and sizes of the image on the same page—for example, on an 8x10 page, you could specify one 5x7, two 2.5x3.5, and four 2x2.5 inch versions.

You can customize the layout and add captions—automated options are any one of file name, copyright notice, description, credit, or title, all picked up from the IPTC metadata, or a custom text string. This is a surprisingly deep little feature.

Web Photo Gallery. This option is like a contact sheet for the Web, but since it's a digital contact sheet, it offers the option of including feedback links. Like Picture Package, this feature has surprising depths, which I'll look at in detail in Chapter 7, *Exploiting Automation.*

All the work you do in the File Browser forms the foundation for future automation. Images are converted using the right Camera Raw settings at the correct orientation, and the converted images contain all the metadata you attached to the original raws. Since this work is so important, you should understand how it gets saved and stored, and that means knowing a little about the File Browser's cache.

The File Browser Cache

Metadata—keywords, IPTC info, Camera Raw settings, and almost everything else that appears on the metadata palette—is stored in the sidecar .xmp files that accompany your raw images. But previews, thumbnails, flag or rank information, rotation, and sort order are saved in the File Browser cache.

The File Browser does a great job of keeping track of everything you do *inside* the File Browser, but it has absolutely no knowledge of anything you do *outside* the File Browser. If you rename a folder outside the File Browser, you'll lose all the flag, rank, rotate, and sort order information, as well as the thumbnails and previews that take time to build. Likewise, if you move a folder (which you can only do outside the File Browser), you'll lose the same information. Fortunately, there's a mechanism that lets you set up folders for work outside the File Browser and that lets you preserve the vital information through renaming or moving; but to understand how it works, you need to know a bit about the File Browser's caching mechanism.

Understanding the Cache

You won't find a file with a name that remotely resembles "File Browser Cache" anywhere on your machine. Instead, the File Browser has its own folder where it stores cache files. On Mac OS, it's the Users/*yourusername*/Library/Application Support/Adobe/File Browser/Photoshop CS folder. On Windows, it's the \Documents and Settings\user\Application Data\Adobe\FileBrowser\PhotoshopCS folder. It's rare that you'll have to interact with the contents of this folder directly, but knowing what they are, where they are, and what they contain will aid your understanding of a process that sometimes seems mysterious, and will simplify troubleshooting on those rare occasions when things go wrong.

The live cache. If you examine the contents of the File Browser's cache folder, you'll find it contains three files for each folder the File Browser has seen.

▶ FoldernameXXX (where XXX is a three-digit number) is the cache for the camera-generated thumbnails

▶ FoldernameXXXM (where XXX is the same three-digit number as the previous file) is the cache for the metadata. It stores the flagging and ranking information along with a copy of the camera-generated metadata. Images that have had metadata added, including Camera Raw settings, have all the *image* metadata stored in sidecar .xmp files that take precedence over the metadata in the File Browser cache, but the sort order, flagging, and ranking metadata exists only in the File Browser cache.

▶ FoldernameXXXT (where XXX is the same three-digit number as the previous file) is the cache for the high-quality thumbnails and previews. It's usually bigger, sometimes much bigger, than the other two files—see Figure 5-21.

Figure 5-21
File Browser cache files

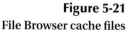

The File Browser creates three cache files for each folder it has read.

These cache files are "live"—they're updated continuously to reflect everything you do in the File Browser. But they have no knowledge of anything you do outside the File Browser—such as renaming or moving folders. If you move a folder to a different location, or rename it, the File Browser thinks it's a new folder. Hence it starts rebuilding all the previews and thumbnails, and it loses any flagging or custom sort ordering you've applied. Fortunately, there's a way to prevent this from happening.

The local cache. The File Browser's Export Cache command writes a copy of the live cache files to the folder in which you're working. The Export Cache feature was designed to let you include the cache in a folder so that when you burn it to a CD or copy it to a different drive or machine, the cache information is already there, so the File Browser doesn't have to spend the time reading metadata and generating previews.

When you export the cache, three files are created in the folder on which you're working. AdobeP8M.md0 holds the metadata information, AdobeP8T.tb0 contains the small thumbnails, and AdobeP8P.tb0 contains the high-quality previews. Whenever you choose Export Cache, all three files are updated to reflect the current state of the File Browser. So, they not only serve as an aid in speeding up the handling of folders transferred to a different location or burned to a CD or DVD, they also provide a useful fallback position if things do, in fact, go wrong—see Figure 5-22.

Figure 5-22
Export Cache

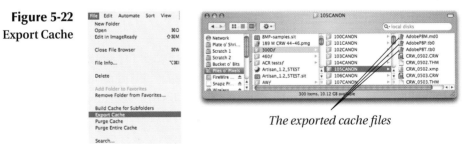

The exported cache files

I think of Export Cache as a "Save As" command for the current state of the File Browser, because while the live cache is constantly updated, the exported cache files are static—they get updated only when you choose Export Cache again or manually delete them outside the File Browser. Export Cache is useful for the purpose for which it was designed, but I've adopted the habit of exporting the cache whenever I do any significant work on a folder of raw images—it takes only a fraction of a second.

The local cache differs from the main cache in one other very important way. It moves with the folder and applies to the folder in which the files are located. So if you plan on moving or renaming a folder, use Export Cache first—that way, when the folder is renamed, the File Browser can use the local cache files to read the thumbnails, previews, and metadata. If this makes your head hurt, a good rule of thumb is, when in doubt, export the cache!

Tip: Recover Lost Camera Raw Settings. The File Browser cache contains image metadata, including Camera Raw settings. But Camera Raw can't read the File Browser cache, only its database and sidecar .xmp files. If you've lost the settings for an image, check the Camera Raw section of the Metadata palette—the settings will almost certainly be listed there, and you can quickly copy them to the Apply Camera Raw Settings dialog box—at least it's quicker than starting over from scratch.

Working with the Cache

Four commands on the File Browser's File menu let you work with the cache in different ways.

▶ **Build Cache for Subfolders.** Choosing Build Cache for Subfolders lets you speed up the initial caching of multiple folders of raw images. Copy the folders full of raws to an enclosing folder, point the File Browser at that enclosing folder, and choose Build Cache for Subfolders. The File Browser then goes to work building a cache for each subfolder. (Don't even try to understand the description of this feature supplied in Photoshop's online help—it's quite inaccurate.) You can also run Build Cache for Subfolders on a single folder, which forces the File Browser to build the cache modally. It's very slightly faster than just pointing it at a folder and letting it do it's thing, and it keeps you out of trouble because you can't do anything until it's finished building the cache.

▶ **Purge Cache.** Choosing Purge Cache purges the live cache for the current folder. It has no effect on local cache files created with the Export Cache command. If you purge the cache and nothing seems to happen, it's likely that you've previously exported the cache to the local folder. As soon as the live cache is purged, the File Browser uses the local cache rather than rereading all the raw and rebuilding the thumbnails and previews.

▶ **Purge Entire Cache.** Choosing Purge Entire Cache purges *all* the live cache files—the entire contents of the File Browser's cache folder—so use it with extreme caution if at all. However, like Purge Cache, it has no effect on local cache files created with the Export Cache command.

▶ **Export Cache.** Choosing Export Cache writes a copy of the live cache to the folder in which you're working. Unlike the live cache, the exported local cache doesn't try to find the folder by path name—it simply applies to the folder that encloses it. If you plan to move or rename a folder, always export the cache first—that way, all the cached information remains intact. You should also export the cache for folders that are destined to be burned to CD or DVD—that way, the recipient won't have to wait while her copy of Photoshop reads all the images, because the cache is already there, in the folder on the CD. In fact, I always export the cache after doing any significant work in the File Browser, just so that I know I have a fallback position if things go wrong.

Make the Work Flow

The File Browser is a deep, complex, and very powerful tool, but unless you take the time to master it, you'll almost certainly wind up spending more time on your work than you really need to. The File Browser lets you do a lot of things once, and once only, so that you don't need to keep doing them over and over again, whether it's applying Camera Raw settings, entering copyright notices, or rotating images. The time you spend in the File Browser will be amply repaid further down the line.

You can make the work flow even faster with a little planning. The File Browser lets you carry out operations in any order you choose; but the most efficient way is to proceed from the general to the specific, starting with operations that every image needs (such as a copyright notice) and continuing with operations required by progressively smaller numbers of images.

Some tasks, such as entering descriptions or captions, must be done image by image, and you'll almost certainly want to fine-tune the Camera Raw settings for your hero images on an individual basis. But you probably don't need to hand-tune every single image that you shoot. Instead, use the File Browser to whittle down the large collection of raws to the images that will make you money, and save the hand work for those.

6 Understanding Metadata

The Smarter Image

Metadata, which literally means "data about data," isn't a new idea by any means. Library catalogs are good examples of long-established metadata systems—the data is what lies between the covers of the book, while the metadata includes information *about* the book—who wrote it, who published it, when both parties did so, what it's about, and where in the library it's located, for starters.

Metadata isn't new to photography either. Photojournalists have long relied on the metadata properties specified by the IPTC (International Press Telecommunications Council) to make sure that their images get delivered correctly with the appropriate photo credit. But two factors are bringing metadata to the front burner for all photographers, not just photojournalists.

▶ Digital cameras embed a wealth of useful metadata right in the raw file.

▶ Adobe is in the process of using its considerable clout to promote XMP (Extensible Metadata Platform) as a documented, open, extensible standard for creating, storing, and sharing metadata.

Digital captures are already rich in metadata straight out of the camera, but one of the problems that has plagued early adopters has been a plethora of proprietary and often incompatible methods of writing and storing metadata. This is an ongoing battle.

The EXIF (Exchangeable Image File Format) "standard," for example, is sufficiently vague that the exchangeability pretty much applies exclusively to JPEGs. Camera vendors are allowed a great deal of freedom ("too much freedom" is a phrase I rarely use, but it applies here) to use private proprietary fields in EXIF to encode important information.

For example, it seems to bring no conceivable benefit to Canon shooters if the image White Balance settings are recorded by the camera in such a way that only Canon software can read them directly, but that's how the current Canon cameras work. This is not to single out Canon—there's more than enough blame to go around, and almost every vendor who produces cameras that shoot raw does something similar with one or another piece of metadata.

The intent here isn't to beat up on the camera vendors (well, not much), but rather to demonstrate just how badly we need a standard framework for handling metadata. That's why XMP is so important to the future not only of photography, but of all the enterprises that consume photography.

What Is XMP, and Why Should I Care?

XMP an Adobe initiative to promote a standard for metadata, but it's not a proprietary initiative. Instead, it's an open standard, it's documented, it's extensible, and it's even somewhat readable by humans. It is, in fact, a subset of XML (Extensible Markup Language), which is turn a subset of SGML (Standard Generalized Markup Language), the international standard metalanguage for text markup systems recorded in ISO 8879.

If you want to delve deeply into XMP, I suggest you start by looking at the available documentation. You can find several useful documents, including one on building custom File Info panels, at www.adobe.com:80/products/xmp/main.html. I'm not going to teach you how to write XML code in this chapter (it's a bit more difficult than writing actions, but a good bit easier than writing JavaScripts), but I *will* show you what XMP metadata looks like and show you some of the ways in which you can work with it.

Growing Pains

Because XMP is relatively new, you'll almost certainly encounter some growing pains if you try to work with a mixture of applications, some that support XMP, and others that as yet do not. There are two things you can do to lessen, if not eliminate, the pain.

▶ Ask the vendors of those applications that don't yet support XMP to do so.

▶ Learn how Photoshop and other Adobe and non-Adobe applications use XMP to record metadata, and find out just which files contain which pieces of information.

The first is up to you. The second is the core topic of this chapter. The metadata that you enter in the File Browser for your raw files will persist through all the converted images that you create from the raw files, unless you take deliberate steps to remove it. This is mostly a huge advantage to photographers—you can enter the information once, for the raw file, and know that it will be present in all the variants that you create from that raw file, not as a sidecar file (those are only necessary with read-only raws) but embedded directly in the .tif, .psd, .jpg or .eps image.

You know that your copyright notice will be embedded in the image, and, even better, you know that if you deliver the image on read-only media like CD-ROM or DVD-ROM, you can prove willful violation of the Digital Millennium Copyright Act of 1998 should someone else remove it. With a little work, you can even put a hidden copy of your copyright and rights notices that will resist all but the most skilled and determined offenders.

However, you may not always want to provide your clients with all that metadata. Some benighted souls still have attitude when it comes to digital capture: it's highly doubtful that they'd be able to identify the source of the image from the pixels, but they can do so straightaway from the metadata. Or maybe you just don't want anyone to know that you shot that image in Program mode....

Metadata may seem mysterious at first, but with only minimal effort, you can gain a great deal more control over it. And if you're willing to do some serious heavy lifting, you can accomplish magic!

XMP Is Text

The first important thing to learn is that .xmp files are simply text files, readable by any text editor or word processor, that conform to a specific syntax and are saved with a .xmp extension. So it's easy to read and, if necessary, edit XMP metadata.

The second important thing to learn is how the user interface in Camera Raw and the File Browser relates to the .xmp files that get stored in various locations on your computer. When you apply keywords or copyright notices, where does that data actually get stored? The answers may surprise you, but if you're at all curious, it's highly instructive to take a peek at sidecar .xmp files, saved Camera Raw Settings and Settings Subsets, Metadata Templates, and even File Browser cache files with a text editor.

For the truly motivated, the third lesson involves the things you can do by customizing .xmp files. For example, when you save a custom Metadata Template, you may be surprised to see all the junk that by default gets saved in it. Judicious pruning with a text editor can make these important files more reliable. If you're really gung-ho, you can actually use XMP to make your own custom File Info panels. Very few photographers have a use for all the fields in the IPTC metadata, for example. With a custom File Info panel, you can hijack the useless ones and turn them into something more useful.

XMP Uncovered

Thus far, the discussion has been a little on the abstract side. So let's bring things down to earth and actually look at some XMP metadata. We'll start with a sidecar .xmp file.

Figure 6-1 shows an image, and Figure 6-2 shows what its accompanying sidecar .xmp file looks like when it's opened in a text editor.

At first glance, the metadata file may seem overwhelming, but once you break it down into its various components, things start to make a bit more sense. So I'll spend the next several pages walking you through the different chunks of text in the sidecar file and showing you the corresponding elements in Photoshop's user interface. Once you see the relationship between the two, things will start to make more sense.

Figure 6-1
The image

©2004 Jack Reznicki

Figure 6-2
The sidecar .xmp file

```
<x:xmpmeta xmlns:x='adobe:ns:meta/' x:xmptk='XMP toolkit 3.0-28,
framework 1.6'>
<rdf:RDF xmlns:rdf='http://www.w3.org/1999/02/22-rdf-syntax-ns#'
xmlns:iX='http://ns.adobe.com/iX/1.0/'>
 <rdf:Description rdf:about=''
  xmlns:crs='http://ns.adobe.com/camera-raw-settings/1.0/'>
  <crs:Version>2.2</crs:Version>
  <crs:RawFileName>May04Workshop_4.TIF</crs:RawFileName>
  <crs:WhiteBalance>Custom</crs:WhiteBalance>
  <crs:Temperature>4800</crs:Temperature>
  <crs:Tint>-5</crs:Tint>
  <crs:Exposure>+1.25</crs:Exposure>
  <crs:Shadows>0</crs:Shadows>
  <crs:Brightness>25</crs:Brightness>
  <crs:Contrast>+95</crs:Contrast>
  <crs:Saturation>0</crs:Saturation>
  <crs:Sharpness>0</crs:Sharpness>
  <crs:LuminanceSmoothing>0</crs:LuminanceSmoothing>
  <crs:ColorNoiseReduction>25</crs:ColorNoiseReduction>
  <crs:ChromaticAberrationR>0</crs:ChromaticAberrationR>
  <crs:ChromaticAberrationB>0</crs:ChromaticAberrationB>
  <crs:VignetteAmount>0</crs:VignetteAmount>
  <crs:ShadowTint>0</crs:ShadowTint>
  <crs:RedHue>0</crs:RedHue>
  <crs:RedSaturation>0</crs:RedSaturation>
  <crs:GreenHue>0</crs:GreenHue>
  <crs:GreenSaturation>0</crs:GreenSaturation>
  <crs:BlueHue>0</crs:BlueHue>
  <crs:BlueSaturation>0</crs:BlueSaturation>
 </rdf:Description>
```

Figure 6-2

The sidecar .xmp file,
continued

```
<rdf:Description rdf:about=''
 xmlns:exif='http://ns.adobe.com/exif/1.0/'>
 <exif:ExposureTime>1/60</exif:ExposureTime>
 <exif:ShutterSpeedValue>5906891/1000000</exif:ShutterSpeedValue>
 <exif:FNumber>13/1</exif:FNumber>
 <exif:ApertureValue>7400879/1000000</exif:ApertureValue>
 <exif:ExposureProgram>1</exif:ExposureProgram>
 <exif:DateTimeOriginal>2004-05-02T15:56:40-07:00</exif:DateTimeOriginal>
 <exif:ExposureBiasValue>0/1</exif:ExposureBiasValue>
 <exif:MeteringMode>5</exif:MeteringMode>
 <exif:FocalLength>70/1</exif:FocalLength>
 <exif:ISOSpeedRatings>
  <rdf:Seq>
   <rdf:li>100</rdf:li>
  </rdf:Seq>
 </exif:ISOSpeedRatings>
 <exif:Flash rdf:parseType='Resource'>
  <exif:Fired>False</exif:Fired>
  <exif:Return>0</exif:Return>
  <exif:Mode>0</exif:Mode>
  <exif:Function>False</exif:Function>
  <exif:RedEyeMode>False</exif:RedEyeMode>
 </exif:Flash>
</rdf:Description>

<rdf:Description rdf:about=''
 xmlns:aux='http://ns.adobe.com/exif/1.0/aux/'>
 <aux:SerialNumber>150657</aux:SerialNumber>
 <aux:Lens>24.0-70.0 mm</aux:Lens>
</rdf:Description>

<rdf:Description rdf:about=''
 xmlns:pdf='http://ns.adobe.com/pdf/1.3/'>
</rdf:Description>

<rdf:Description rdf:about=''
 xmlns:photoshop='http://ns.adobe.com/photoshop/1.0/'>
 <photoshop:Source>Jack Reznicki</photoshop:Source>
 <photoshop:DateCreated>2004-05-02T15:56:40Z</photoshop:DateCreated>
</rdf:Description>

<rdf:Description rdf:about=''
 xmlns:tiff='http://ns.adobe.com/tiff/1.0/'>
 <tiff:Make>Canon</tiff:Make>
 <tiff:Model>Canon EOS-1DS</tiff:Model>
 <tiff:ImageWidth>4064</tiff:ImageWidth>
 <tiff:ImageLength>2704</tiff:ImageLength>
 <tiff:PhotometricInterpretation>2</tiff:PhotometricInterpretation>
 <tiff:XResolution>240/1</tiff:XResolution>
 <tiff:YResolution>240/1</tiff:YResolution>
 <tiff:ResolutionUnit>2</tiff:ResolutionUnit>
 <tiff:BitsPerSample>
  <rdf:Seq>
   <rdf:li>16</rdf:li>
   <rdf:li>16</rdf:li>
   <rdf:li>16</rdf:li>
```

Figure 6-2
The sidecar .xmp file,
continued

```
   </rdf:Seq>
  </tiff:BitsPerSample>
 </rdf:Description>

 <rdf:Description rdf:about=''
  xmlns:xap='http://ns.adobe.com/xap/1.0/'>
  <xap:ModifyDate>2004-05-27T15:23:30-07:00</xap:ModifyDate>
  <xap:MetadataDate>2004-05-27T15:23:30-07:00</xap:MetadataDate>
 </rdf:Description>

 <rdf:Description rdf:about=''
  xmlns:xapRights='http://ns.adobe.com/xap/1.0/rights/'>
  <xapRights:Marked>True</xapRights:Marked>
  <xapRights:WebStatement>www.reznicki.com</xapRights:WebStatement>
 </rdf:Description>

 <rdf:Description rdf:about=''
  xmlns:dc='http://purl.org/dc/elements/1.1/'>
  <dc:creator>
   <rdf:Seq>
    <rdf:li>Jack Reznicki</rdf:li>
   </rdf:Seq>
  </dc:creator>
  <dc:title>
   <rdf:Alt>
     <rdf:li xml:lang='x-default'>Images to Bruce Fraser for RW
     Raw</rdf:li>
   </rdf:Alt>
  </dc:title>
  <dc:description>
   <rdf:Alt>
     <rdf:li xml:lang='x-default'>Image Submit to Bruce Fraser for
     RW Raw</rdf:li>
   </rdf:Alt>
  </dc:description>
  <dc:rights>
   <rdf:Alt>
     <rdf:li xml:lang='x-default'>¬©Jack Reznicki 2004 All Rights
     Reserved</rdf:li>
   </rdf:Alt>
  </dc:rights>
  <dc:subject>
   <rdf:Bag>
    <rdf:li>People</rdf:li>
    <rdf:li>New York</rdf:li>
   </rdf:Bag>
  </dc:subject>
 </rdf:Description>

</rdf:RDF>
</x:xmpmeta>
```

Sidecar .xmp Decoded

The first few lines say that this is a .xmp metadata document, identified by means of a *namespace*. You can think of a namespace as the secret decoder ring for a particular XMP *schema*, which is the collection of properties the document deals with. The use of namespaces avoids conflicts between properties in different schemas that have the same name but different meanings. For example, the "Creator" property in one schema might be the human who created a resource, while I another it might refer to the application used to create the resource.

Schema names look like URLs, but if you point a Web browser at the ones in Adobe .xmps you won't get far. They're actually URIs—Uniform Resource Indicators—that may or may not have an actual Web page attached to them (the Adobe ones currently do not).

The second chunk of text is a little more interesting. It contains the Camera Raw settings that have been applied to the file, in a form that is readable to humans, albeit with some squinting! See Figure 6-3.

Figure 6-3
Camera Raw metadata

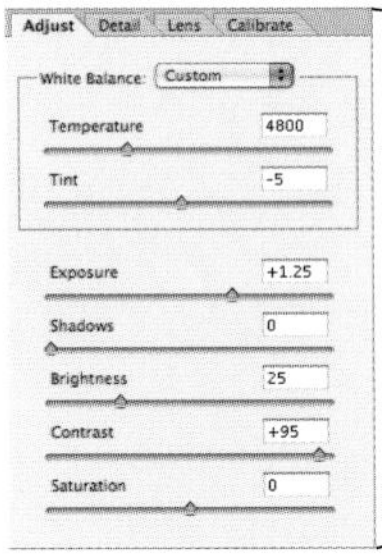

The boxed lines correspond to the Adjust tab settings. The remaining settings are all null, but it should be reasonably obvious that they pertain to the Detail, Lens, and Calibrate tabs, respectively.

```
<rdf:Description rdf:about=''
    xmlns:crs='http://ns.adobe.com/camera-raw-settings/1.0/'>
    <crs:Version>2.2</crs:Version>
    <crs:RawFileName>May04Workshop_4.TIF</crs:RawFileName>
    <crs:WhiteBalance>Custom</crs:WhiteBalance>
    <crs:Temperature>4800</crs:Temperature>
    <crs:Tint>-5</crs:Tint>
    <crs:Exposure>+1.25</crs:Exposure>
    <crs:Shadows>0</crs:Shadows>
    <crs:Brightness>25</crs:Brightness>
    <crs:Contrast>+95</crs:Contrast>
    <crs:Saturation>0</crs:Saturation>
    <crs:Sharpness>0</crs:Sharpness>
    <crs:LuminanceSmoothing>0</crs:LuminanceSmoothing>
    <crs:ColorNoiseReduction>25</crs:ColorNoiseReduction>
    <crs:ChromaticAberrationR>0</crs:ChromaticAberrationR>
    <crs:ChromaticAberrationB>0</crs:ChromaticAberrationB>
    <crs:VignetteAmount>0</crs:VignetteAmount>
    <crs:ShadowTint>0</crs:ShadowTint>
    <crs:RedHue>0</crs:RedHue>
    <crs:RedSaturation>0</crs:RedSaturation>
    <crs:GreenHue>0</crs:GreenHue>
    <crs:GreenSaturation>0</crs:GreenSaturation>
    <crs:BlueHue>0</crs:BlueHue>
    <crs:BlueSaturation>0</crs:BlueSaturation>
</rdf:Description>
```

This chunk of text is what Photoshop and the File Browser use to keep track of the custom settings for each raw image.

The next two chunks of text hold the EXIF data that was extracted from the raw file. They correspond to the second and third entries you see in the Advanced panel of File Info—EXIF Properties, and the auxiliary EXIF information recorded in http://ns.adobe.com/exif/1.0/aux/. Figure 6-4 shows the metadata and the corresponding File Info entries.

Figure 6-4
EXIF metadata

```
<rdf:Description rdf:about=''
  xmlns:exif='http://ns.adobe.com/exif/1.0/'>
  <exif:ExposureTime>1/60</exif:ExposureTime>
  <exif:ShutterSpeedValue>5906891/1000000</exif:ShutterSpeedValue>
  <exif:FNumber>13/1</exif:FNumber>
  <exif:ApertureValue>7400879/1000000</exif:ApertureValue>
  <exif:ExposureProgram>1</exif:ExposureProgram>
  <exif:DateTimeOriginal>2004-05-02T15:56:40-07:00</exif:
DateTimeOriginal>
  <exif:ExposureBiasValue>0/1</exif:ExposureBiasValue>
  <exif:MeteringMode>5</exif:MeteringMode>
  <exif:FocalLength>70/1</exif:FocalLength>
  <exif:ISOSpeedRatings>
   <rdf:Seq>
    <rdf:li>100</rdf:li>
   </rdf:Seq>
  </exif:ISOSpeedRatings>
  <exif:Flash rdf:parseType='Resource'>
   <exif:Fired>False</exif:Fired>
   <exif:Return>0</exif:Return>
   <exif:Mode>0</exif:Mode>
   <exif:Function>False</exif:Function>
   <exif:RedEyeMode>False</exif:RedEyeMode>
  </exif:Flash>
</rdf:Description>

<rdf:Description rdf:about=''
  xmlns:aux='http://ns.adobe.com/exif/1.0/aux/'>
  <aux:SerialNumber>150657</aux:SerialNumber>
  <aux:Lens>24.0-70.0 mm</aux:Lens>
</rdf:Description>
```

The text shown above generates the entries in File Info shown at right.

The next chunk of text is the PDF Properties section. Notice that the File Info contains entries, whereas the metadata does not. The File Info entries are aliased from other areas in the sidecar .xmp file—see Figure 6-5.

Figure 6-5
PDF Properties

```
<rdf:Description rdf:about=''
   xmlns:pdf='http://ns.adobe.com/pdf/1.3/'>
</rdf:Description>
```

The next chunk of text is the Photoshop Properties. Again, note that the metadata contains only the Source and Date Created information. The other information that appears in File info is aliased from other parts of the sidecar .xmp file—see Figure 6-6.

Figure 6-6
Photoshop Properties

```
<rdf:Description rdf:about=''
   xmlns:photoshop='http://ns.adobe.com/photoshop/1.0/'>
<photoshop:Source>Jack Reznicki</photoshop:Source>
<photoshop:DateCreated>2004-05-02T15:56:40Z</photoshop:
DateCreated>
</rdf:Description>
```

Next comes TIFF Properties, where you'll find the camera make and model, the pixel dimensions, and the default resolution for the converted image, set in Camera Raw. Again, the File Info displays some information aliased from elsewhere in the sidecar .xmp file, including any keywords applied to the image—see Figure 6-7.

Figure 6-7
TIFF Properties

```
<rdf:Description rdf:about=''
  xmlns:tiff='http://ns.adobe.com/tiff/1.0/'>
  <tiff:Make>Canon</tiff:Make>
  <tiff:Model>Canon EOS-1DS</tiff:Model>
  <tiff:ImageWidth>4064</tiff:ImageWidth>
  <tiff:ImageLength>2704</tiff:ImageLength>
  <tiff:PhotometricInterpretation>2</tiff:PhotometricInterpretation>
  <tiff:XResolution>240/1</tiff:XResolution>
  <tiff:YResolution>240/1</tiff:YResolution>
  <tiff:ResolutionUnit>2</tiff:ResolutionUnit>
  <tiff:BitsPerSample>
  <rdf:Seq>
    <rdf:li>16</rdf:li>
    <rdf:li>16</rdf:li>
    <rdf:li>16</rdf:li>
  </rdf:Seq>
  </tiff:BitsPerSample>
</rdf:Description>
```

The next two entries record the creation date and, of particular interest to image creators, the copyright flag and copyright URL. You'll find the corresponding entries in the Advanced File Info listing under XMP Rights Management Properties—see Figure 6-8.

Figure 6-8
XMP Rights
Management Properties

```
<rdf:Description rdf:about=''
 xmlns:xap='http://ns.adobe.com/xap/1.0/'>
 <xap:ModifyDate>2004-05-27T15:23:30-07:00</xap:ModifyDate>
 <xap:MetadataDate>2004-05-27T15:23:30-07:00</xap:MetadataDate>
</rdf:Description>

<rdf:Description rdf:about=''
 xmlns:xapRights='http://ns.adobe.com/xap/1.0/rights/'>
 <xapRights:Marked>True</xapRights:Marked>
 <xapRights:WebStatement>www.reznicki.com</xapRights:WebStatement>
</rdf:Description>
```

The remainder of the text contains the Creator, Title, Description, Copyright notice, and keywords. It's the source of the aliased entries you saw in the Photoshop Properties, TIFF Properties, XMP Core Properties, and XMP Rights Management Properties in File Info, and it also shows up in the Dublin Core Properties list in File Info—see Figure 6-9.

Why, you may ask, am I torturing you with this kind of information? My purpose for showing you all this is twofold.

▶ Understanding the contents of the metadata files makes the whole process by which you enter and store metadata a great deal less mysterious.

▶ Use of a text editor is the only way to remove metadata selectively from images with complete control. You can use the metadata palette or the File Info panel to remove some entries, but if you want to strip out some or all of the EXIF metadata, for example, a text editor is your only recourse. (Earlier, I posited the example of removing "Program" from the EXIF data—you'll be glad to know that if you simply cut that line from the EXIF data in the sidecar file, subsequent peeks at File Info show that it's been replaced by the much studlier "Manual.")

```
<rdf:Description rdf:about=''
  xmlns:dc='http://purl.org/dc/elements/1.1/'>
<dc:creator>
 <rdf:Seq>
  <rdf:li>Jack Reznicki</rdf:li>
 </rdf:Seq>
</dc:creator>
<dc:title>
 <rdf:Alt>
  <rdf:li xml:lang='x-default'>Images to Bruce Fraser for RW Raw</rdf:li>
 </rdf:Alt>
</dc:title>
<dc:description>
 <rdf:Alt>
  <rdf:li xml:lang='x-default'>Image Submit to Bruce Fraser for RW Raw</rdf:li>
 </rdf:Alt>
</dc:description>
<dc:rights>
 <rdf:Alt>
 <rdf:li xml:lang='x-default'>©Jack Reznicki 2004 All Rights Reserved</rdf:li>
 </rdf:Alt>
</dc:rights>
<dc:subject>
 <rdf:Bag>
  <rdf:li>People</rdf:li>
  <rdf:li>New York</rdf:li>
 </rdf:Bag>
</dc:subject>
</rdf:Description>
```

Sidecar .xmp files aren't the only kinds of files that you can usefully manipulate outside of Photoshop and the File Browser. Next, I'll show you some more advanced examples.

Meddling With Metadata

Back in Chapter 5, I showed you how to save and use metadata templates. If you save and apply them through Photoshop's user interface, they'll almost certainly work seamlessly better than 99 percent of the time. But if you open one of your saved metadata templates in a text editor, you may be in for a shock.

When you do so, the first thing you'll see is the usual line or two describing what kind of file the template is. The second thing you'll see is a copy of the Camera Raw settings for the image that was selected when you saved the template—Thomas Knoll actually had to build special code into Camera Raw to ignore this entirely bogus data.

Cleaning Up Metadata Templates

Thomas's code is almost invariably pretty darn bulletproof by the time it gets seen by alpha testers, let alone by the public at large, but I dislike the idea of applying bogus metadata to thousands of image—it just seems like a Bad Idea. So let's take a look at a typical metadata template, and go through the process of slimming down so it only contains the information I really need.

When you save Metadata Templates, Photoshop saves them in a dedicated folder. Rather than typing the lengthy path names for both Mac and Windows, I'll show you the simplest way to find your saved templates. Just select a file, choose File Info from the File Browser's File menu, and then, in the File Info dialog box, pull down the flyout menu at upper right and choose Show Templates—see Figure 6-10.

Once you've located your templates, open one in the text editor of your choice. Figure 6-11 shows a newly saved metadata template. All I want it to do is to set the Copyright Status flag to Copyrighted, enter my name in the Author field, and set the Copyright Notice to ©2004 Bruce Fraser. In practice, that is in fact all it does, at least when everything is working properly.

But as computers and software get ever more complicated, we all at some point learn the hard lesson that things don't always work as designed. One rule that's always stood me in good stead is to keep extraneous junk to a minimum. A cursory glance at the metadata template shows a whole lot of extraneous junk!

Figure 6-10
Finding saved
metadata templates

Choose Show Templates
to reveal the saved
template files in the
Macintosh Finder or
Windows Explorer

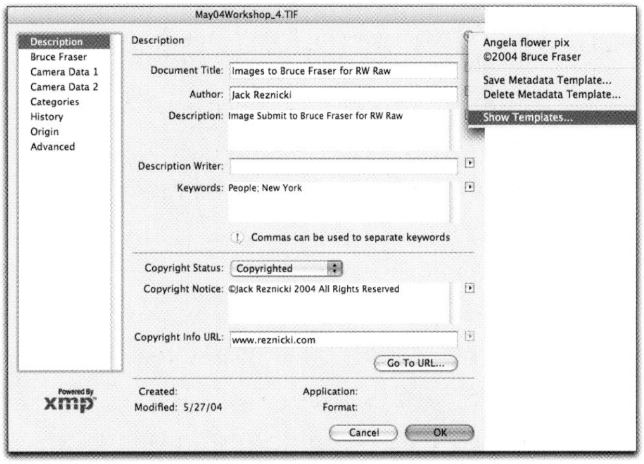

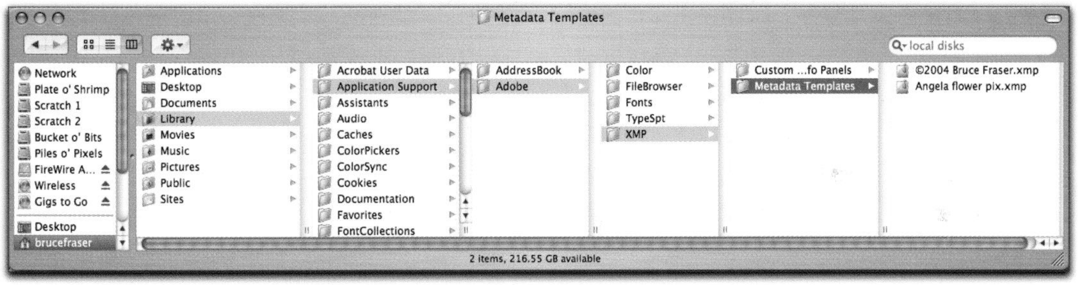

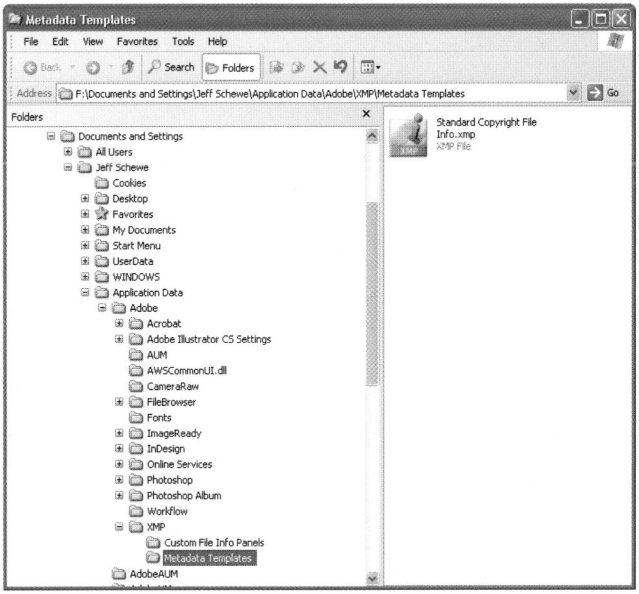

Figure 6-11
Unedited metadata
template

```
<?xpacket begin='Ô ªø' id='W5M0MpCehiHzreSzNTczkc9d'?><x:xmpmeta xmlns:
x='adobe:ns:meta/' x:xmptk='XMP toolkit 3.0-29, framework 1.6'>
<rdf:RDF xmlns:rdf='http://www.w3.org/1999/02/22-rdf-syntax-ns#' xmlns:
iX='http://ns.adobe.com/iX/1.0/'>

 <rdf:Description rdf:about=''
  xmlns:crs='http://ns.adobe.com/camera-raw-settings/1.0/'>
  <crs:Version>2.2</crs:Version>
  <crs:RawFileName>4FCW3895.TIF</crs:RawFileName>
  <crs:WhiteBalance>As Shot</crs:WhiteBalance>
  <crs:Exposure>+0.05</crs:Exposure>
  <crs:Shadows>0</crs:Shadows>
  <crs:Brightness>61</crs:Brightness>
  <crs:Contrast>+33</crs:Contrast>
  <crs:Saturation>0</crs:Saturation>
  <crs:Sharpness>30</crs:Sharpness>
  <crs:LuminanceSmoothing>0</crs:LuminanceSmoothing>
  <crs:ColorNoiseReduction>25</crs:ColorNoiseReduction>
  <crs:ChromaticAberrationR>0</crs:ChromaticAberrationR>
  <crs:ChromaticAberrationB>0</crs:ChromaticAberrationB>
  <crs:VignetteAmount>0</crs:VignetteAmount>
  <crs:ShadowTint>0</crs:ShadowTint>
  <crs:RedHue>0</crs:RedHue>
  <crs:RedSaturation>0</crs:RedSaturation>
  <crs:GreenHue>0</crs:GreenHue>
  <crs:GreenSaturation>0</crs:GreenSaturation>
  <crs:BlueHue>0</crs:BlueHue>
  <crs:BlueSaturation>0</crs:BlueSaturation>
 </rdf:Description>
 <rdf:Description rdf:about=''
  xmlns:exif='http://ns.adobe.com/exif/1.0/'>
  <exif:ExposureTime>1/125</exif:ExposureTime>
  <exif:ShutterSpeedValue>6965784/1000000</exif:ShutterSpeedValue>
  <exif:FNumber>18/1</exif:FNumber>
  <exif:ApertureValue>833985/100000</exif:ApertureValue>
  <exif:ExposureProgram>1</exif:ExposureProgram>
  <exif:DateTimeOriginal>2004-04-22T05:33:30-07:00</exif:DateTimeOriginal>
  <exif:ExposureBiasValue>0/1</exif:ExposureBiasValue>
  <exif:MeteringMode>5</exif:MeteringMode>
  <exif:FocalLength>57/1</exif:FocalLength>
  <exif:Flash rdf:parseType='Resource'>
   <exif:Fired>False</exif:Fired>
   <exif:Return>0</exif:Return>
   <exif:Mode>0</exif:Mode>
   <exif:Function>False</exif:Function>
   <exif:RedEyeMode>False</exif:RedEyeMode>
  </exif:Flash>
  <exif:ISOSpeedRatings>
   <rdf:Seq>
    <rdf:li>100</rdf:li>
   </rdf:Seq>
  </exif:ISOSpeedRatings>
 </rdf:Description>

 <rdf:Description rdf:about=''
  xmlns:aux='http://ns.adobe.com/exif/1.0/aux/'>
  <aux:SerialNumber>152124</aux:SerialNumber>
  <aux:Lens>28.0-70.0 mm</aux:Lens>
 </rdf:Description>
```

All the information here
is irrelevant—it applies to
the file that was selected
when the metadata
template was first saved.

Figure 6-11
Unedited metadata
template, *continued*

```
<rdf:Description rdf:about=''
 xmlns:pdf='http://ns.adobe.com/pdf/1.3/'>
</rdf:Description>

<rdf:Description rdf:about=''
 xmlns:photoshop='http://ns.adobe.com/photoshop/1.0/'>
 <photoshop:DateCreated>2004-04-22T00:00:00Z</photoshop:DateCreated>
</rdf:Description>

<rdf:Description rdf:about=''
 xmlns:tiff='http://ns.adobe.com/tiff/1.0/'>
 <tiff:Make>Canon</tiff:Make>
 <tiff:Model>Canon EOS-1DS</tiff:Model>
 <tiff:ImageWidth>4064</tiff:ImageWidth>
 <tiff:ImageLength>2704</tiff:ImageLength>
 <tiff:PhotometricInterpretation>2</tiff:PhotometricInterpretation>
 <tiff:XResolution>240/1</tiff:XResolution>
 <tiff:YResolution>240/1</tiff:YResolution>
 <tiff:ResolutionUnit>2</tiff:ResolutionUnit>
 <tiff:BitsPerSample>
  <rdf:Seq>
   <rdf:li>16</rdf:li>
   <rdf:li>16</rdf:li>
   <rdf:li>16</rdf:li>
  </rdf:Seq>
 </tiff:BitsPerSample>
</rdf:Description>

<rdf:Description rdf:about=''
 xmlns:xap='http://ns.adobe.com/xap/1.0/'>
 <xap:ModifyDate>2004-05-13T14:44:21-07:00</xap:ModifyDate>
 <xap:MetadataDate>2004-05-13T14:44:21-07:00</xap:MetadataDate>
</rdf:Description>
```

The relevant information
starts here.

```
<rdf:Description rdf:about=''
 xmlns:xapRights='http://ns.adobe.com/xap/1.0/rights/'>
 <xapRights:Marked>True</xapRights:Marked>
</rdf:Description>

<rdf:Description rdf:about=''
 xmlns:dc='http://purl.org/dc/elements/1.1/'>
 <dc:rights>
  <rdf:Alt>
   <rdf:li xml:lang='x-default'>¬©2004 Bruce Fraser</rdf:li>
  </rdf:Alt>
 </dc:rights>
 <dc:creator>
  <rdf:Seq>
   <rdf:li>Bruce Fraser</rdf:li>
  </rdf:Seq>
 </dc:creator>
</rdf:Description>

</rdf:RDF>
</x:xmpmeta>
<?xpacket end='r'?>
```

First is the bogus Camera Raw data. Select and delete it. Next comes some equally bogus EXIF data (it's also from the file that was selected when I saved the template). Select and delete it (including the auxiliary EXIF data). PDF Properties? Nothing of use there, so whack it. Ditto for TIFF Properties. The ModifyDate, MetadataDate, and CreateDate entries were likewise inherited from the file that was selected when I saved the template, and can likewise go in the bitbucket. The remainder of the file contains the entries I actually need, so now I can save the greatly stripped down template.

Once the template is stripped down, it becomes apparent that the easy way to create copyright notices for different years is not to go back into File Info and make the entries there, but simply to change the year on the relevant line using the text editor and then save each one with an appropriate name. Figure 6-12 shows the edited metadata template—it's a whole lot more manageable.

Once you become comfortable with editing .xmp files, you'll find that it's often faster and easier to accomplish your goals using a lowly text editor than it is to do so by tunneling through the many dialog boxes and palettes presented by Photoshop. For example, it's quicker to make multiple Camera Raw settings subsets by editing the values in the text and then saving with the appropriate name.

Custom File Info Palettes

The panels that appear in File Info are actually created by .xmp files. They're stored in Library/Application Support/Adobe/XMP/Custom File Info Panels on the Mac OS, and in Program Files/Common Files/Adobe/XMP/Custom File Info Panels on Windows.

In that folder, you'll find the .xmp files that create the Camera Data 1, Camera Data 2, Categories, and History panels for the File Info dialog box. If you open these in a text editor, you'll get a fairly good idea of the level of complexity you're in for if you want to contemplate making your own File Info panels.

This is not an undertaking for the casual user. The syntax is unforgiving—it's either right or it doesn't work at all—and you'll need to read and digest the documentation referenced earlier in this chapter. But if you're willing to ascend an admittedly steep but fairly short learning curve, you can do some very useful things.

Figure 6-12
Edited Metadata
Template

```
<?xpacket begin='Ôªø' id='W5M0MpCehiHzreSzNTczkc9d'?><x:xmpmeta xmlns:
x='adobe:ns:meta/' x:xmptk='XMP toolkit 3.0-29, framework 1.6'>
<rdf:RDF xmlns:rdf='http://www.w3.org/1999/02/22-rdf-syntax-ns#' xmlns:
iX='http://ns.adobe.com/iX/1.0/'>

<rdf:Description rdf:about=''
 xmlns:pdf='http://ns.adobe.com/pdf/1.3/'>
 </rdf:Description>

 <rdf:Description rdf:about=''
 xmlns:photoshop='http://ns.adobe.com/photoshop/1.0/'>
 <photoshop:Source>Bruce Fraser</photoshop:Source>
 <photoshop:Credit>Bruce Fraser</photoshop:Credit>
 </rdf:Description>

<rdf:Description rdf:about=''
 xmlns:xapRights='http://ns.adobe.com/xap/1.0/rights/'>
 <xapRights:Marked>True</xapRights:Marked>
 </rdf:Description>

 <rdf:Description rdf:about=''
 xmlns:dc='http://purl.org/dc/elements/1.1/'>
 <dc:rights>
  <rdf:Alt>
   <rdf:li xml:lang='x-default'>¬(c)2004 Bruce Fraser</rdf:li>
  </rdf:Alt>
 </dc:rights>
 <dc:creator>
  <rdf:Seq>
   <rdf:li>Bruce Fraser</rdf:li>
  </rdf:Seq>
 </dc:creator>
 </rdf:Description>

</rdf:RDF>
</x:xmpmeta>
<?xpacket end='r'?>
```

Hijacking Useless File Info Fields

Very few photographers have a use for all the metadata fields in File Info.
If a field is useless to you, you can hijack it for your own ends.

Figure 6-13 shows a very simple File Info panel I built for my own idio-
syncratic uses, along with the .xmp file that generated it. The Caption field
is simply picked up from the Description field in File Info's Description
panel, and it propagates through the various other panels. The MISC field
hijacks the Headline field, and the Published In field hijacks the Instructions
field. I have no use for Headline or Instructions metadata, but it's useful to
me to track which of my books a given image has appeared in. So, I use the
Instructions field for Published In.

Figure 6-13
Simple Custom
File Info panel

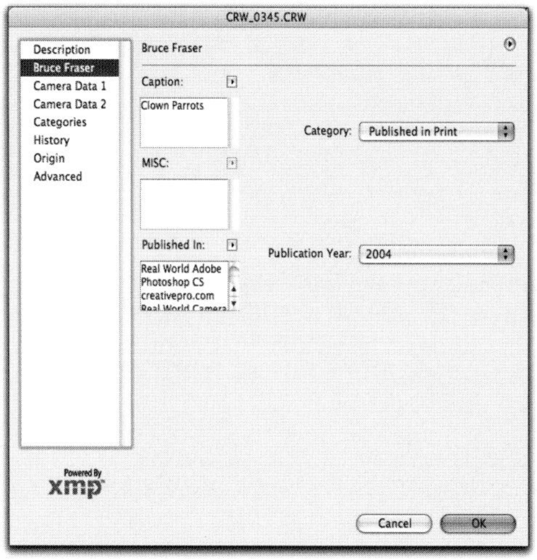

```
<?xml version="1.0">
<!DOCTYPE panel SYSTEM "http://www.pixelboyz.com">
<panel title="$$$/AWS/FileInfoLib/Panels/Categories/PanelName=Bruce Fraser " version="1" type="custom_
panel">
        group(placement: place_row, spacing: gSpace, horizontal: align_fill, vertical: align_top)
            {
            group(placement: place_column, spacing: gSpace, horizontal: align_fill, vertical: align_top)
            {

                group(placement: place_column, spacing: gSpace, horizontal: align_fill)
                {
                    group(placement: place_row, spacing: gSpace, horizontal: align_fill)
                    {
                    static_text(name:    '$$$/AWS/FileInfoLib/Panels/Categories/
                    Category=Caption:', horizontal: align_left);
                    mru_popup(xmp_namespace: photoshop, xmp_path: 'Caption', container_type:
                    single_value, yes_check: true, horizontal: align_right);
                    }
                    edit_text(horizontal: align_fill, height: gTextViewHeight, xmp_namespace:
                    photoshop, xmp_path: 'Caption', v_scroller: true);
                }

                group(placement: place_column, spacing: gSpace, horizontal: align_fill)
                {
                    group(placement: place_row, spacing: gSpace, horizontal: align_fill)
                    {
                    static_text(name:    '$$$/AWS/FileInfoLib/Panels/Categories/
                    Category=MISC:', horizontal: align_left);
                    mru_popup(xmp_namespace: photoshop, xmp_path: 'Headline', container_type:
                    single_value, yes_check: true, horizontal: align_right);
                    }
                    edit_text(horizontal: align_fill, height: gTextViewHeight, xmp_namespace:
                    photoshop, xmp_path: 'Headline', v_scroller: true);
                }
                group(placement: place_column, spacing: gSpace, horizontal: align_fill)
                {
```

Figure 6-13
Simple Custom
File Info panel, *continued*

```
                              group(placement: place_row, spacing: gSpace, horizontal: align_fill)
                              {
                              static_text(name:    '$$$/AWS/FileInfoLib/Panels/Categories/
                              Category=Published In:', horizontal: align_left);
                              mru_popup(xmp_namespace: photoshop, xmp_path: 'Instructions', container_type:
                              single_value, yes_check: true, horizontal: align_right);
                              }
                              edit_text(horizontal: align_fill, height: gTextViewHeight, xmp_namespace:
                              photoshop, xmp_path: 'Instructions', v_scroller: true);
                }
            }
        group(placement: place_column, spacing: gSpace, horizontal: align_fill, vertical: align_fill)
            {
}
        group(placement: place_column, spacing: gSpace, horizontal: align_fill, vertical: align_fill)
            {
                              group(placement: place_row, spacing: gSpace, horizontal: align_fill)
                              {
                              static_text(name:    '$$$/AWS/FileInfoLib/Panels/Categories/
                              Category=Category:', font: font_big_right, horizontal: align_left);
                              popup(items:'$$$/CustomPanels/AWS/Popup1x2= Published in Print{PIP};
                              Published Online{POL}; Unpublished{UPP};',xmp_namespace:photoshop,
                              xmp_path: 'CategoryPopup', horizontal: align_fill);
                              }
                              group(placement: place_row, spacing: gSpace, horizontal: align_fill)
                              {
                              static_text(name:    '$$$/AWS/FileInfoLib/Panels/Categories/
                              Category=Publication Year:', font: font_big_right, horizontal: align_left);
                              popup(items:'$$$/CustomPanels/AWS/Popup1x2=None{None};1994{1994};1995
                              1995};1996{1996};1997{1997};1998{1998};1999{1999};2000{2000};2001{2001};
                              2002{2002};2003{2003};2004{2004};2005{2005};2006{2006};',xmp_namespace:
                              photoshop,xmp_path: 'PubdatePopup', horizontal: align_fill);
                              }
            }
        }
</panel>
```

The advantage of hijacking an existing field rather than creating an entirely new one is that the File Browser's search engine only looks for metadata in its own fields. I can search for "Real World Adobe Photoshop CS" and find all the images for which I've entered "Real World Adobe Photoshop CS" in the Published In field.

Embed Private Metadata

With the fields I've created myself—the Category (Published In Print, Published Online, Unpublished)—I can embed the metadata in the image, but it isn't searchable. It's viewable in the File Info Advanced panel under Adobe Photoshop Properties, but it's only editable in my custom File Info panel or by using a text editor on the sidecar .xmp file.

However, I never send out my raw images, and any image derived from the raw has my metadata embedded directly in the file, where it's safe from geeks with text editors, rather than in a sidecar file. A skilled programmer could remove the metadata, but they'd have to know to look for it in the first place, so it's fairly bulletproof.

Figure 6-14 shows a custom File Info panel developed by my good friend Seth Resnick. It's quite a bit more complicated than the first example, and no, I'm not going to show you the code that created it—Seth put in too much work for me to just give it away, and he built this panel without the benefit of the documentation to which you've been referred. I simply offer it as a useful illustration of just how much you can accomplish with XMP.

There are two significant points to note about this panel. The first is that by default, without any user intervention, a rights notice is embedded in every raw image that's opened in the File Browser—notice that the Rights Management popup doesn't include "none" as an option. The second significant point is that the entries from the Rights Management popup are embedded in any files derived from the raw image, in a form that's uneditable to anyone who isn't either a programmer or a possessor of the custom File Info panel—the File Info panel is the secret decoder ring for this private metadata and offers the only reasonable means of removing or changing it.

Making Images Smarter

Metadata has been around in one form or another for a long time, but in many ways it's still in its infancy. Having a standard in the form of XMP is one factor that will doubtless accelerate its evolution, and the ready availability of basic shooting parameters from the EXIF data is another.

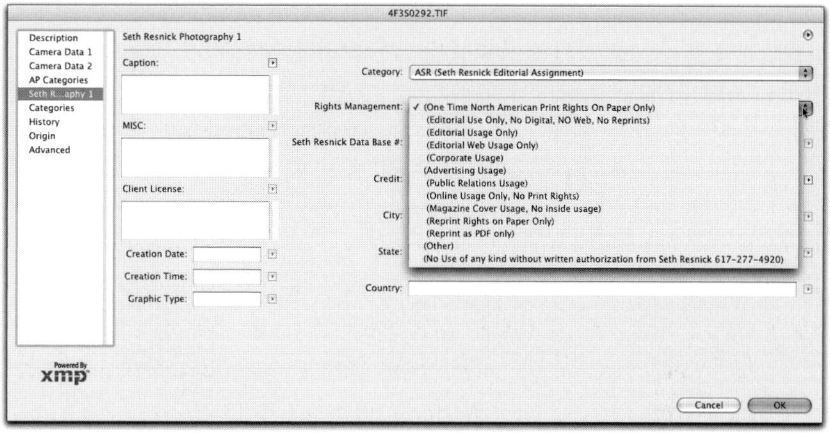

Figure 6-14

Advanced custom
File Info panel

Today, photographers can gain a considerable measure of security by knowing that their copyright and rights management notices are embedded right in the image. In the future, you can reasonably expect to see software that makes more intelligent use of metadata—automatically applying the right lens corrections based on focal length, or the right noise reduction based on ISO speed, for example. You can also look forward to seamless integration with XMP-compliant asset managers and databases.

You'll doubtless encounter speed bumps along the way, but if you understand how image metadata works, you'll be in a much better position to troubleshoot any problems you encounter than those who just treat the whole thing as incomprehensible magic. I hope this chapter provides a starting point for further metadata explorations.

7 Exploiting Automation

Working Smarter, Not Harder

The goal of doing all the work I've discussed so far in this book is to set up your raw images with the correct Camera Raw settings and the right metadata so that you can produce deliverable processed images with the minimum amount of effort. The minimum amount of effort, in this case, means taking full advantage of Photoshop's rich automation features, so that you can simply press a button, walk away, and let the computer do your work for you.

One of the great things about a computer is that once you've made it do something, you can make it do that same something over and over again, exactly the same way, automatically. Tapping the power of automation is key to building an efficient workflow, so in this chapter I'll show you how to leverage the work you've done in the File Browser and Camera Raw to produce deliverable images in a variety of formats.

The File Browser serves as command central for all the operations I'll discuss in this chapter. They all boil down to a two-step process.

▶ You select the images that you want to process in the File Browser.

▶ You run one of the options from the File Browser's Automate menu to produce converted images.

The Automate menu offers a variety of useful routines for creating images in a deliverable form, but by far the most powerful and flexible is the Batch command.

Batch Processing Rules

The Batch command is one of Photoshop's most powerful features. It's conceptually very simple. You point it at a batch of images, it runs an action on them, it (optionally) renames the images, and then it does one of the following:

▶ Saves new files

▶ Delivers open images in Photoshop

▶ Saves and closes, overwriting the source files.

As you'll see shortly, though, the devil is in the details, and some of the details in the Batch dialog box are distinctly counterintuitive. Figure 7-1 shows the Batch dialog box before customizing any of the settings.

Figure 7-1
The Batch dialog box

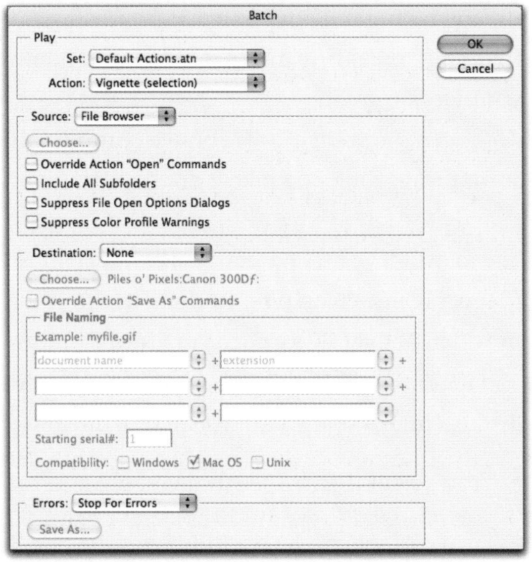

The dialog box is split into four different sections, each of which controls a different aspect of the batch process's behavior.

▶ **Play** lets you choose an action from an action set that will be applied to all the images.

▶ **Source** lets you designate the source—the images on which the batch will be executed—and also lets you choose some very important options whose functionality will become apparent later.

You can run a batch on a designated folder that you choose in the Batch dialog box by clicking the Choose button; on opened files; on images imported through the Photoshop File menu's Import command; or on the images that are currently selected in the File Browser. For processing raw images, the source will invariably be a folder or the selected images in the File Browser.

▶ **Destination** lets you control what happens to the processed images. None delivers them as open images in Photoshop; Save and Close saves and closes the processed images; Folder lets you designate a folder in which to save the processed images. It also includes the renaming features offered by Batch Rename.

When you process raw images, you'll always choose either None or, much more commonly, Folder. Save and Close often ends up being a "hurt-me" button, because its normal behavior is to overwrite the source image. With raw files this is usually impossible and always undesirable. Photoshop can't overwrite files in formats it can't write, including most raw image formats; but if you use a camera that records its raw images as .tif, there's a real danger of overwriting your raws if you choose Save and Close, so avoid it!

▶ **Errors** lets you choose whether to stop the entire batch when an error is encountered or log the errors to a file. I usually stop on errors when I'm debugging an action used in Batch and log them to a file when I'm actually running a batch in a production situation. However, when processing raw files, the batch typically either works on all files or fails on all files.

The difficulties that users typically encounter in running Batch are in the way the selections in the Source and Destination sections interact with the action applied by the batch operation. Here are The Rules. (Note: these are my rules, and I swear by them. They don't represent the only possible approach, but by the time you're sufficiently skilled and knowledgeable to violate them with impunity you'll have long outgrown the need for a book like this one!)

Rules for Opening Files in a Batch Operation

To make sure that the raw files get opened and processed the way you want them in a batch operation, you need to record an Open step in the action that will be applied in Batch. In the case of raw images, you'll want to make sure that Camera Raw's Settings menu is set to Selected Image so that it applies the custom-tailored Camera Raw settings you've made for each image, and you'll also want to make sure that Camera Raw's workflow settings—Space, Bit Depth, Size, and Resolution—are set to produce the results you want.

Now comes one of the counterintuitive bits. If you record an Open step in the action, you must check Override Action Open Commands. If you don't, the batch will simply keep opening the image you used to record the Open step in the action. Override Action Open Commands doesn't override everything in the recorded Open command; it just overrides the specific choice of file to open, while ensuring that the Selected Image and workflow settings get honored.

Some people find this set of behaviors so frustrating and counterintuitive that they latch onto the fact that you can run Batch using an action that doesn't contain an Open step and hence doesn't require messing around with the checkbox. The problem with doing so is that you lose control over Camera Raw's workflow settings—the batch will just use the last-used settings. So you may expect a folder full of 6,144 by 4,096-pixel images and get 1,536 by 1,024-pixel ones instead, or wind up with 8-bit sRGB instead of 16-bit ProPhoto RGB. If you simply follow The Rules, you have complete control over the workflow settings—the correct ones get used automatically.

Rules for Saving Files in a Batch Operation

To make sure that the processed files get saved in the format you want, you need to record a Save step in the action that will be applied in Batch. This Save step dictates the file format (.tif, .jpg, .psd) and options that go with that format—TIFF compression options, JPEG quality settings, and so on.

Now comes the second counterintuitive bit. You must check Override Action "Save As" Commands, otherwise the files don't get saved where you want them, don't get saved with the names you want, or possibly even don't get saved at all! When you check Override Action "Save As" Commands, the file format and file format parameters recorder in the action's Save step are applied when saving the file, but the name and destination are overridden by the options you specified in the Batch dialog box.

Rules for Running a Batch Operation

There are two other settings that commonly trip people up. Unless you check Suppress File Open Options Dialogs, the Camera Raw dialog box pops up whenever the batch opens a file, and waits for you to do something. Checking this option just opens the image directly, like Shift-double-clicking in the File Browser. The Camera Raw settings for each image are used, but the batch operation isn't interrupted by the appearance of the dialog box.

If the workflow settings recorded in the action result in an image in a color space other than your Photoshop working space, you should also check Suppress Color Profile Warnings; otherwise the batch may get interrupted by the Profile Mismatch warning—the day always gets off to a bad start when you find that the batch operation you'd set up to generate 2,000 Web-ready JPEGs overnight is stalled on the first image with a warning telling you that the file is sRGB when your working space is ProPhoto RGB....

Playing by the Rules

If you follow the relatively simple set of rules I've provided, your batch operations won't fall prey to any of these ills, and they'll execute smoothly with no surprises. If you fail to do so, it's very likely that your computer will labor mightily and then deliver either results that are something other than you desired or, even more frustrating, no results at all!

So with the rules in mind, let's look first at creating some actions and then at applying them through the Batch command.

Recording Batch Actions

Writing actions for batch-processing raw images is relatively simple. You don't need to worry about making sure that the action can operate on files that already have layers or alpha channels, or that are in a color space other than RGB. You're always dealing with a known quantity.

Bear in mind that if your actions call other actions, the other actions must be loaded in Photoshop's Actions palette, or the calling action will fail when it can't find the action being called. An easy way to handle this is to make sure that any actions on which other actions are dependent are saved in the same set as the actions that depend on them.

I'll start out with simple examples and proceed to more complex ones.

Simple Action—Save as JPEG

I'll start with a very simple action that opens a raw image at its native resolution and saves it as a maximum-quality JPEG in the sRGB color space.

Creating an action and action set. Start out by creating a new action Set called "Raw Processing" in which to save the actions you'll create in the rest of this section. So the first step is to create a new action set, which you do by opening the Actions palette and clicking the folder ("Create new set") icon and then entering the appropriate name in the ensuing dialog box and clicking OK to dismiss it. The new set then appears in the Actions palette—see Figure 7-2.

Figure 7-2
Creating an action set

To create a new action set, click the "Create new set" icon, enter a name, then click OK. The new set appears in the Actions palette.

Creating a new action. Before creating the action, select a raw image in the File Browser that has already had custom Camera Raw settings applied. That way, once you've created the action, you can start recording immediately without recording any extraneous steps, such as selecting a file, and you can correctly record the Camera Raw Selected Image setting.

Click the "Create new action" icon in the Actions palette, enter the name—"Save as JPEG"—in the ensuing dialog box, and then click Record to dismiss the dialog and start recording the action.

Recording the Open step. The first step is to open the image in Camera Raw, so that you can include the correct Camera Raw settings in the action. When you use the action in Batch, the Camera Raw dialog box won't appear, so it's essential to get these settings right when you record this step. Open the image by double-clicking or pressing Command-O, and the Camera Raw dialog box appears—see Figure 7-3.

Figure 7-3
Recording the Open step

When you record an Open step, it's critical to make sure that the Settings menu is set to Selected Image and the workflow settings are set the way you want them for the batch operation.

You need to record several key settings for this action in the Camera Raw dialog box.

▶ Set the Settings menu to Selected Image to ensure that each image gets opened using its own custom settings.

▶ Set the Space menu to sRGB to produce a converted image that's already in sRGB, the standard color space for the Web.

▶ Set the Depth menu to 8 bits/channel, because you're simply saving JPEGs (which only support 8-bit channels), and this action won't include any operations that could benefit from a higher bit depth.

▶ Set the Size menu to the camera's native resolution (in this case, 4064 by 2704).

▶ Set the Resolution field to 72 pixels per inch to preserve the polite fiction that Web images are 72 ppi.

Then click OK to open the image. (If the Profile Mismatch warning appears, click OK to dismiss it. This doesn't get recorded in the action, and you'll suppress the warning when you use the action in Batch.) The image opens, and the Open step appears on the Actions palette.

Recording the Save step. To record the Save step, choose Save As from the File menu, or press Command-Shift-S. The Save As dialog box appears. The filename and the destination for saving that you enter here will have no impact on the batch process—I usually enter an obviously silly name such as "foo.jpg" (I'm too lazy to type "throwmeaway.jpg") and choose the Desktop as my destination, to simplify cleanup. See Figure 7-4.

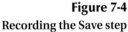

Figure 7-4
Recording the Save step

When you apply the action in a batch operation, the file name and destination will be overridden, but the format options will be applied.

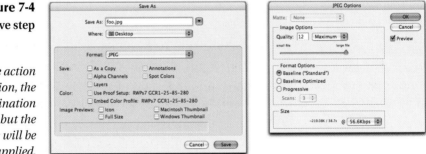

Make sure that the format is set to JPEG, and incorporate any other settings in this dialog box that you want to include in the action. In this case, I'll leave all the options unchecked—any RGB file that I create without an embedded profile can safely be assumed to be sRGB, and I don't care about icons or thumbnails—but if you want any of these options included in your batch-processed files, check them now.

Click Save to proceed to the JPEG Options dialog box, set the Quality to Maximum (12) and the Format Options to Baseline for maximum compatibility with JPEG-reading software, and then click OK. The File is saved on the Desktop as "foo.jpg," and the Save step appears in the Actions palette. Since you don't want the Batch to leave dozens or hundreds of files open in Photoshop, close the image so that the Close step appears in the Actions palette.

Stop and Save. Click the Stop button in the Actions palette to stop recording. Photoshop doesn't allow you to save individual actions, only action sets; so if you want to save an action as soon as you've written it, you need to select the action set that contains it in the Actions palette and then choose Save Actions from the Actions palette menu—see Figure 7-5.

Figure 7-5
Saving the action set

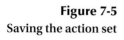

Note that until you save actions explicitly using the Save Actions command, they exist only in Photoshop's Preferences, and Photoshop's Preferences only get updated when you quit the application "normally" by using the Quit command. If Photoshop crashes, or you suffer a power outage, any unsaved actions will be lost. A simple action like this one probably wouldn't have me running to the Save Actions command, but if you make any actions that are even slightly complex, it's a good idea to save them before doing anything else.

If you expand the steps in the Actions palette by clicking the triangles beside them, you can see exactly what has been recorded for each step. When you use this action in Batch with the appropriate overrides selected (see "Batch Processing Rules," earlier in this chapter) the file names and folder locations will be overridden by the settings in the Batch dialog box, and all the other settings you've recorded here will be honored—see Figure 7-6.

Figure 7-6
Save as JPEG action

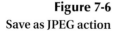

Variants. You can create variants of this action by recording different Open or Save steps. For example, you can create smaller JPEGs by changing the Size setting in the Camera Raw dialog box to one of the smaller sizes, and you can embed thumbnails or create lower-quality JPEGs by making those settings in the Save As and JPEG Options dialog boxes, respectively. To save in a different format, with different options, just choose the desired format and options when you record the Save step.

Complex Action—Save for Edit

The following example is a more complex action that produces 16-bit/channel TIFFs with sharpening applied and adjustment layers set up ready for final editing in Photoshop. It's designed for use on "hero" images that merit individual manual edits in Photoshop. It doesn't actually *do* any of the editing, because the required edits will almost certainly be different for each image in a batch. Instead, it simply does a lot of the repetitive grunt work involved in setting up an image for editing, so that when you open the image, all the necessary adjustment layers are already there, waiting for you to tweak them.

Creating a new action. Record this action in the same set as the previous one, since it's also designed for raw processing. As before, select a raw image that has had custom Camera Raw settings applied before you start recording the new action. Then click the "Create new action" icon in the Actions palette, enter the name "Save for Edit" in the New Action dialog box, and then click Record to start recording.

Recording the Open step. As before, start by launching Camera Raw by double-clicking the selected image. In the Camera Raw dialog box, again make sure that Settings is set to Selected Image. This time, though, you'll make some different workflow settings.

▶ In the Space menu, choose ProPhoto RGB, my preferred working space.

▶ Set the Depth menu to 16/bit channel, because you'll want to make the edits in Photoshop in 16-bit/channel mode.

▶ Set the Size menu to the camera's native resolution.

▶ Enter 240 pixels per inch in the Resolution field, because you'll almost certainly check your edits by printing to an inkjet printer at 240 ppi.

Then click OK to open the image. The image opens, and the Open step appears on the Actions palette.

Adding the edits. This action will add four different editing layers (actually, three layers and one layer set) to the image before saving and closing. First, add sharpening layers using your sharpening tool of choice (mine is PhotoKit SHARPENER from Pixel Genius LLC). Then add a Levels adjustment layer, a Curves adjustment layer, and a Hue/Saturation adjustment layer, as follows.

▶ I apply sharpening by choosing PhotoKit Capture Sharpener Expert from Photoshop's File>Automate menu, selecting Digital Mid-Res Sharpen, Medium Edge Sharpen, and clicking OK. You can substitute your own sharpening routine here, or you can elect to defer sharpening until you've edited the image in Photoshop.

▶ Add a Levels adjustment layer by opening the Layers palette's Adjustment Layers menu, choosing Levels, and then clicking OK to create a Levels adjustment layer that does not as yet apply any adjustments. You'll make the adjustments on an image-by-image basis in Photoshop—the action just does the grunt work of creating the layers.

▶ You need to take care of one small problem here. PhotoKit Sharpener produces an open (expanded) layer set, and the Levels layer gets created inside the set. There's no way to record closing or expanding a layer set, so you need to record a step that moves the Levels layer out of the set and up to the top of the stack. Using the shortcut for Layer>Arrange>Bring to Front only moves the layer to the top of the stack inside the layer set. You have to record dragging it out of the set and putting it on top of the stack.

The step actually gets recorded as "Move current layer to layer 5." Normally I try to avoid recording actions that move a layer to a specific number in the stack because I usually don't know how many layers will be present in a file, and recording a specific layer number can lead to one of two problems. If there aren't enough layers in the stack to move the layer to the specified number, the action fails with an error that states "The Move Command is currently not available." If there are more layers than anticipated, the layer ends up somewhere other than where I want it.

Fortunately, in this case you *do* know exactly how many layers will be there, because this action always starts out with a flat file and always adds the same number of layers. So recording the explicit layer position works for this action. If you start building complex actions, you'll run into issues like these fairly often—you just have to be methodical and keep debugging until you find a workable solution.

▶   Add two more adjustment layers—a Curves layer, then a Hue/Saturation layer—in both cases simply clicking OK when the respective adjustment dialog boxes, Curves and Hue/Saturation, appear. These layers are automatically created in the correct positions in the stack, so you don't need to employ any more layer-moving trickery—see Figure 7-7.

Figure 7-7
Adding adjustment layers

When you open the resulting images in Photoshop, you can start editing immediately by double-clicking the adjustment icon in each adjustment layer without having to do the work of creating them first. If you don't need all the adjustment layers, you can easily throw the unused ones away. All the edits will be performed in 16-bit/channel mode for the best quality.

Recording the Save step. Record the Save by choosing Save As from the File menu. Again, name the file "foo" and save it on the Desktop for easy disposal. This time, choose TIFF as the format, make sure that the Layers and Embed Color Profile checkboxes are checked (creating untagged ProPhoto RGB files is a Very Bad Idea), and check Icon and Macintosh Thumbnail in the Image Previews section. Then click Save to advance to the Tiff Options dialog box.

In the TIFF Options dialog box, choose ZIP for both Image Compression and Layer Compression, and then click OK to complete the save—see Figure 7-8.

Figure 7-8
Save as TIFF

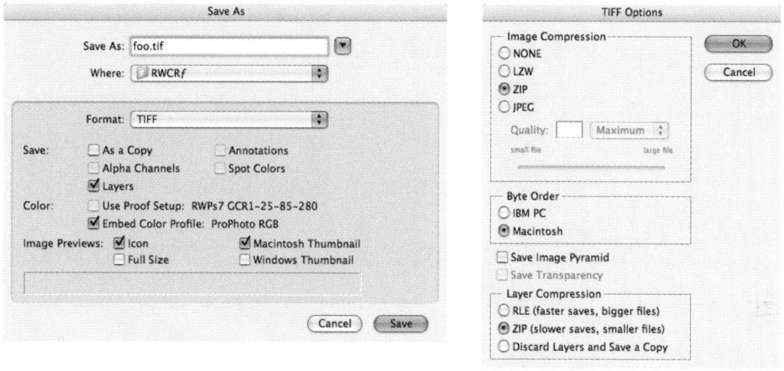

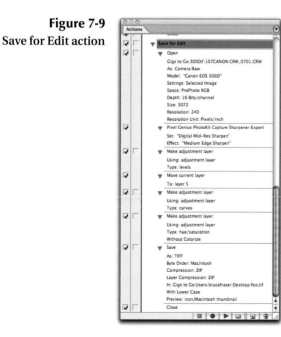

Finally, close the image (so that the batch operation will do so too), and click the Stop button in the Actions palette to stop recording. Figure 7-9 shows the resulting action in the Actions palette with all the steps expanded.

Figure 7-9
Save for Edit action

As with the earlier, simpler action, when you use this action in a batch process with the necessary overrides applied in the Batch dialog box, the file names and locations will be overridden by the Batch settings, while everything else in the Open and Save steps will be honored.

Running Batch

Using the actions I've just shown you in Batch is really very simple—as long as you remember The Rules! (If you need to take another look, refer back to "Batch Processing Rules," earlier in this chapter.) Play by the rules, and all will go smoothly. Violate them at your peril.

Besides the settings in the Batch dialog box, there are three common situations that can cause a batch operation to fail.

▶ There isn't enough space on the destination volume to hold the processed files.

▶ No source files were selected—see "Selecting and Editing" in Chapter 5, *It's All About the Workflow* if you need a reminder on how to select images in the File Browser.

▶ File with the same names as the ones you're creating already exist in the destination folder.

If these points seem blindingly obvious, I apologize. I mention them because they've tripped me up more than once. With those caveats in mind, let's look at setting up the Batch dialog box to run the Save for Edit action you built in the previous section. The key settings in Batch are the overrides in both the Source and Destination sections of the panel.

Source Settings

Whenever you run a batch operation using an action that includes an Open step, you must check Override Action "Open" Commands in the Source section. To process raw images, you also need to check Suppress File Open Options Dialogs—otherwise the Camera Raw dialog will pop up for every image—and whenever you run a batch operation unattended, it's a good idea to check Suppress Color Profile Warnings so that the batch doesn't get stuck on a Profile Mismatch warning.

Destination Settings

Similarly, whenever you run a batch operation using an action that includes a Save As step, you must check Override Action "Save As" Commands in the Destination section; otherwise the files won't get saved. The Destination section also offers the option to rename the files as part of the batch operation. I usually use the raw file name as a base and add a job or shoot designation, "_cvt" to indicate that it's a converted file, and the extension for the file type, but the renaming feature allows many different file naming schemes. See "Sorting and Renaming" in Chapter 5, *It's All About the Workflow*, for the major caveats on file-naming conventions. Figure 7-10 shows the Batch dialog box set up to run the Save for Edit action you created earlier in this chapter.

Figure 7-10
Batch

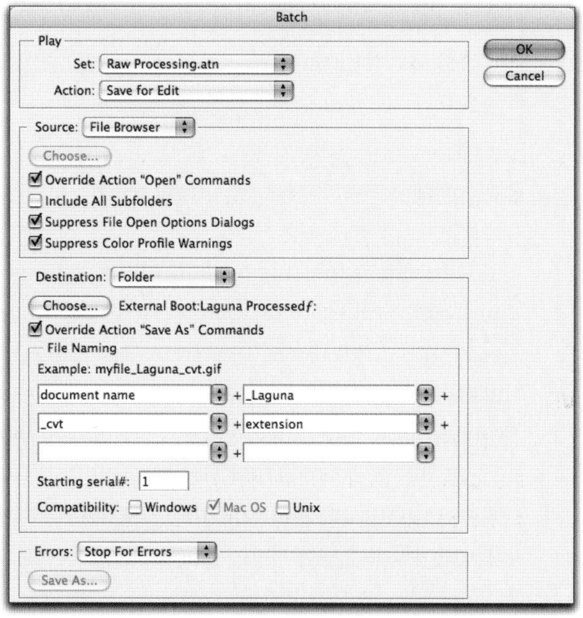

Batch is the most flexible command on the File Browser's Automate menu, but the menu also includes some automation features that are useful for very specific purposes.

PDF Presentation

The PDF Presentation command lets you build very simple slide shows with the Presentation option, or multi-page PDFs with the Multi-Page Document option. Both options build a multi-page PDF with one image per page, but the Presentation option does a little extra work, setting up a transition between pages and making sure that the PDF opens in full screen mode. I almost always use the Presentation option—see Figure 7-11.

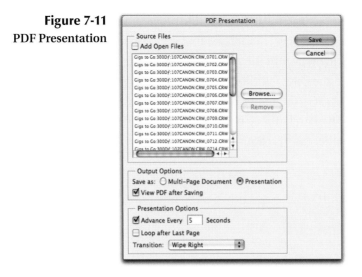

PDF Presentation is fairly limited. It doesn't let you add captions, or copyright notices, or anything else to the image, and it only lets you set a single transition that's used between all the images. It does, however, do the grunt work of getting all the images into a PDF. If you own Acrobat 6.0 Professional, you can add text there and finesse the transitions on an image-by-image basis. The PDF Presentation dialog box also gives you one last opportunity to change the image order by dragging the items in the list, but this is a task that's better done in the File Browser, where you can at least see the thumbnails.

Once you've made your choices in the PDF Presentation dialog box and you've clicked Save, you're prompted for a file name and destination for the PDF; then the PDF Options dialog box appears. Some of the options in PDF Options are irrelevant when you're processing raw files—they can't contain any transparency or vector data—but you should be aware of what the other options actually do (see Figure 7-12).

▶ **Encoding.** This option offers the choice between lossless ZIP compression or lossy JPEG compression, along with a Quality setting for the latter. If the presentation is purely for on-screen use, I recommend JPEG with a Quality setting of no less than 8. If there's a likelihood that you'll need to print the images from the PDF, use ZIP compression instead.

▶ **Image Interpolation.** This option lets PDF-compliant applications use Postscript-based interpolation to upsize the images in the PDF. There are

Figure 7-12
PDF Options

always better and more reliable ways to get a larger image than upsampling them from a PDF presentation, so I don't recommend this option.

▶ **Downgrade Color Profile.** Photoshop CS uses ICC version 4 profiles when they're available, which some older PDF readers can't understand. It's irrelevant for raw file processing because all four working space profiles in Camera Raw's workflow settings are understandable by apps that only understand the ICC version 2 spec.

▶ **PDF Security.** This option is very useful—it lets you set password-protected security at various different levels. You can allow the document to be freely viewed but prevent editing or printing, or you can allow limited editing such as commenting but prevent any of the data from being extracted—see Figure 7-13.

Note, however, that if you set any level of security, you need the password to open the document in Photoshop. Once it's open in Photoshop, it's completely editable—the restrictions apply only when the document is opened in Acrobat or Acrobat Reader. Macintosh users can open the PDF in the Mac's Preview application with no restrictions, so the security is far from bulletproof!

Figure 7-13
PDF Security

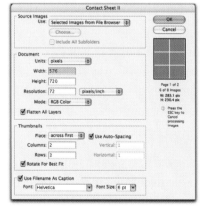

Contact Sheet II

As its name suggests, Contact Sheet II builds virtual contact sheets—pages full of image thumbnails. The contact sheets are built as unsaved Photoshop documents, with a choice to create either a flat file or a layered one with each image (and each image's caption, if included) on a separate layer. Figure 7-14 shows the Contact Sheet II dialog box.

Figure 7-14
Contact Sheet II

The Source Images section of the dialog box lets you choose the images for the contact sheet—in this workflow, you'd use Selected Images from File Browser. The Document section lets you set the size, resolution, and color mode for the contact sheet. (The color is converted to the current working space for the selected color mode.) The Flatten All Layers checkbox, when checked, creates a flat file, and when unchecked, creates a layered file with each thumbnail and each caption on a separate layer—handy if you want to fine-tune the layout in Photoshop.

The Thumbnails section lets you control the size of the thumbnails by specifying how many rows and columns the contact sheet will contain. The page mockup underneath the main buttons shows the layout, and the readout underneath it shows the maximum dimensions of each thumbnail. The Rotate For Best Fit checkbox rotates verticals to horizontal to make bigger thumbnails in the available space. Finally, the Use Filename As Caption checkbox does exactly what it says—it adds the file name as a caption for each thumbnail in your chosen font and size. Figure 7-15 shows a contact sheet generated by Contact Sheet II.

Figure 7-15
Contact sheet

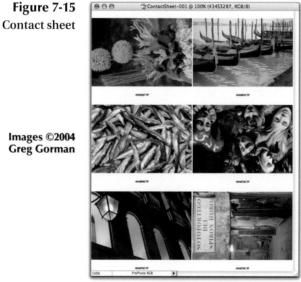

**Images ©2004
Greg Gorman**

Once the contact sheets are open in Photoshop, you can save or print them just as you would any other Photoshop document.

Picture Package

Picture Package is quite similar to Contact Sheet II, except it puts multiple copies of a single image on each page. The Source Images section works identically to that of Contact Sheet II. The Document section also works like Contact Sheet II, with the addition of a Layout menu that lets you choose various different layouts. The Label section offers a little more control over captioning than Contact Sheet II, including the ability to enter custom text (but not, unfortunately, different custom text for each image). Figure 7-16 shows the Picture Package dialog box.

Figure 7-16
Picture Package

Image©2004
Jack Reznici

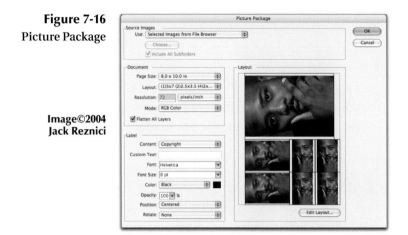

If none of the preset layouts is quite what you need, you can customize the layout by clicking the Edit Layout button to open the Picture Package Edit Layout dialog box—see Figure 7-17.

Figure 7-17
Picture Package
Edit Layout

You can edit the layout either by clicking on the thumbnails and dragging the sizing handles to change size, or by dragging the entire thumbnail to move, or by entering numbers in the appropriate fields. The Add

Zone and Delete Zone buttons let you add and delete thumbnails to the layout. One slightly odd feature is that if you Option-click on a thumbnail, a menu pops up when you release the mouse button, with commands to duplicate or delete the current thumbnail or add a zone using any of the preset sizes.

Like Contact Sheet II, Picture Package creates unsaved documents that are opened in Photoshop, ready for you to save or print.

Web Photo Gallery

Web Photo Gallery is a surprisingly deep feature. It creates a home page with thumbnail images and a gallery page for each image, or a frame-based page that combines scrolling thumbnails with a single larger gallery image. Some of the styles offer a feedback option where visitors to the page can check Approved or Other, or email feedback. Figure 7-18 shows the Web Photo Gallery dialog box.

Figure 7-18
Web Photo Gallery
dialog box

The Site section lets you choose a style for the gallery from the Style menu (the appearance of each style is reflected in the thumbnail that appears below the main control buttons) and enter an email address for receiving feedback.

The Source Images section lets you choose a folder or Selected Images from File Browser as source. It's also, somewhat confusingly, where you specify the destination folder.

All the styles produce the following.

▶ An index file.

▶ A ThumbnailFrame file. Both of the preceding will have a .htm or .html extension, depending on which one you've chosen.

▶ An Images folder that contains the large images and the graphic page elements.

▶ A Pages folder that contains a .htm or .html file for each image.

▶ A Thumbnails folder that contains the thumbnail JPEGs.

▶ A UserSelections.txt file.

The files and folders produced by Web Photo Gallery *always* have these names, so the only way to differentiate between different galleries is by the enclosing folder name. So it's always a good idea to create a new, empty folder and use it as the destination.

The remainder of the dialog box is devoted to the Options panels, of which there are six.

▶ The **General** options let you choose between a .htm or .html extension, use UTF 8 encoding (a Unicode encoding that offers backward compatibility with ASCII-based systems) for the URL, include width and height attributes for the images to speed downloading, and choose the option to preserve or strip all the metadata. (If you only want to strip some metadata, you'll need to edit it using the techniques discussed in Chapter 6, *Understanding Metadata*, before running the automation.)

▶ The **Banner** options let you enter a site name, Photographer, contact info, and date. These entries appear in the banner on each page.

▶ The **Large Images** options let you set the pixel size of the images and the amount of JPEG compression, apply a border, and use selected metadata for titles—the available options vary from style to style.

▶ The **Thumbnails** options let you choose the thumbnail size and, in some styles, layout, apply a border, and use selected metadata for titles. As with the Large Image options, the available options vary from style to style.

▶ The **Custom Colors** options let you choose colors for the background, banner, text, links, active links, and visited links. Again, the available options vary from style to style.

▶ The **Security** options let you place text on the images to prevent people from stealing them. You can choose from various metadata selections or enter custom text, with control over the font, size, opacity, position in the image, and rotation.

If the preset layouts don't do what you need, you can create custom layouts using the presets as templates. You'll need to be comfortable editing HTML, which I confess I am not. But if you are, you'll find a folder corresponding to each of the preset styles in Applications/Adobe Photoshop CS/Presets/Web Photo Gallery (Mac) or Program Files/Adobe/Photoshop CS/Presets/Web Photo Gallery (Windows). Inside each folder you'll find five .htm files.

▶ **Caption.htm** determines the layout of the captions that appear below the thumbnails on the home page.

▶ **FrameSet.htm** dictates the layout of the frame set for displaying pages.

▶ **IndexPage.htm** dictates the layout of the home page.

▶ **SubPage.htm** determines the layout of the gallery pages.

▶ **Thumbnail.htm** dictates the layout of the thumbnails that appear on the home page.

None of these file names can be changed, so if you want to edit an existing style, duplicate the entire folder of the style you want to edit and work on the files in the duplicate folder. When you're done, rename the duplicate folder to the style name you want.

Advanced Automation

You can accomplish a great deal through the combination of Photoshop actions and the built-in features on the Automate menu, but actions do have some limitations. Photoshop has no facility for conditional actions, for example, so if you want to process horizontal images to 800 pixels wide and vertical images to 800 pixels tall, you'll have to segregate them and run separate actions on the horizontals and the verticals.

Some operations can't be recorded in an action—earlier in this chapter, I showed you the problems that can occur when you add an adjustment layer to an image with an open layer set, for example. Usually you can come up with a workaround if you invest enough ingenuity, but sometimes you'll run into the wall. So I'll conclude by pointing out that Photoshop is completely scriptable in AppleScript (Mac), Visual Basic (Windows), or Java (cross-platform).

Inside the Photoshop CS application folder, you'll find a Scripting Guide folder. It contains comprehensive documentation on AppleScript, Java-Script, and Visual Basic scripting for Photoshop; some sample scripts that you can deconstruct; and a plug-in called ScriptingListener that, when loaded, dumps everything you do in Photoshop to a JavaScript log file. (So you only want to load it when you need that data—otherwise you'll make Photoshop run very slowly and create some very large log files!)

For a good example of the power of scripting, check out Russell Brown's excellent Dr. Brown's Image Processor, available either from Russell's web site (www.russellbrown.com) or from the Adobe Studio Exchange at http://share.studio.adobe.com/Default.asp—choose Scripts from the Photoshop Downloads menu, then click Go. You'll find a variety of interesting and potentially useful scripts in addition to Russell's Image Processor.

If I were to attempt to cover scripting in any depth at all, this book would instantly double in length, so I'll content myself with making you aware of the resources that Adobe supplies. Scripting is most certainly not for everyone, but if you've completely digested, implemented, and exhausted all the techniques in this book, and you want more automation, it's the next world to conquer. Good luck!

Image Credits

And Permissions

Earth image used on chapter opening pages, courtesy National Aeronautics and Space Administration.

Page 10. Untitled image.
©2003 Bruce Fraser

Pages 17–26. Clown Parrots.
©2003 Bruce Fraser

Page 31. Untitled image.
©2004 Bruce Fraser

Pages 38–39, 43, 54. Untitled image.
©2002 Greg Gorman,
www.greggormanphotography.com

Page 51, 94. Untitled image.
©2003 Jeff Schewe,
www.schewephoto.com

Page 55. Miami Wall - Palm shadows are cast on this brightly painted wall in South Beach - January 2004.
©2004 Seth Resnick,
Seth Resnick, Co-Founder D-65, LLC
email seth@D-65.com
www.D-65.com

Seth Resnick Photography
www.sethresnick.com
email sethres@sethresnick.com
Pixel Genius, LLC
email seth@pixelgenius.com
www.pixelgenius.com
Editorial Photographers (EP)
www.editorialphoto.com

Pages 61–66. Olé no Moiré Revisited.
Photography by Peter Fox,
www.peterfoxphotography.com

Page 68. Tulips bloom with the first signs of Spring on The Pearl Street Mall in Boulder, Colorado April 2004.
©2004 Seth Resnick,
www.sethresnick.com

Page 75, 77, 85, 88, 91. Untitled image.
©2003 Jeff Schewe,
www.schewephoto.com

Page 78, 81, 83, 87. Window Bottles.
©2003 Jay Maisel,
www.jaymaisel.com

Index

Pixel Genius PhotoKit Plug-in Discounts

www.pixelgenius.com

PhotoKit SHARPENER
A complete Sharpening Workflow for Photoshop

Other products may provide useful sharpening tools, but only PhotoKit SHARPENER provides a complete image "Sharpening Workflow." From capture to output, PhotoKit SHARPENER intelligently produces the optimum sharpness on any image, from any source, reproduced on any output device.

PhotoKit SHARPENER is designed with automation in mind, yet it also provides optional creative controls to address the requirements of individual images and the individual tastes of users.

PhotoKit Sharpener is priced at $99.95.

PhotoKit
Analog Effects for Photoshop

This Photoshop-compatible Plug-in is designed to provide photographers accurate digital replications of common analog photographic effects. PhotoKit is quick and simple, and allows for a greatly enhanced workflow.

PhotoKit is priced at $49.95.

Pixel Genius is offering a 10% discount on any whole order, which must be placed from the Pixel Genius store at: www.pixelgenius.com. This is a one-time discount per email address for any order made from Pixel Genius. This coupon will not work on affiliate sites. Also it cannot be combined with other discounts or programs except for certain cross-sell items. Please note that this coupon will expire upon the next revision of *Real World Camera Raw with Adobe Photoshop*.

Coupon ID: RWCRCPNBF